BERNARDO

Crossroads, Social Center and Agricultural Showcase of Early Texas

by James V. Woodrick

Bernardo
Crossroads, Social Center and Agricultural Showcase of Early Texas

by James V. Woodrick

First Edition, 2011
Second Edition, 2016
Copyright © 2011 James V. Woodrick
All rights reserved

ISBN - 13:   978-1467909693
ISBN - 10:   1467909696

Cover images: Background photo taken of the Bernardo archaeological project. The sketch is an artist's conception of the main house at Bernardo published in "Acco Press", a monthly magazine for the cotton farmer (Houston, June 1936) Vol. XIV No. 6, p. 4.   The image in the upper right of two unidentified women who were former slaves at Bernardo is from this same source. The two images of Leonard and Courtney Groce are photographs of original oil paintings housed in the Briscoe Center for American History at the University of Texas at Austin. The image in the lower left is of Wharton Collins, a former slave at Bernardo. It is taken from a Master's thesis by Frank Edd White, "A History of the Territory That Now Constitutes Waller County, 1821 - 1884", University of Texas at Austin, August 1836.

Table of Contents

Forward	6
Preface	8
About the Author	11
Introduction	12

Book 1 - The Place — 14

Geography and Early Contact	14
Founding of Bernardo by Jared Groce	24
Pioneering the Texas Antebellum Economy	51
Twilight at Bernardo After the Civil War	66

Book Two: The People — 74

Three Generations of Groces	74
Civil War Period	94
Enslaved African Americans	101
Notable Visitors and Events; Groce Texans	114
Aiding the Texas Revolution	125
Family Feud Over Estate Distribution	138
Children of Privilege	145
Descendants of Bernardo Residents	150

Book Three: The Archaeology — 158

Site Identification and Preliminary Fieldwork	158
Creation of the Bernardo Archaeology Project	160
Excavations and Findings	163

Appendix I: Public Business Disputes — 169

Appendix II: Illegal Slave Acquisition — 184

Appendix III: Transportation Links — 188

Appendix IV: Slave Inventories — 204

Appendix V: Clara Chappell Narrative — 225

Research Sources — 228

Bibliography — 231

Endnotes — 237

Forward

On a bitterly cold December morning in 2009, a team of archeologists painstakingly excavated at site 41WL28, the presumed location of the Bernardo Plantation belonging to Jared Ellison Groce II. Earlier that year, the archeological team had conducted magnetometer and ground-penetrating radar surveys in search of the plantation's main house—the home where Groce entertained such Texas heroes as Sam Houston and Stephen Austin. The magnetometer and radar instruments are remote-sensing devices that "see" into the soil and help archeologists decide where to dig. Using these instruments, the team had narrowed down the search area from a few acres to specific targets. Critical clues as to what might lie below came from the voluminous historical information that Bernardo Archaeological Project founder and historian Jim Woodrick had discovered.

Groce was the wealthiest person to join Stephen Austin's 1822 Texas colony, and he built the Lone Star State's first antebellum style plantation, which he named Bernardo. This much was already commonly known about this man. Woodrick, through diligent searching in scattered and sometimes arcane archives, rooted out document after document about Groce and his plantation. He found letters written by Groce, bills of sale for goods bought for the plantation, listings of enslaved workers who cultivated the cotton fields, and—most importantly for archeologists—maps of the plantation and surrounding area drawn by a great-granddaughter of Groce, Sara Wharton Groce Berlet. Woodrick's work added great depth and important context to the archeological work.

Undaunted by the chilling temperature and bolstered by Woodrick's historical data of what might lie below, archeologists continued to excavate. They selected an oval-shaped radar target that was about 3 feet by 6 feet in area. Here, the instrument had located something hard below the ground that prevented the radar's penetration. Initial probing suggested the presence of bricks. As the soil was removed inch by inch, the massive foundation of a brick fireplace was revealed. The bricks where undoubtedly handmade, built by the hands of enslaved Africans and African Americans. Another team of archeologists investigated a cluster of sandstone blocks about 25 feet away. This turned out to be the base of another fireplace. And between the two, a brick skirting was discovered that once hid the crawl space under a large house. Comparison with a plan of Bernardo made by Berlet quickly confirmed that the plantation's main house had been discovered! Now the exact location was known of the parlor where Groce entertained Sam Houston and the dining room where he dined with Stephen Austin. An important Texas archeological discovery had been made—thanks to the exhaustive research by Woodrick.

This book, Bernardo: Crossroads, Social Center and Agricultural Showcase of Early Texas, brings together all of the archival documentation and historical interpretation uncovered by Woodrick for the Bernardo Archeological Project. His book chronicles the story of one of Stephen Austin's most influential settlers, from leaving Alabama to building Bernardo at an important rock crossing on the Brazos River in Texas. He vividly tells the history of the plantation, as it is occupied by successive heirs, faces the Civil War, is impacted by the abolition of slavery, and ultimately fails without the use of an enslaved labor force. For the first time in one place, all of the history of Groce and his dynasty is thoroughly presented. This book will be a classic for historians and archeologists delving into the origins of early Texas.

Jim Bruseth, Director of the Archaeology Division at the Texas Historical Commission.
November 9, 2010

Preface

As an avid student of Texas history I had known about Bernardo for years. My interest in this plantation and the people who made it prominent in early Texas grew during the two years I spent researching and writing the story of my home county, "Austin County - Colonial Capitol of Texas", which I published in 2007. My thirty years as an avocational archaeologist created a desire to visit the site, to see firsthand if there were any visible remains of this storied hub of activities from the earliest days of Austin's Colony. A very fortuitous set of circumstances involving fellow Texas history buff and author Gregg Dimmick led to an introduction to Greg Brown, the current owner of the Bernardo site. We were warmly welcomed by Brown in initial site visits, and enjoyed his continuing active support as Gregg and I engaged others in the archaeological community in an effort that ultimately grew to a major archaeological project. I became the project historian, and this book is the result of my research into the history of Bernardo and the people who made it such a fascinating and unique place in early Texas.

I have worked with many individuals in the course of this effort whose help I acknowledge and sincerely appreciate. Jim Bruseth's early leadership and generous offer to initially evaluate the site using THC resources was critical in launching the archaeological project. A number of references cited in this book were provided by Gregg Dimmick who has a keen knack for searching the internet and locating obscure but pertinent documents. Bob Skiles at the Texas General Land Office provided some excellent research leads. Denton Bryant, descendant of Benjamin Franklin Bryant who was stayed at Bernardo in April, 1836 with the Texian army, provided information on his ancestor. Tom Adolph graciously shared the significant amount of Groce family research he had assembled working with a group of family descendants in 2002. Hempstead resident Clarence Miller compiled a wealth of information about Waller County in his book "Forgotten Places of Waller County", including a very detailed account of all the military activities in the area during and following the Civil War. Miller has spent over two decades locating a number of important historical sites in Waller County and amassing a large collection of artifacts. Much of his research and artifacts reside in the Waller County Historical Museum at 906 Cooper St. in Brookshire. Naomi Carrier, whom I met in the early days of the Bernardo Archaeology Project, has helped me to better understanding the plantation period through the eyes of an African American. Debra Sloan's remarkable abilities in the field of genealogical research were instrumental in tying the pre-Civil War archival records of the enslaved persons at Bernardo to descendants alive today. Jorge Garcia-Herreros graciously provided translations of several letters concerning Jared Groce found in the Bexar Archives. Bill Bishel provided professional editorial suggestions on how to transform my original manuscript, essentially a research report documenting the massive amount of information I had uncovered, into this book. Following the lead by THC, the archaeological evidence at Bernardo has been professionally directed by Robert Marcom, the site's Principal Investigator, and Carol McDavid of Houston-based Community Archaeological Research Institute. A host of enthusiastic volunteers painstakingly uncovered the evidence of past activities at this plantation. Charlie Gordy coordinated the scheduling logistics for these volunteers, most of whom are members of the Houston and Brazoria County and Texas archaeological societies.

One of my goals in writing this book was to present as completely and accurately as possible the stories of all the people who lived at Bernardo and made this such a successful enterprise. As one would expect, information about the plantation owners, the Groce family, was readily available in the historical record. The ability to find detailed information about a group of slaves on a Texas plantation is usually a rare occurrence. As research progressed and more information was compiled, it became apparent to me that two sources of information provided a unique opportunity to see into the lives of the African-American residents who did virtually all of the work that made this plantation successful. Documentation of oral and genealogical history conducted in the early 1900's by Sara Groce Berlet contains descriptions of many of the individual slaves and their role on the plantation. Fortuitously, a nasty estate dispute among Groce family members in the 1840s resulted in over 750 pertinent documents being filed in the county probate court. Among these were several inventories of slaves between 1831 and 1858 which listed individuals by first name, age and family unit. Coupling these two sources of information provides a good understanding of the family evolution of this group of people, some of whom may have arrived in America in bondage from Africa in 1818. Ties have been made between many of the individuals listed in these inventories and their record in the U.S. Census of 1870, where they appear for the first time in a census with their last names. People with ancestors who were enslaved at Bernardo may now be able to trace their genealogy accurately through the plantation period and perhaps even back to their origins in Africa.

The mass of material gathered on Bernardo and its people can be logically divided into three broad topics: the place, the people, and the archaeology. I have presented this material in three "books" following these topics in an attempt to provide the reader with better focus and clarity as the story unfolds. Telling this story necessarily and importantly involves writing about the enslaved African Americans who provided the human energy to operate the plantations. Most historical accounts were written from the perspective of white slaveholders or their descendants, and as such may be offensive to today's readers. I have used these accounts to tell this story, and in most cases chosen the words "slave" or "negro" to refer to the African Americans who resided at Bernardo as found in the archival records, rather than more currently acceptable "bondsmen" or "enslaved persons". I trust the reader will understand that this choice of words in no way justifies the institution of slavery, nor denigrates the people to whom they refer.

This book is dedicated to my grandchildren Jeb and Sadie Armstrong, with whom I have shared the incredible story of Texas.

James V. Woodrick
November, 2011

About the Author

James Victor Woodrick was raised in Austin County, Texas, attended Bellville schools and graduated from high school in 1961. During the next five years he attended the University of Texas at Austin, married Frances Bravenec of Austin County, and graduated with a Master of Science degree in Chemical Engineering from the University of Texas at Austin.

During a 28-year career with DuPont Jim held positions in technology, operations, business and manufacturing management in Victoria, Alvin, Houston and Orange, Texas, and in Wilmington, North Carolina and Wilmington, Delaware. He served eight years as Plant Manager at DuPont's facilities at Chocolate Bayou (Alvin) and Sabine River Works (Orange). After DuPont Jim served for ten years as President of Texas Chemical Council, the trade association representing the state's chemical industry.

His interest in Texas history began as a boy hunting for arrowheads on his parents farm on the old Coushatta trace, only a few miles from San Felipe and the former Bernardo plantation. Family and school trips to the San Jacinto Monument, the Alamo and nearby Stephen F. Austin State Park provided additional foundation for a lifelong interest in history, especially that of Texas.

Jim has a continuing fascination with the descriptions of early travelers in Texas and the evolution of trails to roads to highways as the country became settled. He has published the story of his home county in 2007, "Austin County - Colonial Capital of Texas". "Elusive Dreams - Early Exploration and Colonization of the Upper Texas Coast" was sponsored and published by the Liberty County Historical Commission in 2009. He is one of the founders of the Bernardo Archaeology project and serves as Project Historian.

Jim and Frances have two daughters, Amy (Mrs. Scott) Stevens and Tracy (Mrs. A.W.) Armstrong, and two grandchildren, Jeb and Sadie Armstrong. The Woodricks currently reside in Austin.

Bernardo

Crossroads, Social Center and Agricultural Showcase of Early Texas

Introduction

  The date is April, 11, 1836. Picture a splendid house on a hill, the center of a beehive of activity as preparations are made in anticipation of the approaching Mexican army. Sam Houston is camped across the river with his Texian army, training in preparation for a battle for the freedom of Texas. Two units of cavalry are housed in the cabins of the more than one hundred slaves who operate this, the largest plantation in Texas. The steamboat Yellow Stone is tied up at the river landing, awaiting Houston's orders to transport his men across the Brazos. Men in the blacksmith shop and camped nearby are busy forging iron and melting lead to make equipment and bullets for the army. Women are making bags for sand in case of an attack and helping nurse sick soldiers in the temporary hospital by the main house. The cotton gin stands idle, having completed baling last year's crop.

  The Twin Sisters, two cannons given by the citizens of Cincinnati to Texas, have just been delivered from Harrisburg and are awaiting Houston on the front lawn of the main house. Newly appointed Secretary of War Thomas Rusk has recently arrived and is conferring with Houston regarding battle plans. Scores of refugees have been crossing the river, fleeing the approaching Mexican army. Jared Groce, Jr. is overseeing distribution of corn and beeves to feed the Texian army; he has been entrusted by Houston to care for his prize stallion Saracen while the General trains his troops. Jared Groce Sr., who settled here in 1822 and built the plantation now managed by his two sons, has just arrived from Retreat, the home he built three years earlier when he retired from operating Bernardo.

  It seems as if all of Texas has converged on this once-tranquil agricultural showcase and center of southern hospitality. In two days hence, Houston will cross the river with his men, stay here at the plantation for two days while he reorganizes his army, and depart to meet destiny at San Jacinto.

  Welcome to Bernardo! This book tells the fascinating history of this unique plantation and the people who made it the best known and most prosperous plantation in Texas from the 1820's to the 1850's. Bernardo's history is filled with superlatives. Jared Groce arrived in Texas in early 1822, one of Stephen Austin's Old Three Hundred settlers. He came with some 90 slaves, far more than anyone else. He was granted ten leagues of land because of the resources available to assist in establishing the colony represented by this large number of slaves. Most other settlers received one league of land. An 1825 census listed Groce as owning 90 slaves, some 20% of the total in Austin's Colony at that time. The first cotton harvested in Texas was at Bernardo, as was the first cotton gin in Austin's Colony. In 1829 Groce signed a contract with John Harris to sell around 100 bales of cotton, the first contract of its kind in Texas. This amount represented fully one-third of the total cotton harvested in Texas that year. The income from this enterprise allowed Groce to rapidly accumulate land holdings. Within a few years he owned over 67,000 acres of land in five counties.

Many notable Texans visited Bernardo - Stephen Austin, Sam Houston, Samuel Williams, Jim Bowie, Thomas Rusk, William Wharton, "Mother of Texas" Jane Long, Pamelia Mann whose oxen pilled the Twin Sisters toward San Jacinto, George Armstrong Custer of Little Bighorn fame, and Texas ranger and revolutionary soldier Henry Karnes, just to mention a few. Jared Groce was influential in attracting others to join him in Texas. Among these were Houston, Williams and Philip Cuny, father of Norris Wright Cuney, the most prominent black Texan of the nineteenth century. Several family members also came, encouraged and assisted by the Groces. These included Civil War colonel Jared Ellison Kirby whose Alta Vista plantation became Prairie View A & M University, Edwin Waller and Abner Lipscomb. Waller signed both the declaration of Texas independence and the state's first constitution; he conducted the first surveys to lay out lots in the city of Austin and was its first mayor. Lipscomb was Secretary of State of the Republic and an associate justice of the Texas Supreme Court.

Three generations of Groces and their slaves lived on the plantation. Many of their children remained in the area into the twentieth century. Literally hundreds of people living today have ancestors who were part of life at that fascinating and unique corner of Texas called Bernardo. Enjoy their story!

Book 1 - The Place

Geography and Early Contact

The story of Bernardo begins at the river, and with the Native Americans who knew of this special place for centuries before arrival of the Europeans. The Brazos River is one of the largest in Texas. Crossing the river was always a challenge, even during dry periods when the waters were relatively low. There are only a few natural low-water fords across the lower couple of hundred miles of the river, usually consisting of sandstone outcroppings that provides a firm and somewhat elevated path across most of the river's width. Trade and travel routes of the Native Americans were situated to utilize these crossings. The Brazos leaves the rolling hills of central Texas and enters the coastal plain as it meanders between Austin and Waller counties. One of the most significant natural fords on the lower 100 miles of the Brazos is located in a curve in the river named Raccoon Bend, some 1.3 direct miles downstream of the Highway 159 bridge between Bellville and Hempstead. [1]

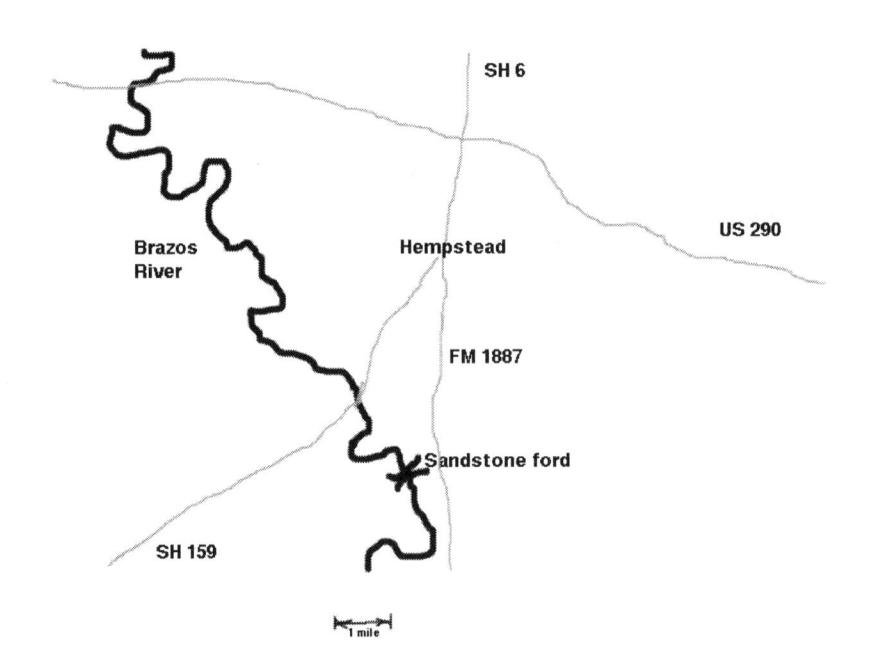

An aerial view of the river at this point clearly shows the rocky outcroppings of this natural crossing:

When the river was too high to ford, travelers for centuries used dugout canoes to cross, or at times made crude rafts of fallen logs.

Álvar Núñez Cabeza de Vaca may have been the first European to visit the Bernardo area. His account of the years from 1529 to 1533 as a slave of the Indians on Galveston Island tells of being allowed to travel between the coastal regions and villages further inland, and that he was given freedom to go "inland as far as I wanted and along the coast I would go as far as forty or fifty leagues." He traded sea shells and sea beans from the coast for animal hides, flint, glue and canes for making arrows, and red ocher and deer hair tassels for personal adornment. He may have crossed the Brazos at this ford during these trading expeditions.[2]

A Spanish expedition in 1718 led by Texas Provincial governor Martin de Alarcón was directed to establish a mission and a presidio on the San Antonio River, to explore upper Matagorda Bay, and to deliver supplies to the recently reestablished East Texas missions. Fray Francisco Cèliz served as diarist for the journey. Alarcón determined the location of the future Villa de San Fernando de Bexar and the Presidio de San Antonio de Bexar on May 5, 1718 at San Pedro Springs, and shortly thereafter placed the location of Mission San Antonio de Valero some two miles down San Pedro Creek. After becoming lost on his first attempt to travel to East Texas, he returned to San Antonio where he reorganized his expedition. His diary indicates that they set out for the second time on September 5, with a total of 53 individuals including Alarcón, Cèliz, church leader Father Antonio San Buenaventura y Olivares and another priest, three Tejas indians, 28 mules and 219 horses. Sixteen of the mules carried supplies for the expedition and sixteen were loaded with provisions and dry goods that Olivares intended to give as presents to the Indians.

Alarcón reached the Colorado River on September 18, where the main body of his group camped near modern Garwood while he traveled down the river and explored the northern reaches of Matagorda Bay. Alarcón then rejoined his group and on September 28 crossed the Colorado and began their journey northward through Austin County to East Texas. After leaving Mill Creek (which he named San Geronimo) he traveled to a point just north of modern Bellville where he was forced to stop when they encountered a large group of peaceful Indian men. Many more soon arrived; Alarcón ordered them to bring their women and children, which they did. Clothing and tobacco were distributed to all, so numerous "that they could not be counted". Conversing through an interpreter, Alarcón learned that six nations were represented, including Sana, Emet, Tayos, Malleyes, Huyugans and Curmicai. These groups requested a mission be established for them on the Guadalupe River some twelve miles below modern Gonzales. Alarcón mentioned killing several buffalo on the next day as he continued his journey to the northeast. Although he did not cross the Brazos in this area, he did pass within ten miles of the future location of Bernardo, and left the first account of the tribes living in the area. [3]

After Cabeza de Vaca and his companions, the earliest European to spend a significant amount of time in the upper Texas coastal region was Frenchman François Simars de Bellisle. Arriving in a ship which grounded in Galveston Bay in August, 1719, Bellisle and four companions went ashore seeking supplies. They were marooned while ashore, their ship having floated free and departed without them. They walked as far east as the Sabine River which they could not cross. They then retraced their route westward, finding a dugout canoe on the way but not encountering any Indians. They rowed upstream on a small creek for eight or nine days, finding nothing at its headwaters. Frustrated, they returned to Galveston Bay from where they ventured west to the San Jacinto river and perhaps as far west as the Brazos. Bellisle's companions died of starvation or exposure during the harsh winter of 1719-20. Back on Galveston Bay mainland he met a band of Atakapan Indians named Caux who took all his clothing and possessions but fed him. He stayed with this group of about twenty adults for almost a year as they hunted for deer and buffalo and dug "wild potatoes," traversing "the most beautiful country in the world." They had no fixed dwellings and did not raise crops but had five or six large dugout canoes. Kept as a virtual slave and frequently beaten by members of the Caux tribe, he was forced to carry large burdens during the next winter. Only the protection of a Caux Indian woman with whom he lived saved him from worse treatment. When a group of Bedai Indians visited the Caux camp, Bellisle was allowed to write a letter to the Europeans living among the Hasinai tribe in east Texas informing them of his whereabouts. The Bedai promised to deliver it as requested.

Of special note during this time is Bellisle's description of a buffalo hunt conducted some forty or fifty miles northwest of Galveston Bay in an extensive and open prairie east of the Brazos River known today as the Katy - Hockley prairie. After killing fifteen bison with bow and arrows from horseback, the Indians spotted smoke from a fire in the distance. Investigating, they discovered the smoke was from a campfire of Toyal Indians, an enemy tribe. In the ensuing attack one Toyal was captured and another killed. Bellisle wrote "When the man [the Toyal] was dead, they loaded him on their horses and and brought him to the place where we had stayed to wait for them. When they returned they threw this Indian on the prairie. One of them cut his head off and another cut off his arms, while they skinned him at the same time. Several of them ate the yellow fat, which was still raw, and they devoured him completely." Upon returning to their main camp and displaying the bones of the enemy, the Caux women danced in celebration. Belllisle did not cross the Brazos River; however his diary does indicate that he was in the general vicinity of Bernardo when his group encountered the Toyals. The letter written by Bellisle reached the French in Natchitoches via the Hasiani Indians, two of whom were ordered by the French to return to the camp of the Caux and rescue Bellisle. This occurred as planned, and Bellisle returned up the Bidai Trail, which has its southern end near Bernardo, to a Hasinai village where he remained for two months before finally arriving at Natchitoches in February of 1721.[4]

Six years later in 1727 Francisco Alvarez Barreiro and 20 soldiers passed through Austin County on a scouting trip as part of an inspection tour of the presidios of Texas led by Pedro de Rivera y Villalón. [5] Barreiro spent a total of thirty-five days in November and December of 1727 traveling over 900 miles on an assignment to explore the coasts, ports, bays, lagoons and the land between his presidio (La Bahía on the Guadalupe) and the Neches River. His effort represented the first significant official Spanish reconnaissance of the mid-upper Texas coastal region. His exact route is unknown and his written description contains disappointingly little detail, but a map he later made based on this scouting trip is quite accurate in many respects and shows the locations of Indian villages and mission settlements.[6] The names of several rivers named by Barreiro were different than we now know them. For example, his *Rio de San Marcos* is today's Colorado River and his *Rio Colorado a de los Brasos de Dios* is today's

Brazos River. This is the logical naming of the Brazos - red or *colorado* after its predominant muddy color. Later Spaniards interchanged the river names; the original San Marcos ended up as the modern Colorado and the original Colorado became the Brazos.

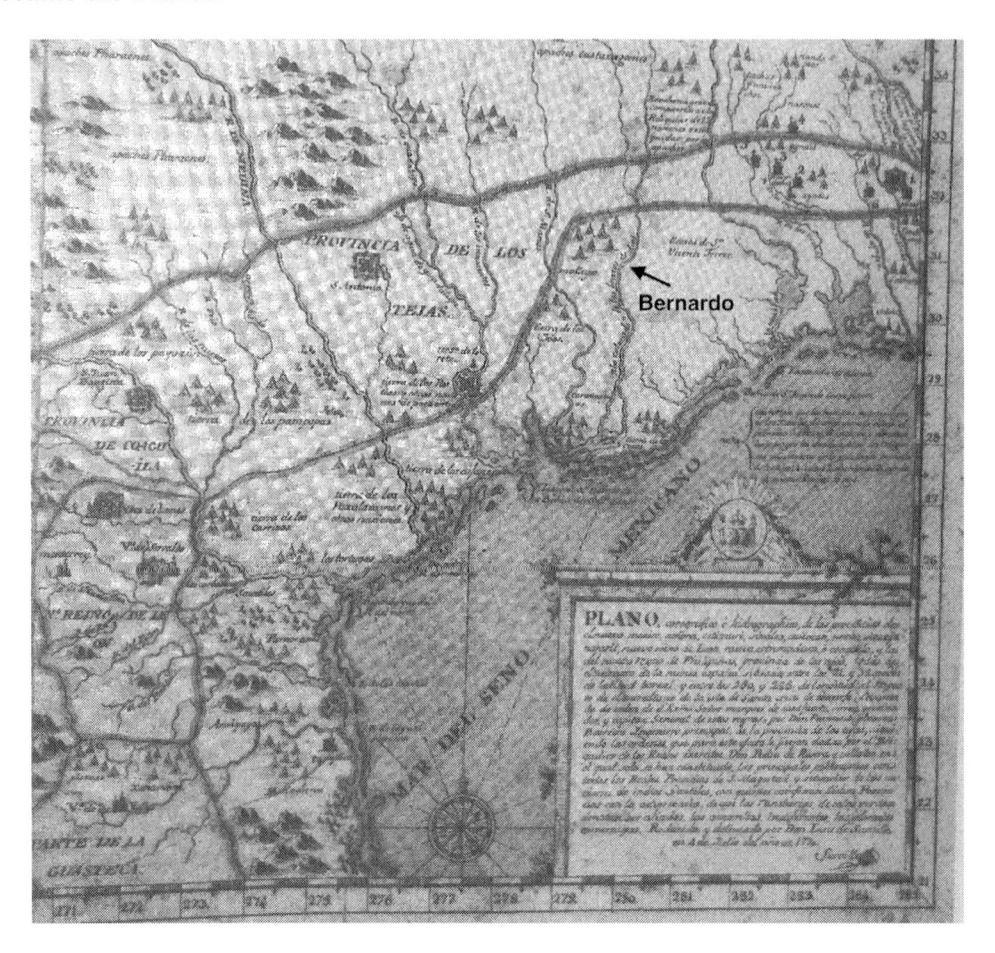

Barreiro accurately showed the Galveston / Trinity Bay system with the major Trinity and minor San Jacinto Rivers entering from the north. A tributary of these bays shown entering from the west is likely either Clear Creek or Buffalo Bayou. The area between the Brazos and San Jacinto rivers is marked "llanos de S[n] Vicente Ferrer", or the plains of Saint Vincent Ferrer. This formerly vast open grasslands is today called the Katy - Hockley prairie. Villages of Malleyes Indians are shown between the Brazos and Colorado Rivers in the vicinity of Austin County. The level of detail on his map suggests that Barreiro visited both sides of the river; his most likely crossing place would have been at Bernardo.

The first Spaniards known to have crossed the Brazos at Bernardo did so in 1746. Rumors of French traders among the Akokisa [7] Indians on the upper Texas coast resulted in an order for Joaquín de Orobio Basterra, captain of the La Bahía presidio (then on the Guadalupe River north of Victoria), to explore the region that, despite the Barreiro visit of twenty years earlier, was still virtually unknown to the Spanish. After an abortive try to reach the upper Texas coast by a water route in 1746, Orobio went up the La Bahía road to Nacogdoches, visited Los Adaes, and then traveled along the Bidai trail to reach the Akokisa villages of chiefs Mateo and El Gordo at a place he named Puesto de San Raphael, in modern Waller County approximately ten miles east of Bernardo. A Bidai village under chief Tomás was also located nearby, on the headwaters of Spring Creek east of Hempstead. The Akokisa confirmed that French traders had visited during the previous year, informed them of their intent to create a settlement near the mouth of the San Jacinto River, and requested them to inform the neighboring tribes of Bidai, Deadose and Tejas that they should bring their animal hides and other trade goods to the prospective French settlement during the next trading season.

Orobio left the Akokisa villages, explored down the San Jacinto River to the purported site of the French settlement where he found no indication of foreign presence and no resources conducive to support a settlement. He then returned home by traveling a new, more direct route due west from the San Jacinto to intersect the La Bahía road some two miles northeast of modern Round Top, and then along this well-known route to his presidio, where he arrived on April 6 to complete his mission. Orobio's reports do not specifically state where he crossed the Brazos; the most logical place would have been the natural ford at Raccoon Bend. On this trip and a followup by Barriero in 1748 as well as several other occasions in the 1754 - 1757 time frame, two tribes of Akokisa Indians and one of Bedias were visited by Spaniards in their villages near Bernardo. [8]

The Spanish established a presidio and mission known as Orcoquisac on the lower Trinity River in 1756 which remained occupied until 1771. During this period food and supplies were brought to the Orcoquisac complex from La Bahía and San Antonio by pack mules over a road created for this purpose known as the Orcoquisac road which followed the route taken by Orobio in 1746, crossing the Brazos at Bernardo. [9]

France ceded Louisiana to Spain in 1763 following the end of the Seven Years War, known in America as the French and Indian War. Texas was no longer a border state. The presidio and missions built in the 1720's in East Texas to guard the border were no longer needed, and Spain sent a military expedition in 1766 and 1767 through the northern frontier led by Marquis de Rubí to make recommendations regarding closing presidios to reduce expenses. Accompanying Rubí was an engineer named Nicolas de Lafora who, along with Rubí, left a diary of the trip. After visiting the Orcoquisac presidio, Rubí traveled toward La Bahía using the Orcoquisac Road. His and Lafora's diary entries for October 20, 1767, describe crossing the Brazos River at the Orcoquisac road crossing by future Bernardo. Rubi described the crossing as follows: "There, as has been the case all along, we saw bear and deer and killed some of them. Entering the thick forest that precedes the Brazos River, we found it to be supremely mucky and troublesome because of the palisade of trees and bogs, and we were forced to make a bridge. Having gone another 3 leagues, we came to the bank of this river that flows in one, united branch at this point, and toward the south. We were able to ford, but with some difficulty because of its great width, rapid current, and irregular, rocky bottom. ...". [10] Lafora wrote: "we forded the river of Los Brazos de Dios on a bottom of flat stone, in water reaching to the holsters of our pistols. Its width, measured straight across, was not less than fifty *toesas*, but it was increased by the obliqueness of the crossing. The passage is made quite dangerous by the narrowness of the channel and the violence of the current which flows south. ..." [11]

A proposed relocation site of the Ocoquisac mission and presidio mentioned by Rubí on October 20 refers to the area surveyed by Bernardo de Miranda in 1756 and named Santa Rosa del Alcazár. The Orcoquisac presidio and mission was to be relocated to this site and a new civil settlement of 25 Spanish and 25 Tlascalan Indian families were to be introduced nearby, creating a settlement similar in scope to San Antonio. The proposed mission, never realized, was to be on the headwaters of Cypress Creek at the juncture of Snake and Mound Creeks at the village of Akokisa chief El Gordo, some ten miles east of Bernardo. The proposed location for the presidio was on Hockley Mound. Neither the mission nor the presidio was ever built. Had they been, it seems unlikely that the Spanish would have opened up nearby lands for settlement by Americans in later years. [12]

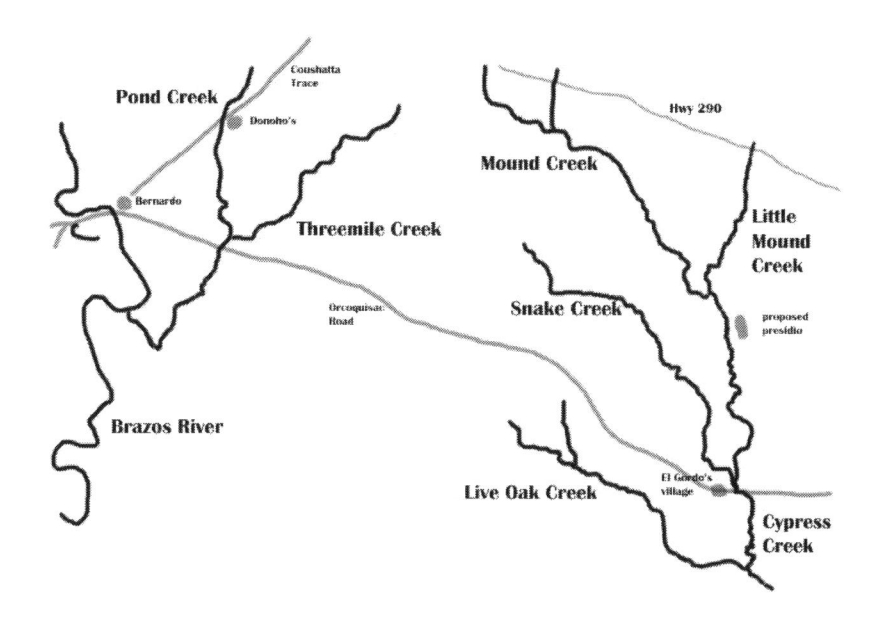

After the abandonment of Orcoquisac in 1771 eastern Texas was once again devoid of Spanish presence, and renewed rumors of foreigners in the area were again of concern to the Spanish authorities. This time, however, it was the English instead of the French who were threatening Spanish sovereignty. Captain Louis Cazorla of the garrison at La Bahía (now on the San Antonio River at Goliad) was ordered by Governor Baron de Ripperda to conduct a military exploration of the lower Brazos, San Jacinto and Trinity Rivers in response to reports of English traders and settlers in that area. He and several of his soldiers left La Bahía on September 18, 1772 and were met on the Guadalupe River near modern Cuero by soldiers from San Antonio. The combined force consisted of a lieutenant, two sergeants, forty soldiers, five Indians who were familiar with the coastal region, and a horse drove of some 300 animals. Cazorla marched up the La Bahía - Nacogdoches road past the Colorado River, then turned east near modern Round Top onto the Orcoquisac road used five years earlier by Rubí.

Cazorla noted in his diary that a short distance after crossing the Brazos (at Bernardo) he encountered a *ranchería*, or group of dwellings of Karankawa, Coco, Bidias and Jaraname indians. This was probably at the former site of El Gordo's Akokisa village. He saw that they had "sailor's shirts, others of fine cloth, red ribbons, and pieces of chintz" which they indicated had been acquired through trade from "foreigners" living above the Orcoquiza presidio and mission on the lower Trinity River. Cazorla also noted that the Indians had English muskets and were at that time involved in killing deer in order to get skins for trading for more powder, bullets and muskets.

Cazorla then went to the Trinity River, interviewed Indians there and explored to the mouth of the Brazos without finding any evidence of foreign activity. Deciding to return home, he wrote: "I resumed my journey on the sixteenth (of October), going back in search of the Orcoquiza road. On this day I crossed the Rio de los Brazos by raft [at Raccoon Bend], and, on the nineteenth, the Colorado [at La Grange]." [13] The Brazos must have been too high to use the natural ford.

Trade between Texas and Louisiana was either banned or severely restricted before 1780. Some smuggling of horses, mules, tobacco and perhaps cattle did occur. In June, 1779, Bernardo de Galvez, governor of Spanish Louisiana, sent a letter to San Antonio requesting permission to buy cattle from the local missions. He needed the cattle to feed his army which at that time was engaged in the American Revolution in campaigns against the British along the Mississippi River and the Gulf Coast. This support was particularly important for the American rebels because it prevented the British from landing forces on the lower Mississippi and attacking the Americans from the west. Texas governor Domingo Cabello y Robles (at San Antonio) asked Viceroy Teodoro de Croix for permission to send the cattle; Croix promptly forwarded the request to the Spanish king, who approved it on May 1, 1780. More than 1,200 cattle were immediately trailed from La Bahía to Opelousas. In July another herd of 2,000 was sent, followed by 1,500 more in September. During the next two years several thousand more Texas cattle were driven to Natchitoches and Opelousas in support of Galvez' army. By the end of the 1780's, however, the British were defeated, the Americans had their freedom, the once-vast herds along the San Antonio River had become depleted and most of the trail drives to Louisiana stopped. The route of these early cattle drives is not precisely known, but probably went using the older Orcoquisac road, crossing the Brazos at Bernardo. Local lore has it that the presence of several very large and obviously old mesquite trees on the Bernardo lands today testify to the earlier passage of Spanish cattle, who ingested the seeds earlier on their journey through the brush country around San Antonio and deposited them along the trails and ultimately here on the Brazos to sprout and thrive! [14]

Spain and the United States nearly came to war in 1805 because of a dispute over the boundary between Louisiana and Texas following the Louisiana Purchase in 1803. The United States claimed the Rio Grande River as the border, based on the French explorer La Salle's occupation of Texas in the 1680's. Spain recognized the border they had established between Spanish Texas and Spanish Louisiana - the Calcasieu River and the Arroyo Hondo near Natchitoches. The United States sent troops to Natchitoches, within their newly-purchased Louisiana territory. Spain garrisoned an older ranch outpost of Orcoquisac on the lower Trinity near modern Liberty named Atascosito. Fortunately, Gen. James Wilkinson and Lt. Col. Simón de Herrera, the American and Spanish military commanders respectively, entered into an agreement on November 5, 1806 that set up a neutral ground between the Arroyo Hondo/Calcasieu River and the Sabine river, thus averting a war between Spain and the United States. The Atascosito garrison remained in place until 1811, during which time it was supplied from La Bahía and San Antonio over the newly developed Atascosito road which crossed the Brazos at San Felipe.

A large group of Coushatta and Alabama Indians had also moved from Louisiana into East Texas in 1805, joining a few of their tribesmen who had made this move to the middle Trinity River some 20 years earlier. They promptly created trails from their new villages to the two Spanish trading posts in Texas at Nacogdoches and La Bahía. The road to La Bahía crossed the Brazos at Raccoon Bend and became known as the Coushatta Trace.[15]

In 1821 Steven F. Austin received permission from the Spanish government to bring 300 American settlers with their families to Texas. Austin and a group of Americans explored the region that he later selected for his colony during September of 1821. Arriving from La Bahía at the Brazos River on the Atascosito Road, Austin split his men into two groups, one proceeding up the west bank and the other up the east bank. They rejoined at the Brazos crossing of the La Bahía Road at the later town of Washington. Austin was with the group who traveled up the east bank (skirting Bernardo); he indicated that they crossed two faint roads which "probably went to Opelousas". These two traces were probably the old Orcoquisac Road and the Coushatta Trace. Those who went up the west bank reported that "the Country they came over was superior to any thing they had seen before in the Province".[16]

Roads in use in the vicinity at and before the time the first American settlers arrived in Austin's Colony are shown on the following map. The unique location of Bernardo as a major crossroads is evident.

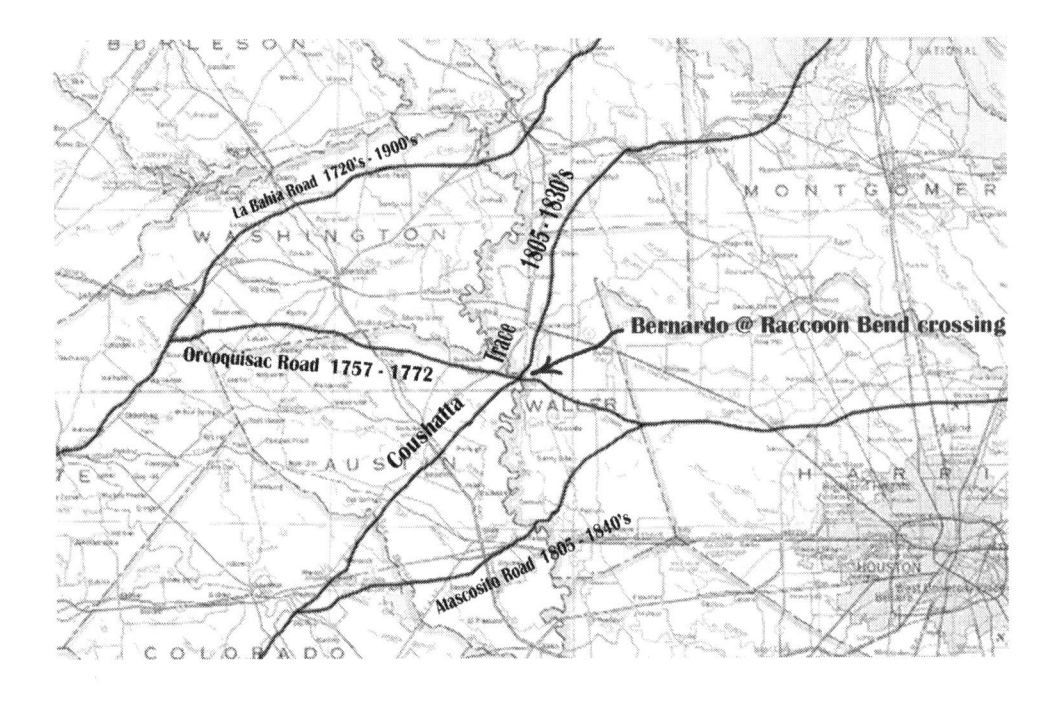

Founding of Bernardo by Jared Groce

The first settlers in Austin's Colony began arriving in late November, 1821, crossing the Brazos on the La Bahía Road. More arrived in December and camped on a stream they named New Year's Creek in modern Washington County while they waited for Austin to bring instructions for settlement. Many more settlers soon followed. By March 3, 1822, there were a reported fifty men on the Brazos and 100 on the Colorado. By the end of 1824 the Brazos was occupied from the coast to present Brazos County.

Jared Ellison Groce, originally from Virginia but then residing in Alabama, heard of the new colony being established by Stephen Austin and decided to move to Texas. Leaving Alabama in late 1821, Groce's first stop was in New Orleans where he purchased extensive supplies for his new enterprise, including farm implements, tools, seeds for planting, sugar, coffee, tea, salt, cloth of cotton, linen and wool, buttons, thread and even patterns for making clothing. His entourage left New Orleans with 50 wagons, extensive livestock, some 90 slaves, his eldest son Leonard and trusted overseer Alfred Gee, who had worked for him in Alabama. This single wagon train was essentially a large cotton plantation on wheels seeking new land, larger by far than anything any of the other early settlers brought to Texas. They crossed streams on portable pontoon bridges carried with them. Needless to say this unprecedented caravan must have attracted considerable attention as it passed through the countryside!

The next stop was in Alexandria. Here Leonard became very sick and they camped for several weeks on Big Creek near the home of Henrietta Wells Fulton Hooper, widow of Alexander Fulton, whose daughter Courtney Ann would later marry Leonard. After Leonard recovered, the Groce caravan proceeded to Texas, passed through Nacogdoches and down the La Bahía road.

Groce reached the Brazos River in early January, 1822. He stopped briefly on the edge of the timber ten miles east of the river to reconnoiter the situation and attempt to confer with Austin. This site was attractive to Jared and would later become one of his first land grants, known as Groce's Retreat. The road through the river bottom must have been nearly impassable due to the winter rains, and the swollen Brazos was a large obstacle for Groce to cross with his extensive caravan. This was probably the reason for his pause on the east side of the river. After a few days Jared II, Leonard and their servants Edom and Fielding crossed the Brazos on the La Bahía road and found the earlier prospective settlers camped on New Years Creek, where they learned that Austin had gone to the mouth of the Colorado to meet the schooner *Lively* which was carrying supplies he had contracted for earlier in New Orleans. Groce then retraced his path back to the camp east of the Brazos where he instructed Gee to have the slaves build temporary log cabins while he continued to explore the territory. Proceeding down the Coushatta Trace, he found attractive land of unsurpassed fertility where that road crossed the Brazos, and decided that this location on the east bank of the Brazos would be his permanent home. Once settled at his new location, Groce sent his son Leonard back to Alabama to continue his education. Jared, Alfred Gee and the slaves set about establishing their new home in Texas.

Among the Groce slaves were skilled craftsmen including carpenters, brick makers, masons and blacksmiths, who promptly built a temporary house for Groce in a grove of walnut trees on a hill overlooking the Brazos bottom just above the Coushatta Trace crossing. This first house was a room 30 by 30 feet, constructed of cottonwood logs. It had two fireplaces and a tamped dirt floor. A wood floor and ceiling were added later. By the end of 1822 a larger, more permanent house for Groce was completed, and the temporary log cabin became known as the Bachelor's Hall or Quarters, housing frequent visitors and travelers during the next several years. Groce named his plantation Bernardo, probably after the former Spanish governor Bernardo de Galvez who played such an instrumental role in assisting in the American Revolution. Galveston Bay (initially called Bernardo) and Island were named in honor of this governor as a result of a thorough exploration of the upper Texas coast made in 1785 at his direction.

Corn was planted that spring by the Groce slaves, but a prolonged drought resulted in failure of the crop. Groce and other settlers were forced to rely on natural resources for their food. Wild game including deer and turkeys were abundant and utilized, but wild mustang horses on the adjacent prairies provided most of the meat. These wild horses were not normally approachable by a man on foot or from upwind on horseback. However, when approached on horseback from downwind, the curious mustangs could not smell danger and allowed the rider to approach within about 50 yards, well within gunshot range. The horse flesh was taken home and jerked by hanging strips of meat on poles, allowing the sun to dry and thus preserve the meat. During 1822 and 1823 most settlers were reported to have subsisted mainly on the flesh of mustangs, "without bread or salt". Buffalo were present in limited numbers and utilized wherever possible. Jesse Burnam, one of Austin's Old Three Hundred settlers, recounted that he bought much-needed powder paid for with a Mexican silver dollar given by Groce to one of his children after he gave Groce some dried buffalo meat. [17]

A cotton crop was sewn and harvested in 1822 despite the drought - the first in Texas and forerunner of the economic engine that drove the Texas economy for a century. Groce's slaves planted corn in the moist bed of a temporarily dry lake across the river from Bernardo in 1823 and successfully harvested a crop in that year of continuing drought. This oxbow lake, a former loop of the Brazos and later named Stone Lake, was the site Sam Houston chose to camp for two weeks in April of 1836 while he trained his army to meet the Mexicans in the campaign for Texas independence. Some of his slaves also performed the role of hunter for the plantation, securing wild game to eat.

Arming slaves was not the norm among settlers; Groce did this out of necessity because of his physical incapacity (he suffered from periodic paralysis of both arms, symptoms suggesting rheumatoid arthritis) and lack of other Anglo adults besides the overseer Alfred Gee to provide food and protection from Indians. Despite their superior numbers, relative freedom to travel alone and being armed, there is no record throughout the plantation period of any insurrection or escape of Groce slaves. While the institution of slavery was a human travesty and can never be condoned, most archival sources state that the slaves at Bernardo were well provided for in terms of food and shelter, not treated with cruelty, and in general were satisfied that their lives at this plantation were better than any other choice they had at that time. Two of the former slaves at Bernardo, Wharton Collins and Clara Chappell, indicated in the 1930's that they were well provided for on the plantation, and in fact struggled more in their lives in the decades after emancipation. [18]

Groce's compound with its relatively abundant resources soon became a favored resting place for travelers. The walls of the main house were of cottonwood logs hewn square and flat on all four sides and about a foot thick. A broad hall fifteen feet wide extended down the middle of the house, with two rooms twenty feet square on both sides. A broad porch supported by polished walnut posts ran across the front of the house. A staircase from the hall led upstairs to two bedrooms situated in the two gabled ends. Each room had a fireplace made of sandstone taken from the Brazos River crossing. Post oak shingles hand-made with a drawing knife covered the roof. Floors were of ash planks planed for smoothness. The kitchen with a large fireplace was built a few feet behind the main house, as was customary at that time as a precaution against a fire there spreading to the main house. Near the kitchen in the back yard were a dairy, a small house for the resident doctor, and Bachelor's Hall, a thirty foot square room with two fireplaces and six beds used to house visiting travelers, friends and relatives. Soon bricks were being manufactured on the plantation as evidenced by their presence in the foundation of the main house and in the kitchen hearth. William Wharton Groce, who was born in this house, described it as being well-made, comfortable and not having the appearance of being a log house. [19]

The following sketches of Bernardo were made by Sarah Groce Berlet, family historian and daughter of William W. Groce, based on his description:

Cotton Field

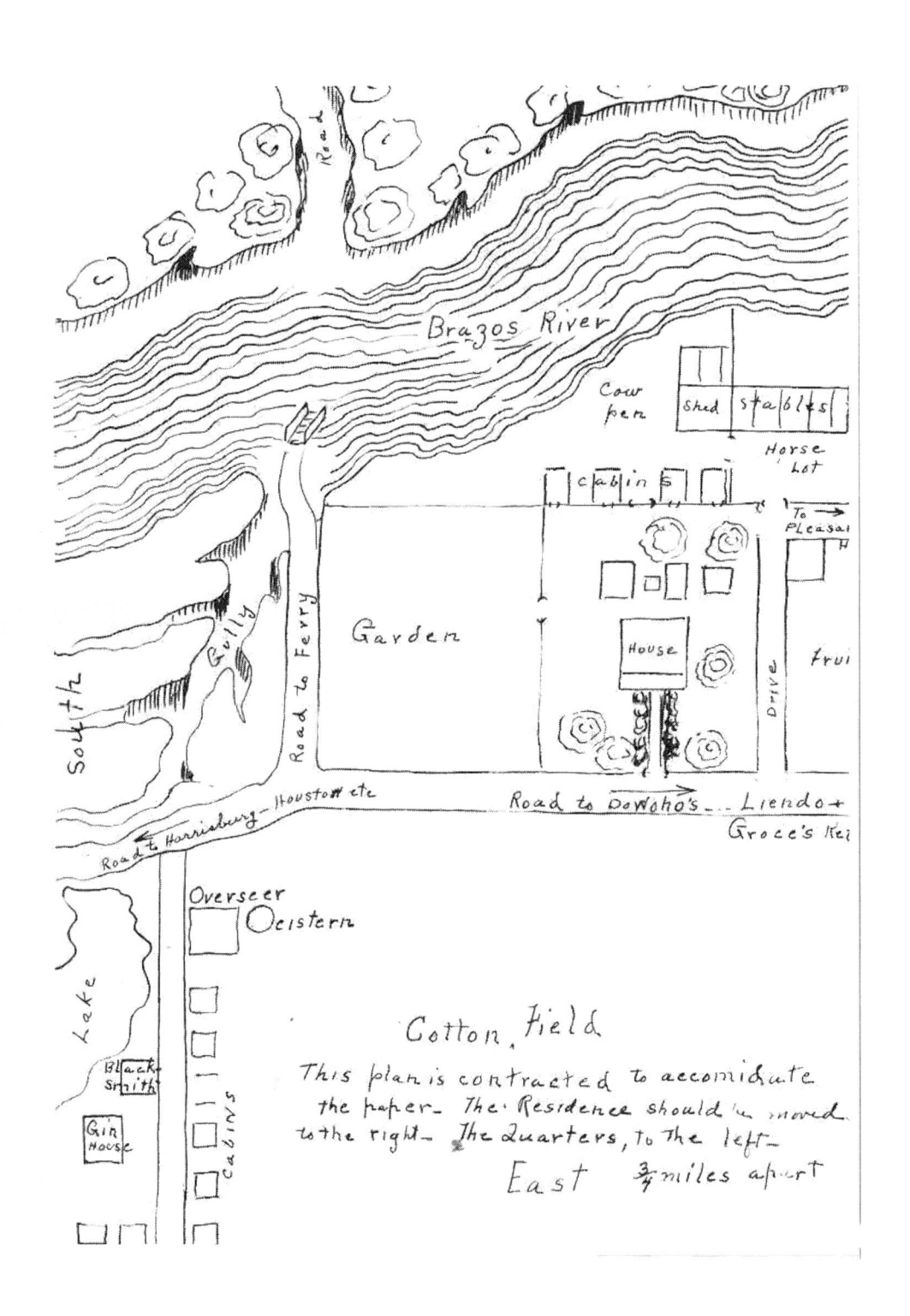

This plan is contracted to accomidate the paper. The Residence should be moved to the right. The Quarters, to the left.

East ¾ miles apart

Bernardo
As described by William W. Groce
Drawn by Sarah Wharton Groce Berlet

Bachelor's Hall 30 x 30 ft

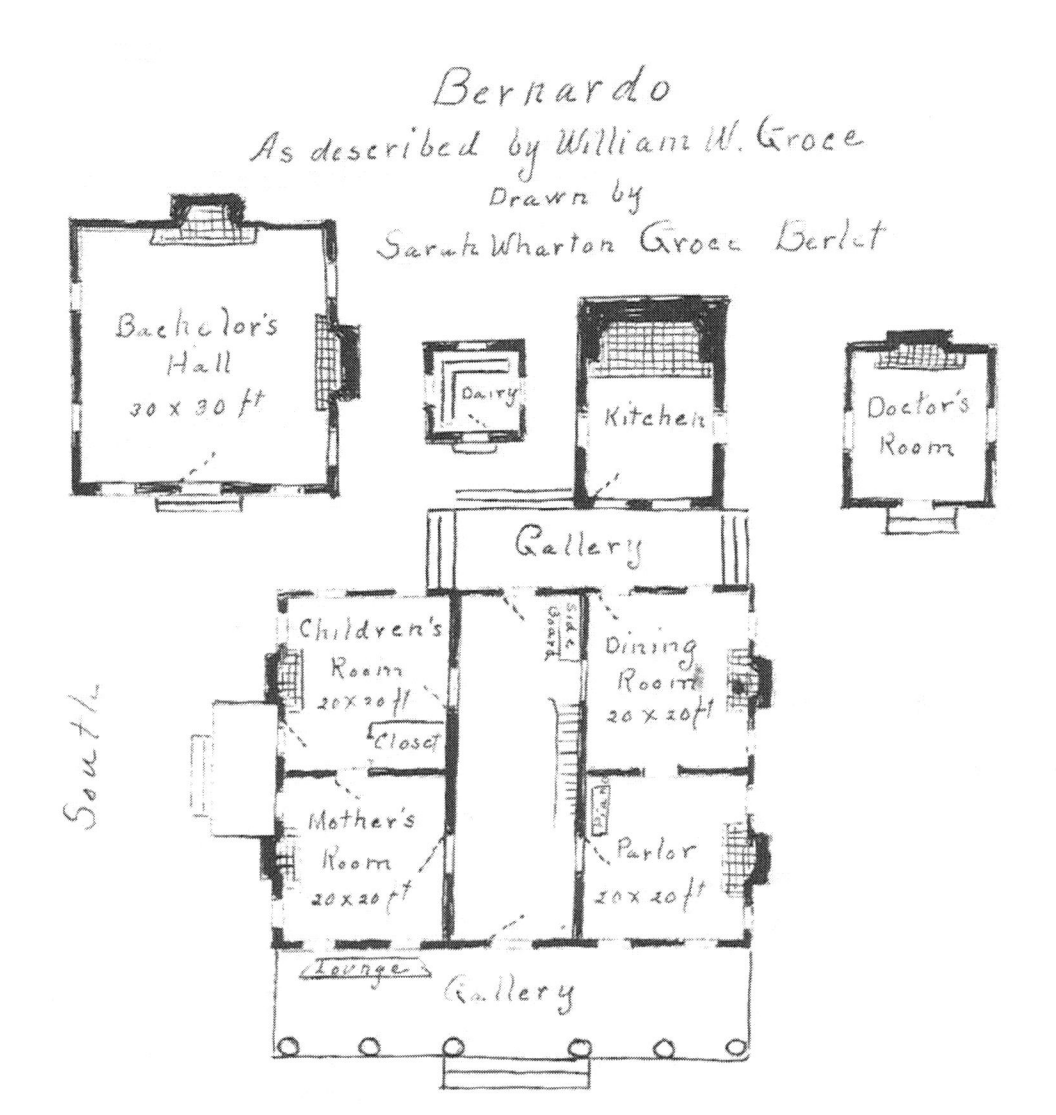

Dairy

Kitchen

Doctor's Room

Gallery

Children's Room 20 x 20 ft

Closet

Dining Room 20 x 20 ft

Mother's Room 20 x 20 ft

Parlor 20 x 20 ft

Lounge

Gallery

South

East

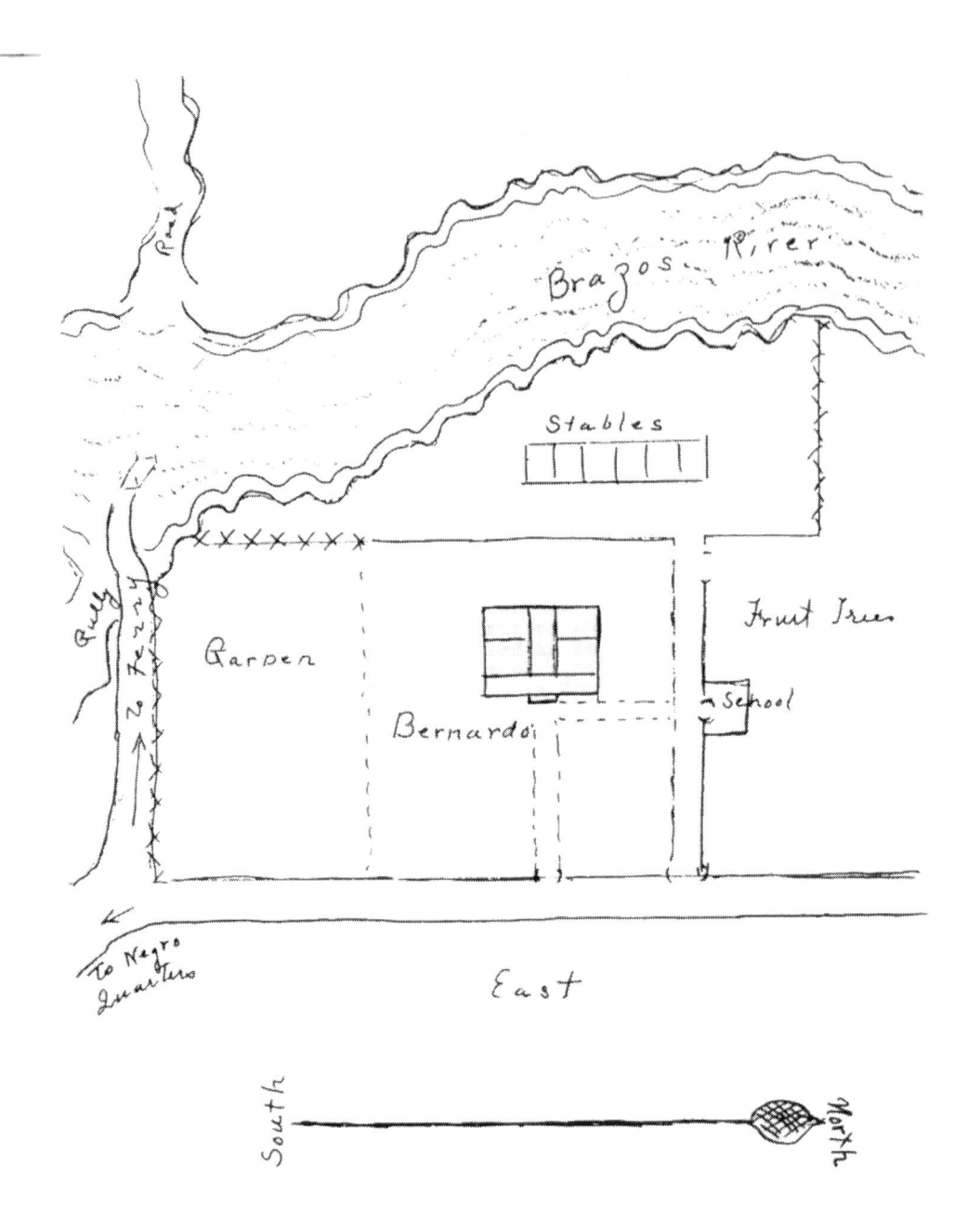

Archaeological evidence suggests that the original main house at Bernardo was of the double dog trot style with two stone fireplaces, and that two more rooms with brick fireplaces were added before William Wharton Groce's birth. One of several sketches of the floor plan of this house by Sara Berlet contains a note which says "modifications and improvements were made in 1838". [20] This is likely the major remodeling in which the two additional rooms were added on the ground floor.

The following image is a photograph of a painting depicting the main house at Bernardo by Mary Groce Mackey, a granddaughter of Leonard Groce. [21] It is titled "Bernardo - 1822" and signed by Mackey, who was born in 1925 and thus never actually saw the house. The basis for her painting was the description of the house as recorded by her aunt Sarah Berlet as well as the artist's rendition sketch shown on the cover of this book as published in a monthly magazine for the cotton farmer in 1936. [22]

Groce and the other American settlers who were the first to arrive in Texas were immediately met with uncertainties concerning their ability to obtain title to the lands they selected. The original colonization agreement had been first made by Moses Austin in 1820 with Antonio Martinez, governor of Spanish Texas. A year later, in August of 1821, Stephen Austin received now-Mexican governor Martinez's permission to act as *empresario* in his deceased father's stead and bring in 300 American settlers. Mexico had achieved her independence from Spain only about a month earlier. Austin's colonists were to receive 320 acres of farming land by running water and 640 acres of pasture land for each head of a family, plus 200 acres for his wife, 100 for each child, and 50 for each slave.

In March Austin went to San Antonio to conduct further discussions with Gov. Martinez. The governor informed Austin that there was considerable turmoil among the leaders of the new Mexican government regarding his colonization plan, and strongly encouraged Austin to personally go to Mexico City to plead his case. Austin responded, leaving San Antonio mid-March and arrived in Mexico City in April. The news of this problem undoubtedly rapidly spread to Austin's colonists, causing great uncertainty about their ability to receive the promised land grants. During the first few months of 1822 Jared Groce received a temporary license from Governor Martinez to settle at the Retreat location. Soon he explored further down the Brazos, found the land at the Coushatta Trace crossing particularly appealing, and redirected his settlement efforts to that location. These lands would later be named Bernardo.

Negotiations were dragging in Mexico City (Austin would remain there until April of the following year), and in July Groce went to San Antonio to secure permanent permission to settle in Texas. It was here, on July 12, 1822, that he signed a letter written for him in Spanish to Governor Martinez requesting a "superior license" or final permission to locate in Texas and survey his lands on the Brazos. In this letter he mentioned his previous temporary license to settle on the Brazos at Retreat, and that he had since reestablished himself further down the river from that location. He also make a similar request on behalf of four other Americans. [23]

The Mexican government appointed Baron de Bastrop as Land Commissioner for Austin's Colony in late 1823. [24] Surveying and granting titles soon began, directed by Stephen Austin. By this time many of the settlers had already claimed their tracts and some had been surveyed, all without specific approval nor title. Of course each settler had selected only prime lands, and the sites were scattered, thus not conforming to Austin's compact settlement pattern. Austin explained to the colonists that "after I returned from Mexico [in 1823] I studied the whole subject with all the attention which my feeble capacity would allow me to devote to one of such importance to settlers" and that rather than running off each tract as selected by the settler, the best plan was to survey systematically the preferred lands on both sides and between the Brazos and Colorado rivers. Thus some of the tracts already "claimed" and surveyed by the settlers were modified by Austin's official surveying of late 1823 and early 1824 before titles were granted. By August of 1824, when Bastrop had to leave the area, nearly all of the Old Three Hundred settlers had their titles. And, due to the more expansive Colonization Law of 1823, these first settlers received several times more land than they had initially expected when they came to Texas.

The original land grant to Jared Groce was authorized on July 29, 1824. [25] Included were 5 leagues on Oyster and Bastrop creeks in modern Brazoria County, 3 leagues east of the Brazos [Retreat, in Grimes County] and 2 leagues east of the Brazos [Bernardo, in Waller County]. The English written field notes to the Bernardo survey refer to a "wild china tree" 12 inches in diameter as one of the boundary markers. [26] Most modern plant taxonomy texts cite the chinaberry tree (*Melia azedarach L.*) as having been introduced to the United States in the mid-1800's as an ornamental. Clearly either the Spaniards or the Coushattas had already introduced this tree to Texas before then, as a mature specimen was found adjacent to an old Spanish / Indian road on the Brazos River in 1824! Additionally, the residence of Gustavus Edwards on the Coushatta Trace at Piney Creek west of the Brazos was known in the 1820's as "China Grove", reinforcing the fact that this species of tree was already established by the time settlers arrived in 1822. The surveyors sketch of the Bernardo tract is shown next. [27]

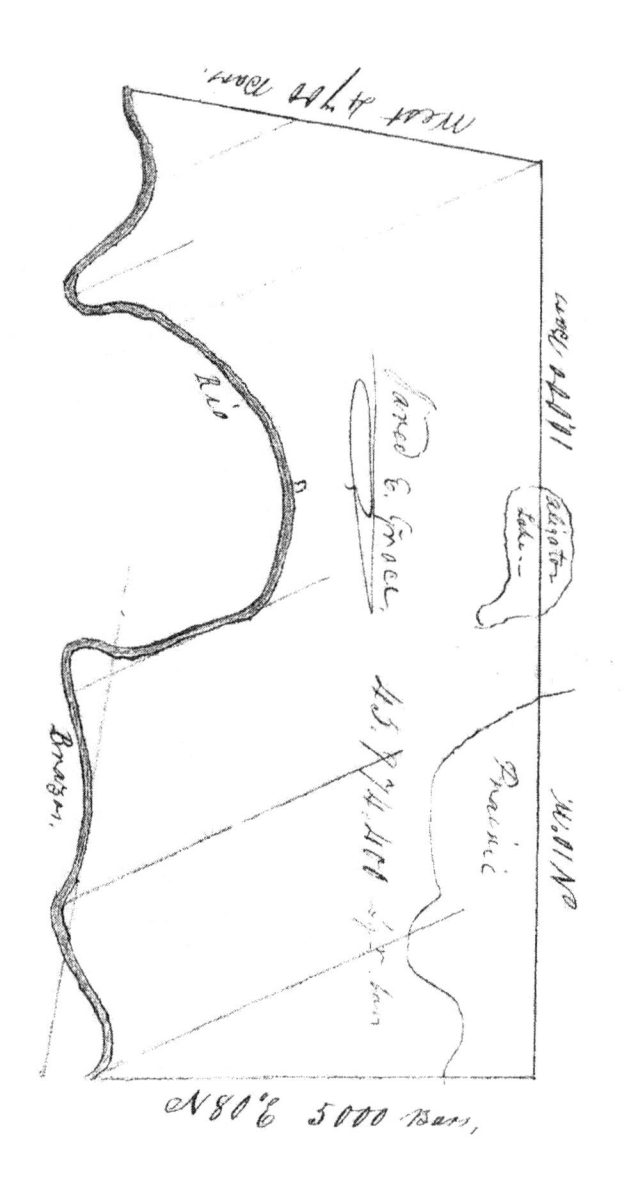

The surveyor calculated the land area of the nominal two league survey survey as 45,974,400 square varas, which equals 8,176 acres or 1.85 leagues using the value of 33 1/3 English inches to the vara as agreed to by Austin and Bastrop at the beginning of official surveying in 1823. Of interest is the unspecified feature on the river appearing as a small square on the east bank below Groce's name which likely indicates the Coushatta crossing, and Alligator Lake as intersected by the

34

eastern boundary. Alligator Lake is the original "Fish Pond" of Pond Creek, today known as Clear Creek. Bernardo Lake is not shown because it was entirely within the survey boundaries.

The grant, written in Spanish on official stamped paper, was written on July 26, 1824 in San Felipe. Groce testified that he was a native of the United States and had moved to Texas with the intention of settling in Austin's Colony. He requested that he be granted "that portion of land which the law allows to colonists, with the understanding that I have close to one hundred slaves and considerable other possessions and that I am prepared to cultivate whatever may be assigned to me, abiding by all the governing laws in all cases, to defend the rights of Independence and the liberty of the Nation." Groce did not sign this document, which was unusual in that most applicants affixed their signature to their request. Perhaps his recurring physical disability prevented use of his hands at this time. Austin added supporting testimony, stating that Groce "is worthy of the favor he requests and can be admitted as a resident of this new colony by virtue of his good qualities and circumstances and well-known application to agriculture, stock raising and industries; and in consideration thereof and of the fact that he has close to one hundred slaves and can be very useful to the new settlement and to the Province on account of the possessions he brought, he can be granted two *haciendas* [ten leagues or 44,280 acres] of land."

The document goes on to "grant and concede unto said Jared E. Groce, his heirs and successors, two *haciendas* of land; one part situated on *Arroyo de Ostiones*, called Oyster Creek in English, on the east side of the Brazos; one part on the east margin of the Brazos at the Co[u]shatta Road Crossing [Bernardo]; and another part at the place where Groce first settled on his arrival, between the La Bahía and Co[u]shatta Roads, east of the Brazos [Retreat], all without facilities of irrigation and only with the use of permanent water ....". Both Bastrop and Austin signed the request. The document further told of interested parties going to survey the tracts, gave the metes and bounds, and indicated that the Oyster Creek tract is five leagues of land, the Bernardo tract is two leagues and the Retreat tract is three leagues. At the end of the document Bastrop and Austin again sign it on the official grant date of July 29, 1824.

The sketch on the next page showing Bernardo and neighboring plantations is from the Sarah Groce Berlet papers in the Brazoria County Museum Library:

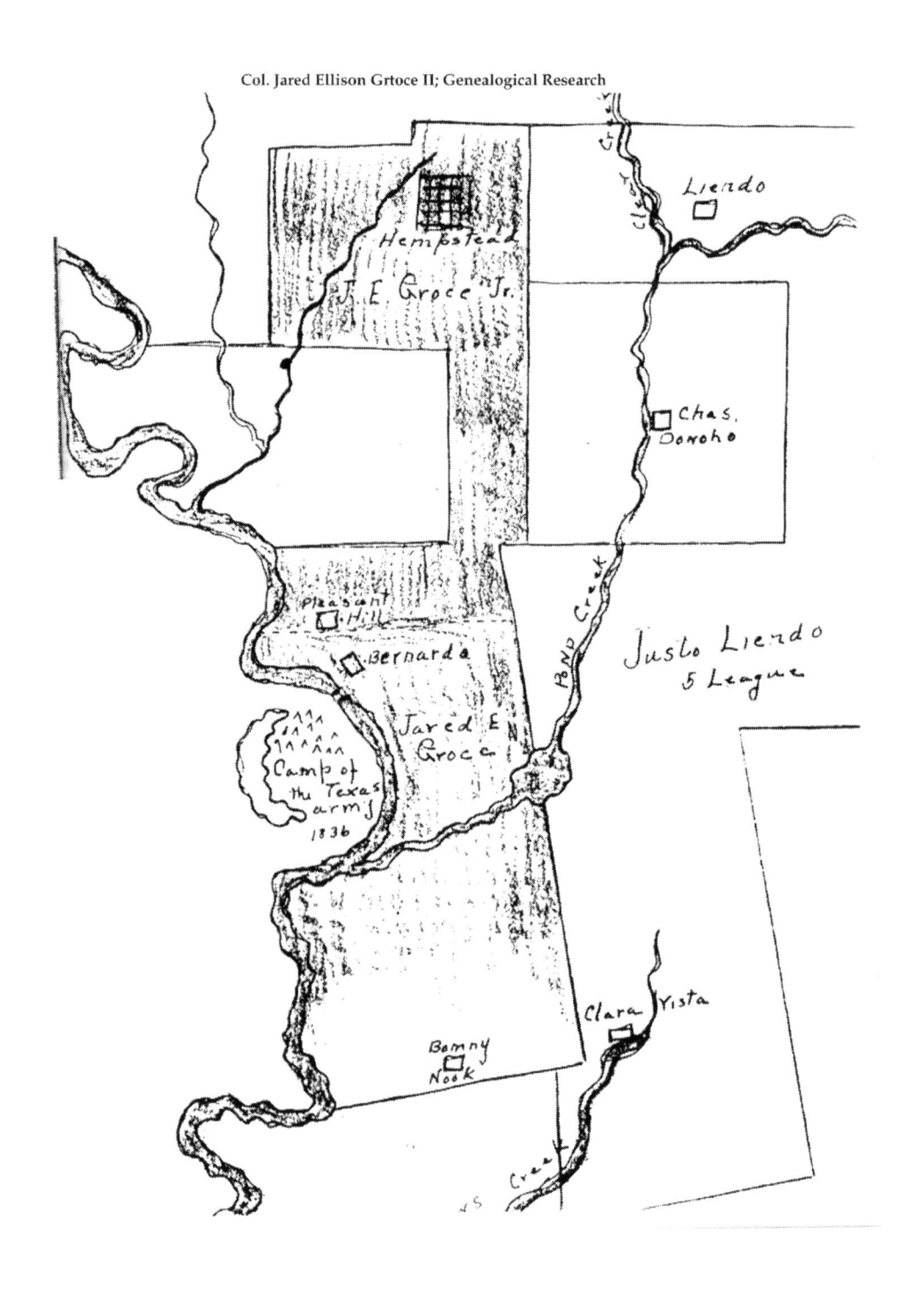

Col. Jared Ellison Grtoce II; Genealogical Research

A doctor was employed to live full-time at Bernardo and care for the slaves and Groce family members. A "Doctor's residence" is shown near the main house on sketches made from family accounts. The first doctor known to have been physically present at Bernardo was Imla Keep of Rapides Parish, Louisiana. Keep was recruited by Groce in July of 1824, perhaps recommended by Samuel M. Williams who was an associate of Keep, or by Thomas Hooper, a Groce acquaintance from Rapides Parish who had married the widow of Alexander Fulton. Keep was hired to become a combination overseer / doctor on one of Groce's nearby plantations. A dispute soon arose in which Groce accused Keep of stealing some $3,000 he had sent with him to buy supplies in New Orleans (see details in Appendix I). If Keep actually served as doctor at Bernardo it was only informally, and only for the first two months of 1824. The first known record of practicing doctors in Austin's Colony are three listed as *Medicos* in the 1826 Census of Austin's Colony; James Phelps of Brazoria County (Orozibo plantation), M.B. Nickols and Francis F. Wells. Phelps arrived in Texas in 1821 already trained as a physician, but his main occupation before 1826 appeared to be farming rather than practicing medicine. It is plausible that the "Doctor's residence" shown on the Berlet sketches of Bernardo represent the first physician's "office" in Austin's Colony.

Jared Groce's economic dominance was characterized in a census of Austin's Colony in 1825. The counted population included 1,347 whites and 443 slaves owned by sixty-nine families. The largest number of slaves, ninety or twenty percent of the total, were owned by Groce. [28]

Indian raids were a recurring problem for most of the early settlers, No raids are known to have occurred at Bernardo, perhaps because of its location beyond the normal Kawankawa territory, or perhaps also because of the large concentration of armed people in this location compared to isolated families of settlers that were the usual targets of Indian raids. Some thefts of cattle and horses did take place in the 1820's on nearby settler's land. Wm. Wharton Groce reported that during the first years of existence, Bernardo was occasionally visited by a tribe of Bedias Indians who lived "within a few miles". They came to beg for corn. When told that they would be given corn in exchange for laboring in the fields, they lost interest and did not often return. A Bedai village had been reported on the headwaters of Spring Creek in 1756. By around 1830 this tribe had removed to the Trinity River and after this no more Indians lived permanently in the Bernardo vicinity.

From its inception in 1821 until 1828 the "government" of Austin's Colony was, except for the laws concerning land distribution, essentially a dictatorship with Stephen F. Austin as sole authority. Texas governor Antonio María Martínez, during Austin's initial visit to San Antonio in 1821, recognized that that he had no means of enforcing laws in a region selected by Austin for his colony that would be a wilderness, uninhabited and without political organization. He made it plain that, for a time, Austin must be responsible for the local government: "You will cause them all [the colonists] to understand that until the government organizes the authority which is to govern them and administer justice, they must be governed by and be subordinate to you." This condition was changed in 1828 with the organization of the *ayuntamiento* of San Felipe de Austin. An *ayuntamiento* was a Mexican form of local government similar to a joint city council - county commissioner's court. After conducting business necessary to organize the new local government and elect officers, the *ayuntamiento* turned its attention to the most pressing issue at hand - improving existing and creating new roads for use by the burgeoning population.

Jared Groce's slaves were ready resources, and were promptly utilized in early 1829 by the new government: "The *ayuntamiento* passed to the consideration of the condition of the road from here [San Felipe] through the woods on the other side of the river, and agreed that all the [nearby] inhabitants of that side of the river ... shall work the said road and put it in condition for carts and wagons. ... It was also agreed that the *Atravesia* [Spanish for "crossing over"] road, known as the Madelana road, which crosses the river at Jared E. Groce's house, shall be worked by the said Groce with his negroes, according to the instructions of the *ayuntamiento*, from his place to the intersection of the road that runs from here to Gustavus Edwards's". Edwards was an early settler who lived on Piney Creek in modern Austin County at the intersection of the Coushatta Trace and the newly laid out road from San Felipe north to Washington. Groce was ordered to maintain the Coushatta Trace from his home to that of Edwards. In lieu of property taxes, public works such as roads were assigned to be built by landowners of means through whose land the roads traversed. [29]

The names of the road that crossed the Brazos at Bernardo were often related to that of Cypress Creek, presumably dating from the days of the Orciquisac road which went from the Brazos to the headwaters of this stream and along it to the San Jacinto. The original Spanish name for modern Cypress Creek was Magdalena, and this was also the Spanish name for the road in the 1800's. Later the American settlers changed the name of the creek from Magdalena to Raccoon, as seen on the following segment of a map made in 1836. [30] During this period the river curve by Bernardo acquired its modern name - Raccoon Bend.

Maps made during the 1840's began to use the name Cypress Bayou for the stream we know today as Cypress Creek.

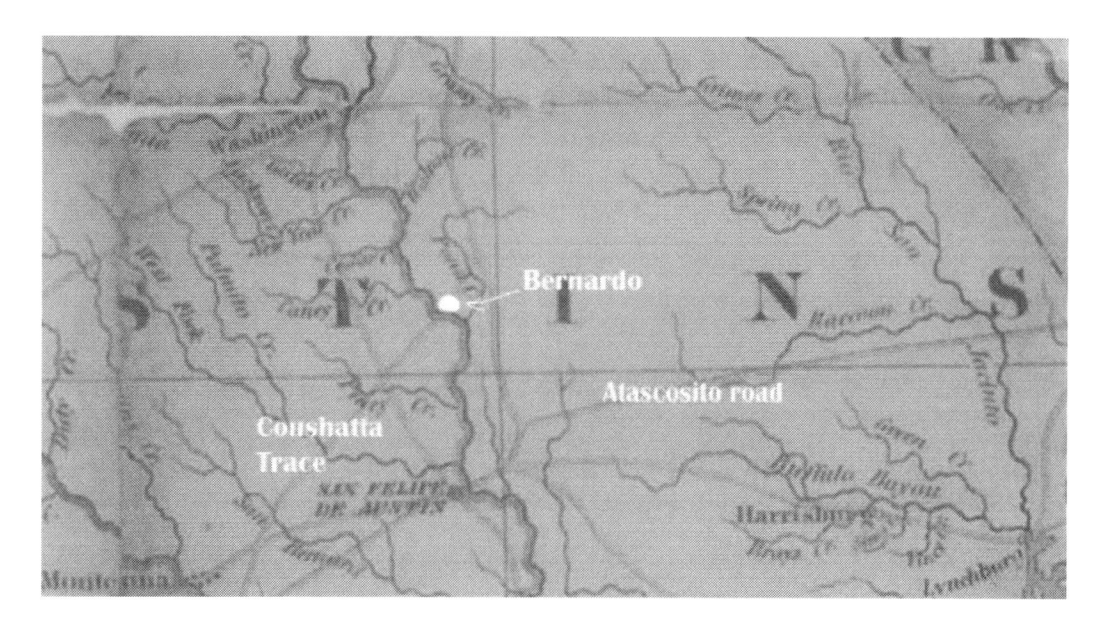

Terms of settlement in Austin's Colony remained fluid during its first two years. Laws were finally passed by the Mexican government in 1823 spelling out the final terms of settlement and the amount of land to be granted to each settler. Arriving heads of household were to receive one league (aka. *sitio*, 4,428 acres) if they planned to raise livestock, or one *labor* (177 acres) if they planned to raise crops - a substantially larger land allotment than initially expected. Most of course stated that they would both farm and ranch, and received a league and a *labor*. Because of his extensive assets in slaves and agricultural equipment, the Mexican government granted Jared Groce II ten leagues of land (two *haciendas*) instead of the usual one league received by the other settlers. Austin later indicated to disgruntled settlers who received "only" one league that "in the case of Groce, the political chief of the Province himself, by whose orders I [am] bound to obey, designated 10 leagues as the smallest he ought to have." [31]

Groce transferred title to 1 1/2 leagues on the south boundary of Oyster Bayou on April 26, 1827 to his wife's nephew William C. White, whenever White might request it. On March 24, 1828, White sold this instrument to Stephen F. Austin for $500, and on March 24, 1828, Groce executed the promised deed to Austin, leaving Groce with 3 1/2 acres on Oyster Bayou. Near this same date Groce acquired White's league across the Brazos from Bernardo, suggesting a trade between the relatives.

A new Jurisdiction of Austin's Colony was created on November 1, 1830. Named Viesca, Its boundary began at the crossing of the Coushatta Trace at Bernardo on the east bank of the Brazos River, then in a direct line to the Atascosito at a point four leagues from the Brazos, along the Atascosito road to the divide between the San Jacinto and Trinity rivers, northward on the divide to the Old San Antonio Road, along the San Antonio Road to the Brazos, and down the meanders of the Brazos to Bernardo. This political boundary dividing Bernardo disappeared with the creation of Austin County in 1837.

Significant changes in the management of Bernardo came in 1831, associated with the marriage of Leonard Groce. Jared II increasingly relied on his two sons to manage the operations of the plantation. Leonard and his new wife lived in the main house at Bernardo, with his father and bother. Jared II decided to begin planning for his retirement. He liquidated all of his real and personal property in a series of documents filed at Bernardo May 24, 1831, citing his wish to "make a public sale of all of my property to the last and highest bidder, with a view to convert the same into money to enable me to adopt a course of life more congruent to my feelings and interest, and also to get clear of the trouble incident to the management of a large number of slaves …". These records list all of his lands and the 117 slaves, by name, owned at that time. Most of the land and slaves were bought by business associate Zeno Philips and Groce's son-in-law William Wharton, but Phillips was apparently only an intermediary as in the same bills of sale all of the slaves became jointly owned by Leonard, Jared Groce III, and Wharton. These legal proceedings may also have been a means for Groce to create a firm title to any of his slaves that he acquired after they were illegally imported from Africa in 1818. The slave listing is given in a later chapter of this book titled "Enslaved African-Americans". [32]

The list of livestock, personal possessions and land sold in this auction, in addition to the 117 slaves listed elsewhere, represent the largest net worth of a single individual in Texas at that time. The livestock included 74 horses and mules, over 600 cattle and some 600 hogs. Over 60,000 acres of land and extensive farming implements were sold.

On the same day Groce sold to Zeno Phillips for $40,000 ("and for the faithful payments of same") 1000 acres on the west side of the Brazos River [in Brazoria County] known as the Sugar Plantation, including all appurtenances, the lower half of a league lying on the San Bernardo River "near the [Damon] mound", one league on the east side of the Brazos granted to John Irons, the Wm. White league across the river from Bernardo, another unnamed league across from Bernardo. Phillips must not have made the required payments because these tracts of land were listed as Groce property in later years. [33]

Zeno Philips, one of the "Old 300" colonists, received a title on July 19,1824, to a *sitio* of land in what is now Brazoria County known as the Waverly Place plantation on the San Bernard River. The census of March 1826 classified him as a farmer and stock raiser, a single man aged between twenty-five and forty, with one servant and twenty-two slaves. In March 1829 Philips and John R. Harris acted as partners in the first purchase contract for cotton in Texas, when they bought about 100 bales from Jared Groce. Philips was a lieutenant colonel in the local militia in August 1829. He married Elizabeth (Eliza) Martha Westall, the widow of James E.B. Austin (Stephen's brother), who had died in 1829. Phillips died in 1835. The 1840 census shows W.G. Hill as administrator of his estate, consisting of 8,706 acres of land and 8 slaves. Hill had married Zeno Phillip's widow in 1836.

An extensive description of Bernardo in 1831 was provided by Wm. Wharton Groce. He indicated that many improvements were made to the main house at Bernardo in preparation for the arrival of Courtney as Leonard's wife and mistress of the household. The exterior was painted a dark red. Brick gateposts replaced wooden ones, and a brick sidewalk from the gate to the house were added. Walls were plastered, new silk damask curtains hung, and the floors in the rooms were covered with new thick piled carpets below and rag carpets above. New rosewood furniture and a piano were placed in the parlor, a mahogany table in the dinning room, and a large sofa on the gallery porch. And old sideboard with decanters of whiskey and wine was placed in the hall near the dining room door. All the furniture was upholstered in black hair. The long dining table was beautifully set with china glass and silver. In warm weather two negro boys stood at each end of the table, and fanned the guests with fans made from the feathers of resident peacocks. [34]

Windows were without screens but flies were not a problem as cooking was done outdoors and many servants kept the house spotless. Beds were four-poster affairs tall enough to require small steps to enter. Mosquito nets were essential during the summer. Mattresses were of cotton or wool; feather beds were added on cold nights. Oil portraits of family members were hung, and a large wall clock was in the hall. Hooked and braided rugs were used. There were no guns or horns hanging on the walls nor animal skins on the floors, as wealthy planters wanted their houses to appear like those in the civilized East and not like a frontier hunter's cabin.

The office was in the yard, and was where Jared and later Leonard received the overseer each morning to issue orders and consult with him about the plantation. The overseer never entered the house as an equal. The hall on the second floor was used as a school room for the younger children, where a governess presided. The older children attended the a little white school in the yard, until old enough to be sent to college. Several cousins, and young friends attended this school too, which was taught by a Mr. Deans, an eminent teacher recruited by Leonard Groce from New York who later opened a school in Galveston. [35]

Shortly after his marriage in 1833, Jared III built a new frame house about a half-mile north of the main house at Bernardo, located about midway between the road and the river. It was painted white with green blinds and had rock chimneys and a full length gallery or porch along the front side. The slave quarters were about one half mile north from the house, and the barns and stables were between the house and quarters. There was a local source of lumber that could have been chosen for Pleasant Hill. James Cummings, two brothers and a sister Rebecca arrived in 1822 and settled on a five league grant straddling the major creek that enterer the Brazos just upstream of San Felipe - known then as Palmetto and later Mill Creek. Cummings established a water powered mill to grind corn into meal and to saw logs for use in house construction. Most of the lumber in early frame structures built in San Felipe came from this source. William B. Travis wooed Rebecca Cummings, who lived at the mill site, for a year and a half before he went to the Alamo in early 1836. They became engaged just before he departed. The Cummings mill closed in late 1836 after James' death.

Pleasant Hill began as a two story frame house as sketched by descendant Mildred Lee Clarke:

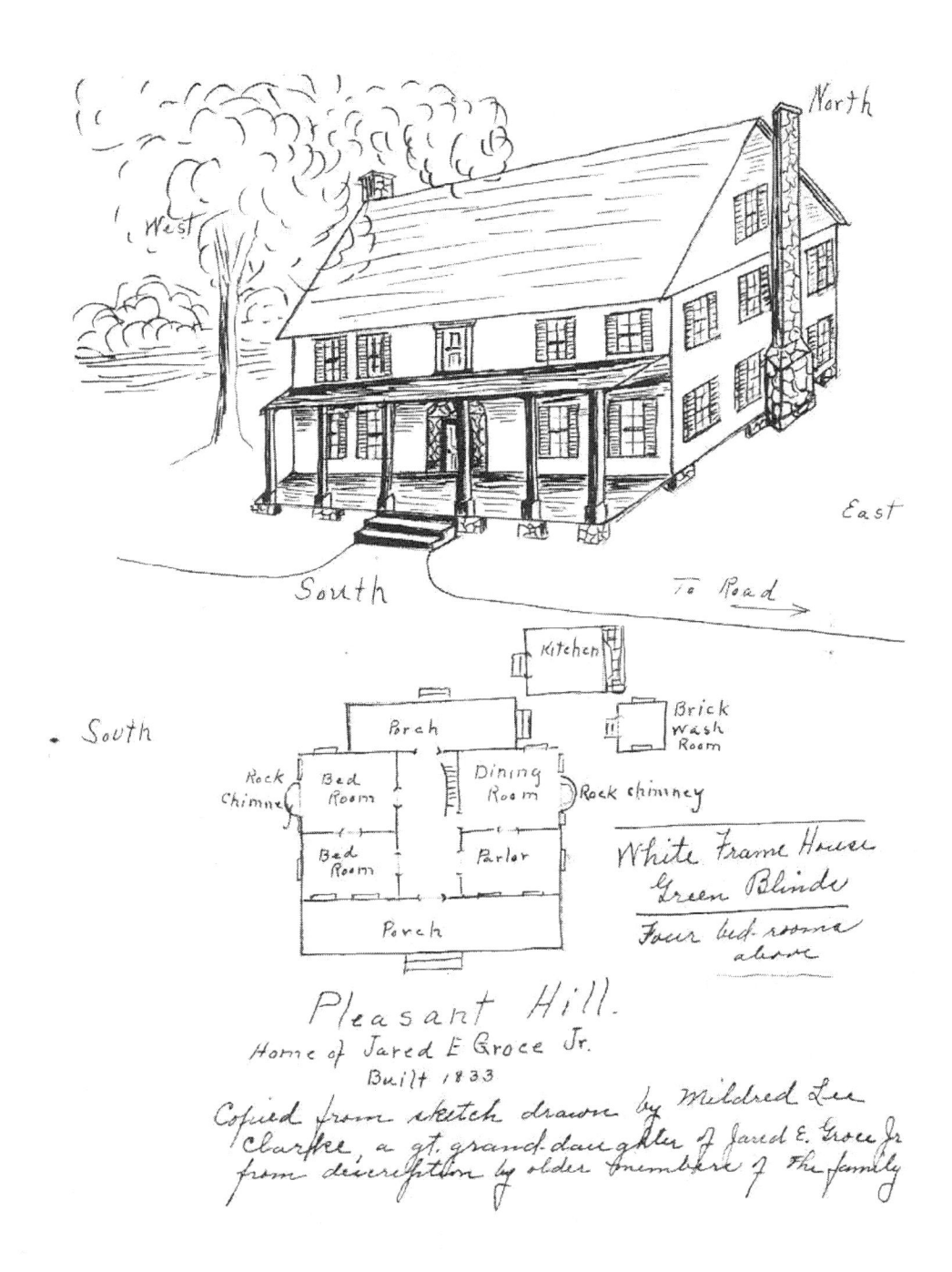

Pleasant Hill.
Home of Jared E Groce Jr.
Built 1833

Copied from sketch drawn by Mildred Lee Clarke, a gt. grand-daughter of Jared E. Groce Jr from description by older members of the family

White Frame House
Green Blinds
Four bed rooms above

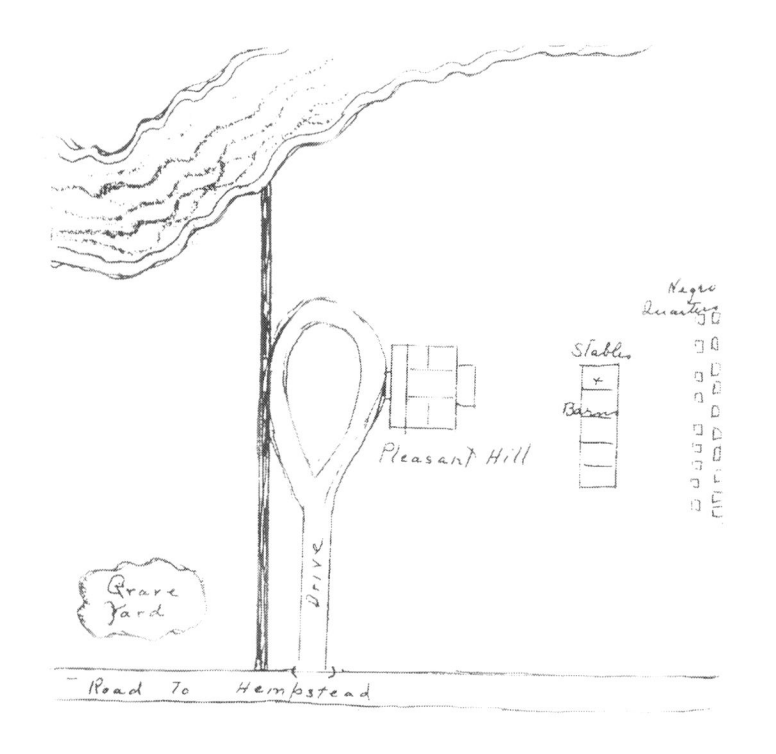

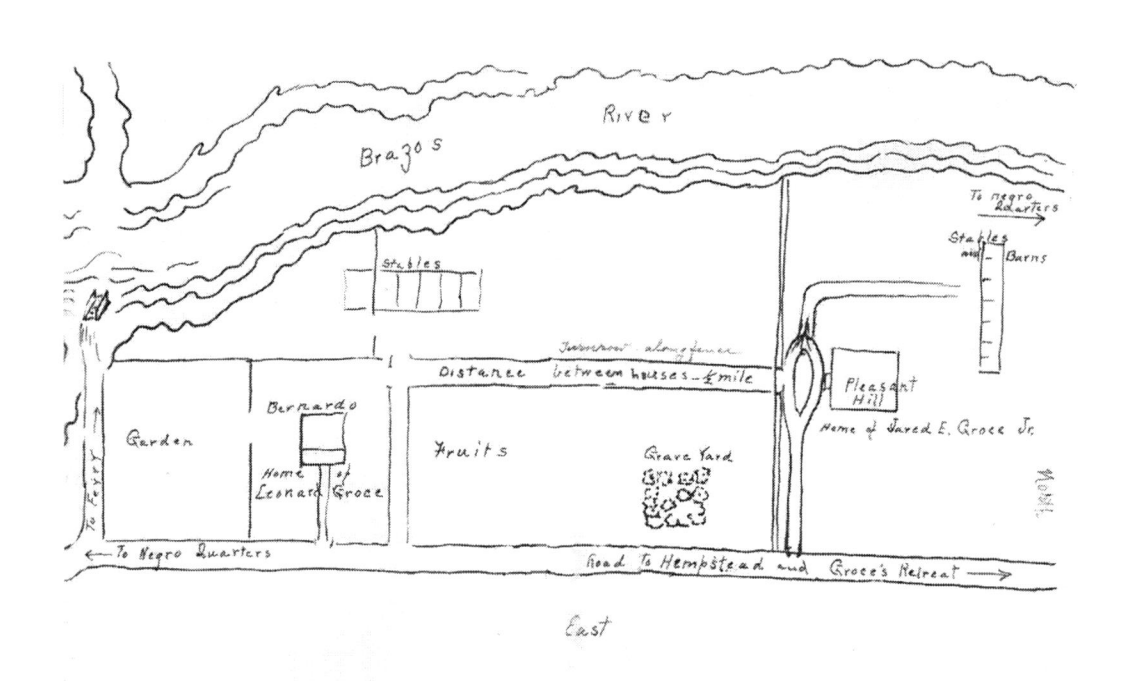

On January 17, 1835, Jared II transferred title to virtually all of his holdings to his two sons, including tracts he had sold to Zeno Phillips in 1831, suggesting that Phillips, who died in 1835, had not been able to pay the $40,000 debt he incurred when he bought the land in 1831. Jared gave the lower quarter of the Smithers league to his sister-in-law Pamelia (Mrs. James) Foster, and 400 acres in the White grant to Julia (Mrs. McLin) Bracey, Pamelia's daughter. [36] Jared III was given six tracts totaling some five leagues or 21,700 acres for which he paid $22,220. [37] Leonard was given six tracts totaling about three and one-half leagues for which he paid $17,300 [38] The Bernardo two league grant was transferred for $15,000 to Leonard and Jared III in joint ownership. [39] Slaves were not included in these 1835 transactions as they had been conveyed in 1831 to his two sons and son-in-law.

Groce had acquired the Smithers league from J. Parker on June 21, 1828, for a horse, saddle and $25. Parker had apparently decided to return to Alabama, he had purchased the league from Joseph Callaghan on June 14, 1825, who had acquired it from Smithers on April 21, 1825. [40] Pamelia Foster later gave her land to daughter Emeline Cochran for the use of her three sons. James Foster was granted 3/4 of a league of land west his wife's land gifted from Groce. The Austin County community known today as Cochran evolved from these early settlers.

This image is of the signature of Jared E. Groce II (Sr.) from the January 17, 1835 deed in which he conveyed the Bernardo Two League grant to his two sons.

Following the death of their father in 1836, Leonard and Jared III consolidated their holdings and decided to operate Bernardo and Pleasant Hill in a partnership. The contract for this partnership was signed on January 27, 1837. It stated that both parties had previously acquired various tracts of land, individually and jointly, from purchases, grants, gifts and inheritance. All of their lands were pooled into joint ownership by this contract with the exception of the Bernardo two leagues, which was intended to be divided between them in a separate instrument. Any proceeds from sales of the jointly-held lands were to be shared equally. The separate instrument mentioned in which they planned to divide Bernardo has not been located. [41]

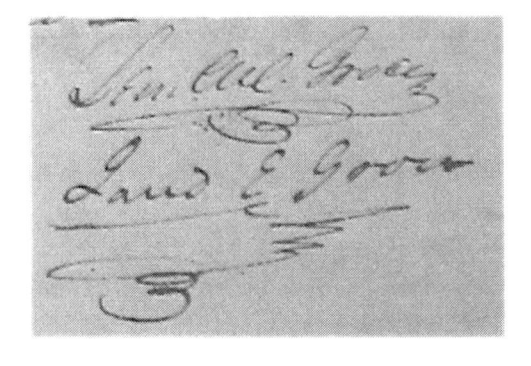

This image is of the signatures of Leonard and Jared Groce on this document.

In October 1836 Columbia became the first capital selected by an elected government of the Republic of Texas. It remained so for three months, during which time the government sought a new site for a temporary capital. The Groce's petitioned for Retreat to be the site selected. The new village of Houston was picked instead, and President Sam Houston ordered the government to move there on December 15, 1836. Houston expressed the notion that if not for his namesake town being on the ballot he would favor Retreat's petition for the new capitol. This was the first of several attempts by the Groce's to either site the state capitol, or a county seat, at a location on their land holdings. [42]

The Telegraph and Texas Register on January 3, 1837 editorialized against the Retreat location. Reasons cited included lack of housing and accommodations, a "remote" inland location hindering communications from coastal hubs, and a view that the climate was unhealthy. The main motive for the newspaper's owners objections was, of course, to keep the government in Columbia, where the newspaper was printed at that time.

In early 1838 the new government of the Republic of Texas formed a committee to solicit offers from citizens for land on which to permanently locate a new state capital. The Groce's and their brother-in-law William Wharton responded along with scores of other Texan landowners. In a letter dated April 5, 1838, they offered to give to the Republic 4,200 acres of land on the Brazos in modern Grimes County, part of and adjacent to the Retreat grant given to their father. [43] Their proposal was not accepted. Had the Retreat site been selected, the capital was to be named San Jacinto. Instead, the committee selected a site near La Grange, Fayette County, in 1838; Congress passed a bill to build the capital there, but Houston vetoed it. The village of Waterloo, soon renamed Austin, was proposed for the capital site by Mirabeau Lamar, Houston's successor as President, and approved on January 19, 1839.

On October 5, 1837 the Groce land holdings were inventoried by the Austin County tax assessor for state and county tax purposes at over 68,000 acres, consisting of 23 tracts of land in five counties. [44] Each of Jared II's original grants, Bernardo and Retreat, are show as one league each, instead of the actual 2 and 3 leagues respectively. A note by the tax assessor dated Aug. 22, 1838 states that these lands were submitted by the Groce's, in addition to their plantation tracts and other taxable property, suggesting the latter may have been counted in another place or treated in a different manner. A tax report of 1838 sets the Groce acreage at 67,152 in five counties, and this did not include the Brazoria County properties previously given Sarah Ann Wharton.

Jared entered into a contract with Alfred Gee on August 25, 1838 for Gee to be the Pleasant Hill overseer for two years, beginning January 1, 1839. Gee was the overseer for Bernardo who came with Jared II to Texas in 1822. Payment was specified as title to 1/4 league of land above the Yegua Creek and near the Brazos, being part of the John W. Mitchell grant, or if not this then $1280 per year. Gee was obligated to manage the negroes "with humanity" and tend to the horses, cattle, hogs and farming utensils of the plantation. On June 25, 1841, Leonard Groce conveyed title to the 1/4 league to Gee. [45]

Jared Groce III died in 1839. His brother Leonard then managed both Bernardo and Pleasant Hill, provided assistance to Jared's widow and her family, and began the process of administering Jared's estate. The Republic of Texas Census of 1840 shows that Leonard W. Groce had 8,120 acres (of presumed improved land since his total was much greater), 66 slaves, 4 saddle horses, 30 horses, 1 4-wheeled carriage and 1 gold watch. As administrator of J.E. Groce III he reported that Jared's estate had 2,200 acres, 63 slaves, 3 saddle horses, 23 horses, 1 carriage. L.W. Groce and Co. had 21,500 titled acres plus 4,428 with title pending and 600 cattle. McLin Bracey was listed with his wife's 400 acres across the river from Bernardo, and by this time operating a ferry over the Brazos with four slaves. [46]

In a document dated October 24, 1841 and executed at San Felipe, Leonard Groce reiterated his marriage pledge of $10,000 to Courtney Ann plus the receipt from her guardian (apparently her father-in-law Thomas Hooper) of $5,500 of her inheritance from her father. He conveying Bernardo and his slaves in a deed of trust to Young Gaines Lipscomb on Courtney's behalf, and specified that upon Courtney's request, Lipscomb was to sell at public auction enough of the property in tis trust to pay her the $15,500 from her marriage, plus interest. Any excess from the sale was to go to their children.

The years 1841 and 1842 were ones of continuing prosperity for Bernardo. The Pleasant Hill house was expanded. A large amount of lumber was purchased on May 18 - 512 (board) feet of ceiling plank, 1,032 feet 1¼" plank, 530 feet "rough edge". The ceiling plank would have been sufficient to cover two rooms of fifteen feet on each side, and the 1¼" plank enough to sheath the exterior wall of a house eight feet high and forty feet on each side. A well was dug in

November in "Mrs. M.A. Groce's yard". The construction continued into the next year as John W. McCloskey was paid $417 by Leonard on behalf of Jared III's estate for 50 1/2 days of work "on Mrs. Mary Ann Groce's house, etc. - gallery, ceilings, etc." This implies that a large covered front porch was either redone or added at that time. Family oral tradition indicates that the Pleasant Hill main house was significantly remodeled at an unknown date after Mary Ann's 1843 marriage to Richard Peebles. Two brick chimneys were added and the house floor plan was expanded, apparently enclosing the gallery built in 1841.

The following sketch by Mildred Lee Clarke shows the house after it had been remodeled:

White frame house with green blinds

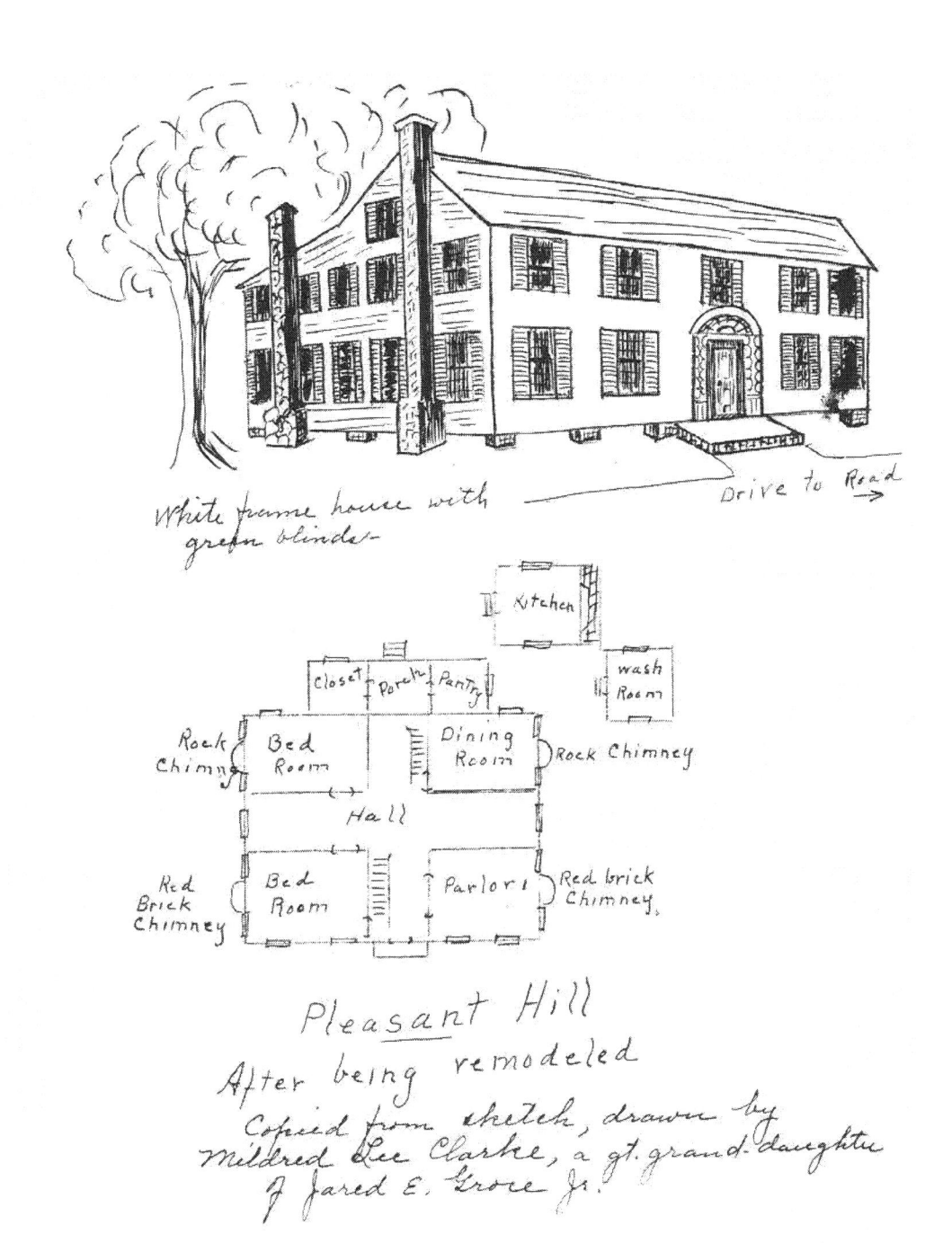

Drive to Road →

Pleasant Hill
After being remodeled
Copied from sketch, drawn by
Mildred Lee Clarke, a gt. grand-daughter
of Jared E. Groce Jr.

Leonard hired Joseph Fessenden to be the overseer of Pleasant Hill during 1843, but ended the contract upon the marriage of Mary Ann Groce and Richard Peebles. In a note dated June 11 of that year Fessenden acknowledged receipt from Leonard of $100 on behalf of Jared's estate as "payment in full for disappointing me in not continuing me as the overseer of said house and plantation of said estate during the present year ." A tombstone for a Joseph Fessenden, age 31, with death date of Dec. 31, 1841 is in the Groce family cemetery at Bernardo. This suggests that the overseer mentioned here in 1843 was the father of the man who died in 1841, and that Fessenden Sr. had been overseer at Bernado or Pleasant Hill in 1841. The tombstone reads: "Joseph Fessenden native of Boston, Mass. who departed Dec. 31, 1841 Aged 31 years 8 months 17 days." A newspaper entry indicates that Fessenden's death occurred in Galveston. The younger Fessenden is known to have fought at the Battle of Velasco. The elder Joseph Fessenden had previously owned land in Brazoria County and had connections to the Groce family, as indicated in a Telegraph and Texas Register issue of November 10, 1838, in which Edwin Waller offered to sell Fessensen's Brazoria County plantation of 1,111 acres. Waller was apparently administrator of the Fessenden estate. John Wharton was given as an alternate contact.

The cemetery at Bernardo had been established in 1836 with the death of Jared Groce II. Leonard and Courtney's daughter Sarah was buried there in 1839, and others followed in the 1840s. When the land containing the cemetery was finally sold out of the family by Leonard Jr. in 1878, the remains of Jared II and Sarah were moved to the city cemetery in Hempstead and placed by the graves of Leonard and Courtney. In addition to Fessendon, two other tombstones are present in the Bernardo cemetery today, with tombstones reading as follows: "In memory of John Powell, son of Gen. P and Eliza L. Cuny. died July 17, 1843 aged 1 year and 7 months" and "In the memory of Mrs. Jane C. Reid, wife of the Rev. H. Reid who died on the 8th of April, 1844. Aged 53 years, 4 months and 25 days". The grave foot-stone has initials JCR. The Cuny's were owners of the neighboring Sunny Side plantation downriver from Bernardo. Jane Cuny Reed was Courtney's cousin. A Houston newspaper article dated April 17 states that Mrs. Reid died at the Leonard Groce residence. Rectangular brick outlines without tombstones of at least two other graves in this cemetery probably indicate the original burial sites for Jared II and Sarah. Another cemetery plot is shown on the Berlet sketches as being on Pleasant Hill property, likely being created for Jared III. His remains were also later relocated to the Hempstead cemetery. The cemetery for the slaves at Bernardo was in woods about 1/4 mile from the main house, according to William Whaton Groce. A likely location would be on the south side of the creek that separates the main house from the negro quarters, close to the Groce family cemetery. African tradition called for cemeteries to be located on the east (sunrise) side of a stream of running water. No stone markers were used for these internments, so nothing remains on the surface today.

The inventory and appraisal of the assets held in the Groce brother's partnership was completed and listed in a memorandum from Leonard in August of 1843. The items owned jointly included carriages, wagons, cattle, hogs, 30 head of sheep, 12 horses, 8 mules, 3 stock horses and 4 colts, 1 double barreled gun, 1 carriage and horses, 1 saddle horse, farming utensils and 2 horses. One hundred head of cattle were sold separately from the partnership to B. Gayle for $400. Leonard kept half of these assets and Peebles paid him $3,500 for the other half.

Following the division of the partnership lands and the closure of the estate of Jared Groce III, Leonard Groce operated Bernardo and then Liendo without significant changes until the end of the Civil War. He did have family members living in the Bernardo house after his move to Liendo in 1853. Similarly, Richard Peebles operated his wife's Pleasant Hill plantation as a separate entity from Bernardo until the late 1850's when Jared III's two children came of age and claimed their half of their father's estate.

Pioneering the Texas Antebellum Economy

Cotton was king in Texas, and Bernardo was the pioneer of this backbone of the plantation-based agricultural economy that defined the state through the Civil War. The first cotton crop in Texas was harvested at Bernardo in 1822, and the first cotton gin in Austin's Colony was built at Bernardo in 1825. Bernardo led the state in this commodity for some forty years. Texas was admitted to the United States in part because of the importance of the cotton economy. The foundation laid by Bernardo ensured that cotton would typify the state's economy until it was displaced by oil production in the 1930's.

It all began on the banks of the Brazos River by Jared Groce and his slaves. Groce was widely acclaimed for his pioneering role in Texas agriculture. The December 13, 1836 edition of the *Telegraph and Texas Register* wrote: "Colonel Groce's extraordinary success in cultivating the growth of cotton, first engendered the surprise of the planters of the West, to whom the highly exuberant quality of Texas land was little known, and then was ancillary by the comparative excellence of the article in its quality, in encouraging the emigration of neighboring planters." An 1853 periodical about Texas agriculture recognized Groce's leadership in planting, shipping and ginning cotton in Texas. [47]

The first cotton contract in Texas was made by Jared Groce. Dated March 27, 1829, the contract stated that John Harris, founder of Harrisburg, would purchase 90 - 100 bales from Groce. Zeno Phillips, a Groce associate, was a partner in the transaction. Final payment from Harris to Groce was set for January 10, 1830. A cotton trade magazine mentioned this transaction, stating that the cotton was hauled by ox cart from Bernardo to Harrisburg, then shipped down Buffalo Bayou and on to New Orleans. The article indicated that this was the "first shipment of cotton ever made from Texas." The author probably meant first water-born shipment, as Groce had hauled cotton overland to Mexico since 1822. The article also noted that the total production of cotton in Texas that year was 331 bales, indicating that Bernardo accounted for around one-third of the entire state's cotton production at that time. [48]

One observer wrote: "It took the spirit of a sturdy pioneer, and a few pounds of cotton seed and a small amount of corn to establish one of the greatest agricultural districts in the world. By this act, Colonel Groce started the foundation for the backbone of Texas prosperity, as well as founding the power that would sway the destiny of Texas. He therefore won for himself the title of Father of Texas Agriculture." [49]

Several historians have indicated that the importance of Texas as a cotton growing region attracted the attention of Great Britain and made possible the diplomacy which resulted ultimately in annexation of Texas to the United States. Anson Jones, in his farewell address as the last president of the Republic of Texas, stated: "We have sent the best possible negotiator to England, a ship loaded with cotton, the staple production of the country. It was cotton that attracted the interest of England, and it was England's interest that alarmed the United States and brought about the move toward annexation." As the largest cotton producer in Texas for over two decades, the Groce family through the labor of their slaves played an important role in the evolution of Texas from a Spanish colony to a Republic to one of the United States.

Slave labor was essential for the large scale production of cotton, and Jared Groce owned more slaves by far than anyone else in Texas for at least a decade. From its inception in 1821 until Texas became an independent republic in 1836, the issue of slave ownership was under constant challenge from the

Mexican government. The colonization law passed in 1821 prohibited importation of slaves into Spanish territory; all slaves brought to the area were to be freed. This edict was put on hold when Mexico achieved her independence from Spain that same year. Groce had a vested interest in this institution, and most of his political involvement dealt with protecting his right to own slaves. The leaders of Austin's Colony were involved early in trying to clarify the Mexican laws pertinent to slavery in Texas. The first Mexican Colonization law was passed on January 3, 1823. Article 30 of the law inferred permission for immigrants to bring slaves into Texas, but declared children of slaves born there would be freed at the age of fourteen. Domestic slave trading was prohibited. Austin knew that there was sentiment in Mexico to ban slavery; he also knew that continuation of the institution was of prime importance to his settlers. He called a general meeting of the colonists which was held at San Felipe on June 5, 1824. There, Jared Groce and three other prominent settlers presented two petitions to the Mexican government. The first requested permission to raise tobacco, an activity that was carefully regulated by permit and taxed, and only accorded to a few select jurisdictions. The second petition concerned slavery issues, reflecting the recently-enacted Mexican emancipation law. They stated that they had brought slaves to the new colony in accord with the colonization law that existed at that time, and that these slaves had all been born in the United States and were intended for use as personal servants and in agricultural activities, without which the settlers would be unable to clear and plant fields and begin agricultural operations. They specifically requested that the first 300 settlers of Austin's Colony be exempted from the emancipation law and that their existing slaves and their descendants be slaves for the rest of their lives. If their request were not granted they requested permission to remove their slaves from the country. [50] The document was sent to the provincial delegation in San Antonio; it is not known if it was forwarded to Mexico City. There was no known response.

    The settlers efforts were not entirely successful. A law proposed on July 13, 1824 prohibited 'commerce and traffic' in slaves, and declared slaves introduced after this decree be immediately freed. This proposal either did not pass or was soon reconsidered. The state colonization law of March 24, 1825 merely said that the introduction of slaves would be regulated by existing laws. Austin obtained a legal interpretation that the state law was too indefinite to mean anything and that the Federal Act of July 13, 1824, could reasonably be interpreted as only prohibiting the slave trade, causing Austin to conclude that colonists could bring slaves in for their own use. In August, 1825, Austin sent an elaborate memorial to the governor proposing that until 1840 colonists, but no others, should be allowed to bring slaves to Texas for their own use and property and that the grandchildren of slaves so introduced would be freed at age 25 for males and 15 for females; still no response from the governor. In July, 1826 Austin was informed that work on the state constitution was approaching a critical stage. He heard that emancipation would pass but colonists could sidestep it by liberating their slaves and then getting a contract with them to be indentured servants until they could repay their owner for their initial cost - essentially meaning for life. The situation regarding slavery in Texas continued to remain in flux.

Introduction of additional slaves into the state of Coahuila y Tejas was outlawed by the legislature in 1827, and freedom was granted at birth to all children born to a slave. The new laws also stated that any slave brought into Texas should be freed within six months. Clearly, Groce and his fellow slaveowners were threatened by the Mexican laws dealing with slavery, but the importance of the agricultural economy in Texas prevented the Mexican government from taking immediate action to enforce their slavery laws.

Mexico again passed an edict in 1829 outlawing slavery, but granted Texas a one-year exemption based on an appeal from the governor of Coahuila y Tejas. Mexican president Anastasio Bustamante finally ordered all slaves to be freed in 1830, causing many Texas settlers to convert their slaves into indentured servants for life to circumvent this law. No records have been found indicating that Jared Groce took this action. This tactic was outlawed in 1832 by prohibiting worker contracts from lasting more than ten years. Despite these laws, the numbers of slaves in Texas increased from about 440 counted in an 1825 census of Austin's Colony to an estimated 5,000 in 1836. Some of this was by natural increase; some 500 slaves were estimated to have been illegally imported in the first half of the 1830's. Although certainly not the only issue, one of the key drivers which led Texans to revolt from Mexico and form an independent republic was to maintain the ability to continue slave ownership and the associated cotton economy. [51]

The large number of slaves on Bernardo plantation represented an opportunity to institute efficient practices not available to the smaller slaveholder. One, begun in 1824 by Groce, involved hiring a full-time doctor to be resident on the plantation to provide health care for the slaves, and for the Groce family as well - another first in Texas. With a market value greater than that of his land, Groce's slaves represented his largest asset and he, as any good businessman would, saw to it that these assets were maintained in their most productive state. Groce's treatment of his slaves was lauded by many as exemplary. The motivation to maximize long term productivity of his human chattel surely also influenced his management practices. He also was the first to employ a community kitchen and dining hall for food preparation and distribution. This practice spread to other large plantations in Texas as they developed in the 1850's.[52]

Family accounts of the first few years of cotton marketing from Bernardo indicate that the raw cotton was taken to market in the interior of Mexico on mules. Two packs of about 75 pounds each were hung over the sides of each mule and a sack of feed was strapped on top. One man could manage 10 to 12 mules, and the caravans could travel up to 20 miles each day. Jared Groce led each caravan but because of his crippled arms much of his work, including guarding the money, was left to his manservant [initially Edom, later Kelly]. Few problems were reported with Indians along the way; some believed they were afraid of the black-skinned men. The entire expedition was heavily armed. Once the cotton was sold the group would return to Bernardo with packs laden with coffee, tea, clothing and other goods not able to be produced on the plantation, and sacks full of Mexican silver dollars received in payment. Two documents support this family story of early cotton sales. Groce was in La Bahia on October 19, 1822, where he paid duty to export goods to the villages along the Rio Grande. He was in San Antonio on November 30, 1823, where he obtained an import permit to bring seven crates of clothing into Texas y Coahuila. Presumably both of these documents relate to his trips into Mexican territory below Texas to market his cotton and bring back goods needed at Bernardo. [53]

The money accumulated over the early years at Bernardo as most necessities were self-produced and there were few luxuries readily available. Buying more land was also relatively cheap. Within a few years flatboats called *chalans* by the Mexicans were built at Bernardo and used to transport cotton bales down to Velasco where they were sold and loaded on sailing ships for New Orleans and other ports, ultimately to textile mills in the United States and Europe. These same flatboats were occasionally used to transport travelers across the river at Bernardo, leading to the term "Groce's Ferry". By the 1840's steamboats were engaged on the Brazos to provide transportation for passengers, cotton and other goods - when river levels permitted.

Some of the cotton crop remained at Bernardo and was spun and woven by the women for use in clothing, called "homespun". Sheep were raised and the wool was also used to make clothing, bed covers, and for knitting socks and sacks. Hogs by the hundreds were raised for their meat and lard. Groce family members also imported fancier cloth and clothing from New Orleans for their use.

Leonard Groce completed is education in 1824 and returned to Texas, arriving at Bernardo at Christmas of that year. Accompanying them on this trip was his future step-father-in-law Thomas Hooper and Dr. Imla Keep of Alexandria, who Groce had arranged to be his first plantation doctor. Leonard soon took over most of the business duties previously performed by his father, whose health continued to deteriorate. In May of 1825 Leonard returned to New Orleans and arranged for a horse-powered cotton gin to be shipped to Velasco and then freighted to Bernardo, where it was installed near the slave quarters. This is reported by most historians as the first cotton gin in Texas, although a more technically correct statement would be that it was the first gin in Austin's Colony. The Groce gin was apparently second in Texas by a few months to one built by John Cartwright in the "Redlands" region of East Texas. John Cartwright moved to Texas in 1819 and settled in the Ayish district. He was an expert ironsmith and carpenter and built a cotton gin and mill that was in operation by 1825, the same year in which the Groce gin was established. [54]

The census of Austin's Colony enumerated in March of 1826 lists Jared E. Groce as a widower, age 25-40, occupation farmer & stockraiser, 4 children (2 males ages 7-16, 1 male age 16-25, 1 female age 7-16) 5 servants (*journleros*) and 90 slaves for a total of 100 persons, with a note stating that he had constructed a cotton gin (*tiene fabricado un Molino p. despepitas Algodon sobre los Brazos*). At the time of this census Leonard was the only Groce child in Texas. Jared listed his other three children even though they were living outside of the state at that time. Stephen Austin's brother John E.B. Austin was also listed in this census as having a cotton gin. It apparently was constructed several months after the one at Bernardo. The total population of Austin's colony in this census was 1,800. [55]

Detailed descriptions of Bernado and its resources were recorded in three diaries of Mexican officials participating in an inspection of Texas in 1828. Although the Adams-Onis Treaty of 1819 between Spain and The United States established the lower Sabine River as the international boundary, the treaty had not yet been ratified by either country, and the longitudinal line running north from the Sabine to the Red River had not been surveyed on the ground. Mexican General Manuel de Mier y Teran was appointed a Boundary Commissioner to lead the inspection. In addition to investigating the boundary, Teran was charged with compiling a report on the natural resources of Texas, its agricultural, mining and commercial possibilities and the history of its settlements. Accompanying Teran and each writing diaries were draftsman Jose Maria Sanchez y Tapia and botanist/zoologist Jean Louis Berlandier. [56,57,58] On the outward-bound leg of their trip they passed up the east bank of the Brazos from San Felipe and camped at the intersection of the older Orcoquisac road, naming it *Campo de la Virgen* and noting that this was the place that the road (the Orcoquisac) entered from Bernardo, which they knew as the *Camino de la Magdalena.* Berlandier described the very muddy conditions on the road up from San Felipe, and noted the extensive display of wildflowers on the prairies.

Sanchez was dispatched to Bernardo to obtain food for themselves and corn for their horses. After setting up camp under some nearby trees they were met by Leonard Groce, Wm. Wharton and a doctor whom he described as a *pedant*, or person obsessively concerned with making a show of his learning. They were served bacon, milk and coffee and briefly conversed with difficulty through signs and written Latin phrases. Jared Groce was very ill, upstairs in his bed and unable to move. They secured the corn but were not given food "because there is nothing but bacon or ham (for the family) to live on". The cotton operation at Bernardo was noted, indicating that 116 slaves had made a large harvest, and that two pieces of machinery were used to treat the raw cotton - the gin to remove seeds and a comb also used to grind corn. More than 40,000 pounds of cotton had been loaded on flatboats for shipment to New Orleans. Sanchez was offended that his men were not offered lodging in the house, and later became even more irate when called back to the house "for the sole purpose of showing us the wealth of Mr. Groce and to introduce us to three dogs called Ferdinand VII, Napoleon, and Bolívar. The indignation at seeing the name of the Colombian Liberator thus debased, caused Mr. Chovell to utter a violent oath which the impudent fellows did not understand or did not wish to understand." Sanchez's description of Groce's operations were quite unflattering, reflecting his indignation at not being offered food and shelter: "Groce … came from the United States … in order to avoid paying the numerous creditors that were suing him. He brought with him 116 slaves of both sexes, most of which were stolen [referring to the illegally imported and obtained Africans]. These wretched slaves are the ones who cultivate the corn and cotton, both of which yield copious crops to Mr. Groce. Likewise, he has a great many head of cattle, innumerable hogs, and a great number of horses; but he is a man who does not enjoy his wealth because he is extremely stingy, and he treats his slaves with great cruelty."

On his return trip to Mexico, Teran came down the Coushatta trace arriving at Bernardo on January 29, 1829 and staying three days before his party was barged across the river by Groce's slaves to allow him to continue his journey. Teran described Groce as the richest property owner in the Austin colony, with "105 slaves of all ages and both sexes, whose estimated worth is 100 thousand pesos. His main crop is cotton, of which 600 *fardos* [bales] of 500 pounds each already ginned. He transports it by *chalán* [flatboat] to the mouth of the river, where he ships it for storage in New Orleans, and it is sent to England. The owner says that the price of 20 reales per [*arroba]* that it commands now in that city is low, and he hopes that it will rise to one real per pound." Teran further described in detail the cotton gin at Bernardo. [59] He also noted that extensive cultivated fields stretched along the banks of the river were enclosed by wooden fences, and that more raw land was being prepared for cultivation as evidenced by hundreds of girdled trees posing "a melancholy appearance because of the enormous skeletons of trees that still stand." [60] Teran's views on Groce's lifestyle and treatment of his slaves were decidedly different than those expressed by Sanchez: "This settler, despite the vast assets he enjoys, seeks very few comforts for himself. He lives with a young man, his son, and another white man [overseer Alfred Gee] among the huts of the Negroes, whom he seems to treat well. At least, nowhere around the house are there cages, prisons, or any other sign that force is necessary to subordinate so many slaves. Furthermore, the latter appear well dressed, with indications that they enjoy abundance. The annual cost of each negro is set by Gros at 75 pesos, the cost of all the different items with which he feeds and clothes them. He obtains the food from the land itself, where he grows corn and raises many cattle and hogs. On this evening the black men and women gathered at the master's house and held a dance, which I am told is customary every Saturday night. ..."

Jared Groce II attended the First General Convention of 1832 as a representative of Viesca, a short-lived political subdivision that had been created in 1830 and included part of Bernardo. Jared chaired the committee which produced a resolution that was adopted recommending import tariff exemptions be extended for three years on farming implements & machinery, clothing, household and kitchen furniture, tobacco, ammunition, medicines and stationery, explaining that they were the principle imports needed in Texas. Wm. Wharton also wrote an opinion against the Mexican act of 1830 barring new immigration. Jared was a delegate to the Second General Convention of 1833 that drafted a constitution for state of Texas within the Mexican federation. Wm. Wharton was President of this Convention and Jared & Leonard signed it. [61]

After the town of Houston was established in 1836, Leonard Groce transported his baled cotton to the Buffalo Bayou docks on wagons pulled by oxen, where it was shipped to Galveston and then New Orleans and beyond, bringing an estimated annual income of $80,000 - 100,000 dollars.

The cattle brands used on the Bernardo and Pleasant Hill herds were recorded in the Austin County courthouse in Bellville:

May 8, 1848 to L. W. Groce

**May 27, 1858 to J.E. Groce IV
used by his father since 1836**

April 30, 1859 to Wm. W. Groce

Many details regarding the cotton enterprise at Bernardo from 1839 to 1843 are preserved in the Austin County Probate records as court documents related to the estate dispute between Leonard Groce and Mary Ann Peebles, widow of his deceased brother Jared who had married Richard Peebles. A few of the hundreds of these documents provide good insight into the commercial activities of a large Texas planter in the 1840's.

For example, one document dated July 3, 1839 indicates that 105 1/2 bales of cotton were sold by Leonard Groce and delivered at New Orleans from Mobile on the steamboat *Isabella*. Net proceeds after shipping, handling and sales expenses was $3,261, nearly enough money to buy a league of land in Texas at this time.

Another similar document shows cotton sales activities in 1838 and 1839 with McKinney & Williams Co. of Galveston in which 232 bales selling for $7,092 was shipped to Baltimore, Liverpool and New York. Groce had a running account with McKinney & Williams and other merchants through which money was added from the sale of cotton and groceries, clothing, farming supplies and cash were drawn as needed, often through friends or agents authorized to access the account. Merchants served many of the functions of banks, which were rare or nonexistent at that time. There are several other similar documents in the probate files.

A contract dated December 28, 1840 between Leonard and Futrel Hall detailed the terms of Hall's employment as Pleasant Hill overseer for $750 for the year 1841. It specifically stated that Hall was to "make as good crops of cotton, corn etc. as is possible to be done, treat the negros with humanity but to see that they all obey him strictly as overseer - he is also to attend and keep the plantation in god repair - attend to the stock - & to the negros strictly when sick". Hall "shall have no control over the household servants of Mrs. Groce [Mary Ann], whilst in her yard or on business, but if they or any others be in the quarters at undue hours they must be treated as others - and the said Hall is to use every exertion to get on in peace, & is to furnish Mrs. Groce with a cook or washerwoman. In case of sickness - of hers - or any other servants she may want to supply the deficit by sickness."

McLin Bracey was paid $100 in April of 1840 for "carrying down their two crops from Groce's Landing to Columbia - one half being for the estate". The mode of transportation was presumably by flatboat, although Bracey also preformed wagon hauling services. Leonard received his license to practice law in 1840 but he continued to spend most of his time running the plantation. The Austin County tax records for 1840 show Leonard and Jared Groce III owning 129 slaves.

From the earliest days Bernardo was noted for its agricultural prowess. The *Telegraph and Texas Register* of May 4, 1842 reported that cotton on Bernardo was ready to bloom, that Leonard Groce and a neighbor had over 500 acres in cultivation, and that the prospects seemed good for an excellent crop.

The rivalry among planters as to who could grow the best cotton and be the first to get it to market in the new season was also mentioned. [62]

Later in 1842 Houston merchants award silver and gold cups to Leonard for the first twenty bales of cotton delivered that year. This article appeared in the *Telegraph and Texas Register* on August 17, 1842.

For the Telegraph.
HOUSTON, AUG. 12th 1842.

LEONARD W. GROCE, ESQ., Austin County.

Sir:—It affords us much gratification to acknowledge that we received from your plantation, on the 29th day of July, the first five bales of cotton being the growth of the present year, and the requisite number entitling you to the Silver Cup, according to the original resolutions offered by the merchants of this city; as also the first twenty bales thereafter, which we acknowledge having received in full on the 6th day of August, consequently, entitling you to the Gold Cup offered in the same resolutions — Both of which premiums we do cheerfully and cordially award, as a satisfactory evidence that the merchants of this city will, at all times, be ready and willing to support the most noble exertions of the Planter, and the merited reward of Industry.

In the name of the merchants, I beg most Respectfully to subscribe myself
Your ob't. serv't.
A. S RUTHVEN,
Chairman of the meeting.

This silver cup was held by Barbara Groce of Hempstead, daughter of Dr. Leonard W. Groce, in the 1930's. It is shown in this photo resting on top of the Groce family bible from 1752. The gold cup, if ever actually awarded, has apparently disappeared.

The cotton business continued to flourish. A letter dated April 17, 1843 from J.W. Robinson in Houston described how eight bales were sold for $149.76 and credited to the Estate, while seven bales belonging to Leonard were yet unsold and that he would wait until Leonard came to Houston to do so. Robinson also mentioned that "there is not a keg of Buckwheat in this town" and "there has not any Goods arrived for you from New Orleans." It is apparent that Robinson was acting as an agent for Groce during this time, and that Houston was beginning to rival Galveston as a center of commerce in the region. James W. Robinson had been in Mexico in December, 1842, having been captured by Adrian Woll in September in San Antonio. Here he opened a clandestine correspondence with Santa Anna and reached an agreement by which he [Robinson] was to be released from prison and allowed to return to Texas with terms for a truce between Texas and Mexico. Robinson reached Galveston on March 27, 1843, conferred with Sam Houston at Washington, conveyed Santa's Anna's proposal and may have been responsible for the ensuing armistice between Texas and Mexico that lasted for several months. The timing indicates Robinson may have stopped by Bernardo on the way from Washington to Houston and was charged by Leonard to attend to his cotton sales there. [63]

The letter from Robinson included this drawing of the mark that was used by Leonard to identify his cotton bales as they traveled from Bernardo to their ultimate market destination.

Receipts from B. and D.G. Mills dated October 2, 1843 shows that twelve bales of cotton from the Jared Groce estate were shipped from Houston on the *Touladons*, and eight bales were shipped from New Orleans on the *Ocean Queen*. The Mills acted as agents for Groce. The mark used to identify cotton from the estate contains the initials "GE", presumably for Groce Estate.

Richard Peebles followed the lead of the Groces in advancing agricultural technology in Texas. An article appearing in the Houston Telegraph datelined Hempstead, March 27, 1858, reported on experimental sheep at Pleasant Hill. The reporter mentioned that Peebles had recently imported two Merino sheep from New York at $300 for the pair. Shorn fleece weighed about 20 pounds each, valued at 55 cents per pound. By comparison, Texas "improved" sheep at that time, when shorn, had fleece weighing about four pounds, worth 25 cents per pound. Peebles was noted as having a flock of 400 - 500 head at that time, and that Leonard Groce and several others nearby had bought some of the Merino variety for their plantations. [64]

The Texas population rapidly expanded each decade between 1840 and 1860. Many more plantations were formed, and several other men acquired land and slaves in numbers that rivaled Bernardo and Pleasant Hill. The relative importance of the original Bernardo plantation had been diluted, but was still of consequence. Slaveholders like Leonard Groce, Richard Peebles and others dominated the state's economy, controlled its politics and occupied the top rung on the social ladder. The Particular Institution influenced and shaped virtually every aspect of life in the Lone Star state. In 1850, slaveholding households constituted 30% of the total in Texas, and owned 72% of the property. Similar statistics were recorded in 1860. [65] Jared Groce at Bernardo had shown the way, and others had responded. Texas, east of San Antonio, felt like one of the states of the Old South from which it had been derived.

Twilight at Bernardo After the Civil War

Life changed markedly for both the freed slaves and their owners after the war. One of the first orders of business by the Union occupiers was to pardon former Confederate supporters. On December 8, 1865, President Andrew Johnson issued a Warrant of Pardon for Leonard Groce. Leonard swore his amnesty oath and accepted the pardon in a April 6, 1866 letter to secretary of State Wm. H. Seward. Another key governmental role following the war was to assist the freed slaves in finding ways to independently support themselves. Economic disruptions of the Civil War followed by loss of slave labor and the tangible value they had represented depressed property values made the immediate post-war days very financially difficult for former plantation owners. An 1873 article aptly described the situation, indicating that land values had dropped from one-fifth to one-tenth of their market value before the war. An estimated half of the agricultural labor had been provided by slaves and "that labor was at first almost lost to the country by emancipation". Because of the labor shortage most of the cotton, sugar and corn fields previously planted fell fallow. The resulting loss of income forced thousands of planters to offer improved lands that had been worth fifty dollars an acre for sale at $5 to $10 per acre. The article did note that in recent years much of the idled land was being placed back into cultivation by the flood of new immigrants coming from Europe to Texas. Former slaves also began increasingly to return to the fields: "There has also been considerably improvement in the labor of the freed men, who as a general rule, perform far more labor than after the first emancipation. Having been disappointed in their first anticipation of support by the government, they have been compelled by necessity to labor enough for their own support." [66]

Hempstead became a hotbed of unrest in the county during the reconstruction period. The *Texas Countryman* newspaper, which had been moved from Bellville to Hempstead by its publisher John Osterhout, reported twenty-five incidents of violence in the two-year period after 1867. Nearly one-half of these involved both races, and thirteen whites and eight blacks lost their lives. Two Federal soldiers were slain after attacking a Negro woman. An ordinance in 1867 outlawed carrying deadly weapons but was not successful in stemming the violence. An out-of-town writer referred to Hempstead as the "fighting village of Texas" and the town became known by its neighbors in Bellville as "Six-Shooter Junction". Blacks could carry firearms and would gather in groups, where they were sometimes aided by the Union Loyal League, a political organization comprised largely of blacks and led by reconstructionist whites in the area. The Ku Klux Klan and similar secret groups organized in early 1868 and terrorized freedmen. Nearby, a riot was started by Federal troops in Millican and a fire in Brenham was attributed to arson. By 1868 Hempstead residents were thankful for the occupying Union military presence as a protecting force from local violence. In March 1868 Osterhout wrote commending the "gentlemanly" and "fair dealing" soldiers for limiting their authority to enforcement of municipal laws, and that the imminent departure of the Union officers prompted "universal regret".

Leonard Groce tried to continue operating his plantation by contracting with the former slaves to work for him, but this was ultimately not successful. The Freedman's Bureau was instrumental in encouraging such contracts. [67] A contract between Groce and Lewis Baker indicated the nature of these agreements, which basically paid the former slaves to do the work they had previously done, as directed by the planter. Dated January 13, 1866, the contract specified that Lewis and his wife Francis will work for the year 1866, "obeying all reasonable orders of said Groce or his wife". For the year's work Baker was to receive $100 and 20 acres of land, plus room, board, two suits of clothes and any needed medicine. Baker was also allowed time off without pay to "hunt his children" who had apparently been separated from the family. The Baker's were allowed free time on Saturday afternoons, unless Groce needed them to work and allowed extra pay. The Bakers agreed to "bind themselves to be polite and respectful to said Groce and family", and if any problems arose between the contracting parties the local Freedman's Bureau would mediate. On the back of this contract Leonard Groce wrote "Settled in full… Perfectly satisfactory. LWG January 7, 1867." Lewis and Francis Baker were former slaves at Bernardo; the names Lewis and Fanny appear in the Groce probate inventories. Frances was the daughter of Courtney's maid Harriet and was the seamstress at Bernardo. [68] One would guess that this couple was chosen so that Frances could continue to make dresses for Courtney.

One example of the financial loss incurred by Leonard Groce as a result of the emancipation of the slaves is given by the statement of his property rendition in 1865. The Tax Assessor / Collector for Austin County certified that in April of 1865 Groce reported 135 negroes at $500 each for a net worth in slaves alone of $67,500; in 1866 this element was zero. The value of his land also plummeted after the war and most was not cultivated. Thousands of owners offered their best lands for any price they could get; Leonard Groce suffered the same fate. Sarah Berlet wrote: "His generosity had gone beyond his hospitality. Among his remaining papers are notes of loans of thousands of dollars, which were never repaid because of a law passed by the Government which repudiated all debts made prior to the war." The tax appraisal confirms that Leonard Groce had not significantly dispersed his slaves before or during the war.

Leonard Groce decided to move to Brazil in 1866 in hopes of escaping the financial turmoil surrounding him in Texas, and to be able to continue to live the life to which he had become accustomed in another country that still allowed slavery. Other planters he knew were doing likewise. He moved his family to Galveston while he wound up his affairs. A letter dated March 6, 1866 by attorney Marcus Fulton Mott of Galveston (Courtney's nephew) records that he purchased on his aunt's behalf Lots 4 and 5 in Block 327 in Galveston for $1,800 in gold. Of this total $1,500 was "from her individual money" with the remainder coming from Leonard; the lots became Courtney's "separate and individual" property. Leonard continued to divest himself of his properties whenever he could find a willing buyer. On October 6, 1866, Leonard and Courtney sold the portion of Bernardo they still owned, less the half-acre containing the family cemetery, to Wm. Ahrenbeck for $25,000 to be paid to Courtney in American gold. It seems that Jared IV preferred not to act as trustee for Courtney as had been arranged the year before because the trustee for this sale to Ahrenback was Marcus Mott. Ahrenbeck was not able to come up with the gold down payment required for the sale, and ownership of Bernardo reverted to Leonard. During this time a headline in the Galveston newspaper stated that Brazil had abolished slavery, so Groce informed his family they they would not move to South America after all. On December 15, 1866, he and Courtney sold Liendo to Dr. P.S. Clarke and wife Barbara Mackall Groce for $2,000 down and two notes of $4,000 each, all to be paid in American gold. In a diary entry for January 9, 1867, Leonard stated: "W. Harris has at last secured for us a shelter at $5,000 - my wife and I have signed papers. Place is well improved and on Market St. [in Galveston]".

The regard that his fellow Texans had for Leonard Groce is seen in a letter of recommendation written for him in anticipation of his moving to Brazil: "Austin 27 Oct. 1866 The undersigned members of the Legislature & citizens of Texas learning that Col. L. W. Groce of Austin County contemplates leaving Texas - While we regret his determination we are pleased in testifying to his high tone & honorable bearing that during a residence of over forty years we are sure not one act of his could be pointed to which does not do him credit. No man has ministered more to the comfort of others than Col. G and his family. No man has more cheerfully discharged all the duties of a good citizen than Col.

Groce & he and his noble lady & children will be a valuable acquisition to any people or country." This letter is signed by 28 senators. Gov. Wm. Throckmorton added a supporting note.

Sarah Berlet indicated that her grandfather Leonard Groce was a meticulous keeper of diaries. She indicated that most of these had been lost or destroyed but one remained - a single, leather-bound memorandum book with entries from November 24, 1866 to January 31, 1867. The majority of the entries chronicle visits with family and friends, routine and local activities, including cordial relations with Mary Ann and Richard Peebles and their children. Later entries mention sales of furniture and other assets, preparing to move, closing the sale of Liendo to Clarke, moving to Galveston and buying a house. On December 16 he wrote: "I am sad at the idea of giving up my old home, with all its comforts, but such is the fate of War." The last entry in this diary (Jan. 31, 1867), mentions selling $1,925 worth of corn and livestock to Clarke. Leonard was forced into bankruptcy in 1868. A notice from U.S. Marshal's Office in Galveston April 18, 1868, declared him bankrupt and ended with a list of 22 creditors being owed a total of $36,448. Among the creditors were Courtney A. Groce ($9,787.48), Jared E. Groce IV ($9,000), and E.M. Pease, then Governor of Texas ($7,500 for "purchase of negroes").

Leonard and Courtney had a close personal connection to John Harris, son of the family from whom Harrisburg and Harris County derived their names. They named their youngest son John Harris Groce. On June 17, 1854, Leonard gave 100 acres out of the Liendo tract to David Harris. In 1866 when Leonard was in Galveston contemplating moving to Brazil, William Harris found a house for the Groces to buy on Market St. in Galveston.

Like so many other planters after the war, Dr. Clarke was not able to turn a profit raising cotton with hired labor, and he defaulted on the payments for Liendo. Groce repossessed the property on October 23, 1868 and his family moved back to their former home.

The following images of Courtney and Leonard Groce were taken late in 1868. [69]

Courtney Ann Fulton Groce died on July 14, 1869 while visiting her sister Eliza Mott in Galveston. Leonard Waller Groce died on August 29, 1873. Wm. Wharton and Kate Groce had moved from their Bonny Nook plantation, on the southern margin of the original Bernardo, to Houston in 1873, then to Eagle Island at the urging of his aunt Sarah. Sarah Ann Groce Wharton died on February 11, 1878, ending the second generation of the Groce dynasty in Texas. She left her home and 200 acres, all that was left of Eagle Island, to her nephew William Wharton Groce.

Leonard Waller Groce Jr. graduated from a medical college in New Orleans and practiced as a physician in Bryan for a few years. He returned home and married Florence Herndon, a niece of Mary Ann Peebles, on December 23, 1873. Following his father's death in that year, Leonard Jr. conveyed the 1,350 acre Bernardo Plantation to trustees Thomas M. Jack and James B. Stubbs on July 14, 1874. A month earlier (June 24, 1874) Leonard Jr. filed a promissory note for $4,000 in gold to his younger brother Ellison K. Groce in exchange for Ellison's interest "in our deceased Mother's estate", to become due when Ellison "became of lawful age". The Bernardo of this date, reduced considerably in size from its original two leagues, was bounded on the north and northeast by the Hempstead tract of R.R. Peebles and Mary Ann Peebles, on the west by the Brazos River, and on the south and east by Fish Pond Creek "save and except the one half acre including the family Graveyard of L.W. Groce Sr.". The deed of trust to Jack and Stubbs served as collateral for the loan. [70]

Leonard Jr. built a new frame house at Bernardo at a location about half way between the original house site and the slave quarters. A frame house showing in a 1939 aerial photograph between the graveyard and the modern highway is probably that built by Leonard, Jr. He lived there until 1878 when he moved to Hempstead. Three of his children were born at Bernardo; two more in Hempstead. Tragically, his son Leonard III was executed in Nicaragua as a young adult. On March 7, 1878 Thomas M. Jack, trustee, conveyed Bernardo to Ellison K. Groce. [71] Ellison and Marcus Groce were living with their brother Leonard Jr. in 1880.

Leonard Jr. reacquired Bernardo between March 7, 1878 and June 9, 1880 because on that latter date he sold two tracts of inherited land including Bernardo to Mrs. B.M. (Barbara Mackall) Herndon, his wife's sister. The price for Bernardo's remaining 1,350 acres was $3,000. The document states that Bernardo at that time was encumbered by a deed of trust to E.B. Wilson of Austin County to secure payment of a $680 loan to Leonard Jr. [72]

By 1882 the identity of the original Bernardo plantation was lost. Peebles owned the north portion until around 1900 when it was sold into smaller tracts. A.S. Fletcher of Hempstead owned a few acres in 1931, including the site of the old house and the graveyard. A colony of Italian immigrants owned another portion. Some portions of the southern portion had become split into smaller lots and other portions merged with lands owned by a man named Steele. A state prison was established on Steele's lands and the convicts were used as laborers on the farm. In 1903 Steele's estate sold his holdings to R.W. Hardy of Beaumont. An article in the January 8, 1903 issue of the Houston Post indicated that the 3,000 acres known as Bernardo was sold for $32,000, and was "one of the finest tracts of land in Waller County."

Rufus Hardy eventually acquired large agricultural land holdings four and a half miles south of Hempstead on FM 1887 which contained the eastern portion of the original Bernardo survey. Hardy drained Fish Pond Lake in 1928 by plowing a trench from the lake or marsh at that time due west across FM 1887 to the edge of Lake Bernardo, then southwest to the river. This action also effectively drained what was left of Lake Bernardo. [73]

Sarah Berlet wrote two letters describing visits to Bernardo in the 1931 and 1936. In them she mentioned that only a few pieces of sandstone, a large brick cistern which was falling down, and some crepe myrtles remained at the home site. At the slave quarters only the base of the old gin was visible. They visited the family cemetery and noted several tombstones including one for Philip Cuny, his wife and child, dated 1819, and speculated that their remains had been brought from Louisiana. Based on the death date, this Philip Cuny would have been an uncle of the Philip Cuny who owned neighboring Sunny Side plantation. All the tombstones and remains of the Groce family buried at Bernardo had been removed to the Hempstead City Cemetery after the Civil War. Berlet noted in 1936 that Bernardo Lake had been recently drained into the Brazos.

Sarah Berlet also wrote in the 1930's that after the death of Richard Peebles, his unmarried daughter Sammie (Sarah Marshal) inherited Pleasant Hill, and "It burned to the ground many years ago." Peebles died in 1893, suggesting that the Pleasant Hill house burned around 1900. Berlet also indicated that on the night of the great 1900 hurricane the house of her aunt burned to the ground, destroying many old letters, silver and antiques, and several old portraits including the only oil painting of Sarah Ann Groce Wharton. Fortunately, William Wharton Groce had sent the portraits of William and John Wharton to the state capitol several years before.

Bernardo and Pleasant Hill had been part of Austin County since the initial organization of Texas counties in 1837. Residents of the northern portion of Austin County east of the Brazos, led by Richard Peebles, Edwin Waller, Jr., and Leonard Groce, had petitioned the state legislature several times to separate from Austin and form a new county. In one unsuccessful petition in 1869, the new county was to be named Peebles. An earlier one proposed Groce as the county name. In 1873, during the last political gasps of Reconstruction, the Radical Republicans, of which Peebles was an active member, were rapidly losing control of the state government. In an effort to gerrymander votes in their favor, the Radical Republicans proposed to create a new county from Austin County lands east of the Brazos, to be named Hempstead County. The Democratic Party, consisting largely of pre-Civil War residents of Texas and rising to power in Texas, initially opposed the bill because they did not want to confer the name of a Unionist, Hempstead, on a new Texas county, and because the original bill included the eastern part of Harris County in the new county. The bill was amended to eliminate the portion from Harris County and to name the new county Waller, after Edwin Waller who had signed both the Declaration of Independence in 1836 and the new state constitution in 1846. Although strongly opposed by most residents of Austin County, political gerrymandering triumphed and the bill passed both houses of the legislature.

Governor Edmund J. Davis, a Radical Republican, opposed the bill on the grounds that the two counties would be too small - in fact less than the constitutional size requirement for a county - and thus would be hard pressed to raise sufficient taxes for courthouses, jails and other public necessities. He also opined that the majority of county residents would not support the division, and requested that the matter be put forth for a public vote. Despite his sound advice, party politics prevailed and the legislature failed to reconsider the bill. Governor Davis did not sign the bill but it became law instead on April 28, 1873, by his lack of a veto. [74]

In 1951 a visitor to Bernardo noted that an immense brick cistern, located near the overseer's house, was in a very good state of repair, except it was no longer utilized for the storage of water and was filled with scrap iron and other recent junk. [75]

An aerial photograph taken on October 1, 1939 clearly shows the outline of Lake Bernardo prior to being drained eleven years earlier. [76]

Book Two: The People

Three Generations of Groces

The first Jared Ellison Gross was born in or near Newcastle, England around 1740. Their Gros ancestors were originally Frenchmen who according to family lore came to England with William the Conquerer. The middle name Ellison refers to ancestors by that surname who were landed gentry in England. Jared immigrated with his brother to America before 1764, settling first in Surry County, North Carolina, then moving to Halifax County, Virginia before 1774. He married Sarah Shepperd of North Carolina in 1767. They had nine children of record.[77] During the American Revolutionary War Jared was sympathetic to and fought with the colonists. His brother remained a Royalist, prompting Jared to change the spelling of his last name to Groce to distinguish himself from his brother. Deed records in Virginia spell the surname both ways - Gross and Groce. Jared, Sarah and family moved to Lincoln County, Georgia in 1789. In 1798 he became a delegate to the convention that drafted the Georgia constitution. Jared I made his will December 3, 1803, and died within the next two months.

Jared Ellison Groce II was born in Halifax County, Virginia, on October 12, 1782. Around age ten he made his first dollar building a chicken coop for Col. Leonard James Waller, a neighbor and his future father-in-law. In 1802 he moved to South Carolina where he acquired valuable property and on August 29, 1804, married Mary Ann Waller of Virginia, a relative of future Texas pioneer Edwin Waller. The Waller family had aristocratic roots tracing back to Nottingham, England in 1183. Col. John Waller came to the United States in 1686 where he was a sheriff in Virginia and a delegate to the House of Burgesses. They were related to three presidents, James Madison, Zachery Taylor and John Tyler. The Wallers were Baptists in South Carolina.

Jared and his new wife soon moved to Lincoln County, Georgia, where he purchased a large estate. Here he expanded his holdings and acquired his first fortune. A few years later Mary Ann's family relocated from Spottsylvania County, Virginia to Abbeville District, South Carolina, just across the Savannah River from the Groce plantation. Four children born in Georgia to Jared II and Mary Ann Groce lived to adulthood - Leonard Waller (born September 27, 1806) , Edwin (born 1808) , Sarah Ann (born February 12, 1810) and Jared Ellison III (born September 5, 1811). The birthplaces of Sarah Ann and Jared III are recorded as being in South Carolina because, as was the custom of that time,

Mary Ann went to stay at her mother's home nearby when it came time for their children to be born. Leonard was born in Lincoln County, Georgia, likely before the arrival of his Waller grandparents. Mary Ann Waller Groce died on November 7, 1813, at the Cambridge, South Carolina home of her parents.

Jared II then married Annie Waller, sister of his first wife, in November of 1814 and moved to Alabama where he invested in cheap timber lands on the Alabama River about 20 miles upriver from Mobile. Here he put his slaves to work clearing the fields for cotton and corn. Several Indian raids by Choctaw Chief Red Eagle (Billy Weatherford) threatened the security in the area, resulting in the fortification of the Groce home which became known as Fort Groce after its builder. Jared and Annie had two children who died young. [78] Augmenting his agricultural activities, Jared II directed his slaves to harvest timber on his lands and he made another fortune within a few years.

While in Alabama in 1817, Groce received title to nine slaves, apparently in settlement for a debt relating back to his residence in South Carolina. The 1817 deed record expressly says these were "only mortgaged". Some apparently did not make the move with Groce to Texas; others did. [79] During the winter of 1817 - 1818 Jared Groce II acquired 47 enslaved Africans who had just been illegally imported to the United States. With this new labor force he was able to expand his operations in Alabama. Presumably some of this group came with Groce to Texas in 1822. [80] During this same period Groce also sold lands in South Carolina, as recorded in the same deed records of Edgefield County, S.C. [81] Groce's youngest child died in Alabama, followed shortly by the death of his second wife in 1818.

About this time, Groce invested in a mercantile business in Augusta owned by Andrew Erwin. The partnership was named A. Erwin, Groce and Co. and included Erwin's son James. Erwin had similar interests in mercantile businesses in other towns but apparently Jared Groce's interest was only in the Augusta enterprise. The business failed during the Financial Panic of 1819, the first financial crisis in the United States. In a letter to S.F. Austin in 1825, Erwin indicated that he had lost $100,000 and Groce $50,000. Erwin entered bankruptcy and did not emerge from this state until 1825. Around 1820 Groce and the two Erwins reached an agreement with their Augusta creditor Col. McKinni to settle the affairs of the business. Each of the three debtors made a note payable to McKinni for $10,000, with each being jointly and severally liable for the total $30,000 debt. Groce agreed to pay his in two equal installments of $5,000 each after the next two cotton crops were harvested. He apparently did not pay these debts on time, leading to an extended and bitter dispute with the Erwins.

A letter from Andrew Erwin to Groce dated April 6, 1833, records that he finally did pay Erwin $6,086 in that year and that the longstanding debt was then paid in full, finally closing the affairs of A. Erwin, Groce & Co. Detailed records pertaining to the several-year dispute between Groce and the Erwins pertaining to their failed business are included in Appendix I.

Already a wealthy planter in Alabama, widower Groce read about Stephen Austin's new colony advertised in New Orleans newspapers in the fall of 1821. Austin's descriptions of the soil and climate attracted Groce, and he decided to relocate to Texas. He may have even met Austin in New Orleans as both men were known to have been in that town in November of 1821. The death of his then-youngest daughter in October of 1821 left him a widower with four children and likely contributed to his decision to leave Alabama. Groce's move to Texas was also likely influenced by the unpaid $10,000 debt to Mckinni which, had he stayed in the United States, might have led to bankruptcy and seizure of his property. The Erwins accused Groce of "running away" to Texas to avoid having to pay this debt, which Andrew Erwin was forced to pay on Groce's behalf. A Mexican official named Jose Maria Sanchez y Tapia who met Groce briefly in 1828 similarly indicated that Groce came to Texas "in order to avoid paying the numerous creditors that were suing him." Additionally, he knew that the dubious legal status of the 47 slaves he had obtained in 1818 would pose no continuing problems in Mexican Texas.

Groce placed his sons Jared III and Edwin in boarding school living with relatives in Georgia and his daughter Sarah at school in Nashville until he could establish his new homestead. He, son Leonard and overseer Alfred Gee left his Alabama home for Texas around the first of November, 1821. He arrived at Bernardo in January of 1822. Shortly after arriving he sent his son Leonard with his manservant Fielding back to the United States to finish his education, where he roomed with his aunt Sarah Harper Kirby in Augusta from 1821 to 1824. Leonard completed his education near the end of 1824 and set out to join his father in Texas. On the way he stopped at the Fulton home in Alexandria where he observed Courtney Ann growing into a young woman. The Fulton - Groce connection grew as Courtney's step-father Thomas Hooper became interested in Texas colonization and traveled to Bernardo with Leonard.

Upon Sarah Ann Groce's graduation from a young ladies seminary in New York in 1827, Jared II sent Leonard to that city to bring his daughter, then aged seventeen, to Texas. The return journey was accomplished by stage to Alabama for a visit with relatives, then by boat to Velasco without mishap. The Bernardo household was abuzz in anticipation of her arrival. Jared had not seen his daughter since she left Fort Groce for Tennessee before he came to Texas. Myra, long-time head housekeeper for the Groce family, was looking forward to having a Groce mistress at home for the first time in over a decade and wanted very much to impress her upon her arrival. Concerned that their fancy china had long ago been broken, Myra proposed to Jared that they acquire new serving dishes, preferably in silver. William C. White, Jared II's wives' nephew and silversmith who was a guest at Bernardo, overheard the conversation regarding silver dishes. He indicated that he could make some if he had silver. Jared accepted the offer and provided access to the bags of Mexican silver dollars that still remained from the earlier cotton sales. White went to the blacksmith shop and turned out a fine set of serving dishes including bowls, pitchers, platters, mugs, cups and saucers, which remained in use in the family for years. William C. White was in Texas at least by 1824, as he was awarded a league of land across the river from Bernardo during that year, no doubt with encouragement and assistance from Jared. He was a witness to the first Groce deed. White and his wife Eliza Picket White lived in San Felipe in 1827 where he practiced his metalworking trades of blacksmith and silversmith.

As Sarah Ann settled into her new role as mistress of Bernardo, she decided they needed some silver knives and forks to go with the new serving pieces. Jared again provided a number of the Mexican dollars which were sent to a New York jeweler and converted to silverware.

Following approval of the annexation of Texas to the United States in late 1845, Sarah Ann Wharton gave a silver pitcher made at Bernardo in 1827 to President Tyler after having it embossed with a Lone Star. She was distantly related to Tyler. Her letter stated: "We firmly believe that to you, Texas is indebted for this great measure. Texas, no longer a lost Pleiad, has returned to take her place in a bright and beautiful constellation." [82]

William and John Wharton moved from Nashville to Texas in 1827. Shortly after his arrival, William came to Bernardo to do some legal work for Jared Groce II. There he encountered Groce's daughter Sarah Ann and a rapid courtship followed. These two may have met or at least new of each other earlier in Nashville as one of Sarah's closest friends and classmates at the boarding school there was Betsy Wharton, sister of William and John. William and Sarah married at Bernardo on December 5, 1827. Jared gave his daughter a wedding present consisting of 3 1/2 leagues of his land holdings in Brazoria County, including slaves and a working plantation known as Eagle Island. After their wedding the Whartons returned to Nashville where William resumed his legal practice. Their only child, a son named John Austin Wharton, was born in

Nashville on July 3, 1828. The Whartons were encouraged to return to Texas by personal letters from Steven Austin and from Jared, who offered to build them a new home if they returned. They finally agreed to move back to Texas, and did so in 1829. The new home promised by Jared was built at Eagle Island in Brazoria County and rapidly became another of the grand plantations in Texas.

Organizing a militia was also a high priority for the new government of Austin's Colony. Leonard Groce was appointed as Lieutenant in the civil militia organized at San Felipe in 1829. [83]

Jared Ellison Groce III came to Texas in 1830 at age 18 to join his family at Bernardo. He, his brother Leonard and Thomas McKinney formed a partnership in which Leonard ran the operations of the plantation and Jared III and McKinney handled the marketing of the cotton in Mexico and elsewhere.

Edwin Groce came to Texas in 1831 after having lived with relatives in Alabama since late 1821. [84] Soon after his arrival at Bernardo, he set out with his sister to visit her home in Brazoria County, and drowned in a boat accident crossing the Brazos River. [85]

The relationship between Leonard and Courtney Ann Fulton blossomed and they were married in Louisiana on November 17, 1831. Courtney was the daughter of Alexander Fulton and Henrietta Wells. Fulton was a cousin of Robert Fulton, the inventor of the steamboat, although the two apparently did not have a close relationship. Fulton moved to Louisiana in 1797 where he purchased land from the Choctaw, Biloxi and Pascagoula Indians and founded the town of Alexandria which he named either after himself or a daughter who died young. Henrietta's father was one of the early settlers in Rapides Parish, working for the Spanish and French governments before 1803, and the Americans after the Louisiana Purchase.

Courtney was 15 and Leonard was 25 years of age when they married. Marriage Bond Court Records from New Orleans show that Leonard gave her $10,000 as a wedding dowry. The money owed by Leonard, plus $5,000 that Courtney received from her father's estate a few years later and was used by Leonard, was handled as a promissory note because it is mentioned in the context of a "payable", still owed from Leonard to Courtney, many years later in both of their wills and in several land transactions in which Bernardo was placed with a trustee to assure Courtney received the dowry. After a short stay in New Orleans, the newlyweds arrived at Bernardo on January 8, 1832, after which a second wedding was held at Bernardo, presided over by Catholic priest Miguel Muldoon.[86] Mexican Law required all residents to be Catholic, and a wedding in this faith was necessary to assure any heirs could legally inherit the land.

Muldoon was the first Catholic priest resident in Austin's Colony and was known to perform mass weddings of couples who had "wed" before a member of the clergy was available. Muldoon served in Austin's Colony from April, 1831 to August, 1832, when he returned to Mexico. His influence on Texas continued; in 1837 he helped William Wharton escape from a prison in Matamoros.

Over the next 23 years, Leonard and Courtney had eleven children. [87], Sarah Berlet recounted that Courtney taught her children to swim in the Brazos River before they could walk.

Jared Groce III married Mary Ann Calvit on October 1, 1833. She was the daughter of Alexander and Barbara Mackall Calvit of Ever Green Plantation, located adjacent to Eagle Island in Brazoria County where Jared had spent much time visiting his Aunt and Uncle Sarah Ann and William Wharton. The Calvits had moved to Texas from Alexandria, Louisiana where they were closely associated with Courtney Fulton's family. A Certificate of Baptism for Mary Ann Calvit performed by Father Muldoon dated April 1, 1832 and written in Latin and Spanish is among the Groce Family Papers. Mary Ann's baptismal sponsors included her aunt Jane Wilkerson Long (aka. the "Mother of Texas") and Sarah Ann Groce Wharton. Jared III and Mary Ann promptly built their home about a half mile north of Bernardo, naming it Pleasant Hill. Mary Ann had a younger sister Sarah Jane Wharton Calvit who married John Sharp on October 25, 1836. Their mother Barbara Mackall Wilkinson Calvit was a sister to Jane Wilkinson Long. John Sharp, originally from Scotland, came to Texas in 1833 and settled at Brazoria. He was a First Lieutenant in Capt. Robert J. Calder's Company at San Jacinto. In 1837 he was a passenger on the schooner Julius Caesar when she was captured by a Mexican squadron, taken to Matamoros where he spent time in prison with Wm. H. Wharton. Sharp died at Velasco on August 17, 1840. Later his widow Sarah married Robert S. Herndon, brother of John Herndon who had earlier married her sister Barbara Mackall Calvit. [88]

Jared III and Mary Ann had three children. [89] Their first daughter Frances Ann may have been the first family member to be buried in the Pleasant Hill cemetery shown as the "graveyard" on sketches of that plantation.

Jared Groce II moved to Retreat with 20 slaves in 1833, citing deteriorating health and a desire to be free from the fever and malaria-prone Brazos River bottoms. George Childress wrote the draft of the new constitution for the nascent nation while staying at Retreat during the weeks prior to the declaration of independence from Mexico by Texas in March, 1836. After the formation of the Republic of Texas, all of the newly-elected officials stayed for three days at Retreat on their way to Harrisburg. On July 2, 1835, Jared and other Retreat neighbors signed a petition to James B. Miller requesting a new jurisdiction of Washington, wanting to split the territory that later became Grimes County from Montgomery County.   Jared had long been in poor health, but insisted on being brought to Bernardo during the April, 1836 events that took place there during the Texas revolutionary campaign. He never recovered from the physical decline he experienced as a result of this trip.   As he neared death from "consumption" (tuberculosis), he called to his bedside Methodist doctor and preacher Rev. W.P. Smith, M.D., who lived near Independence some twenty miles west of Retreat. Groce was baptized and comforted by Smith. He had not been active in a church during his life in Texas, nor before; few such opportunities were available on the frontier. Jared Ellison Groce II died at Retreat on November 20, 1836. He was buried at the family cemetery at Bernardo. When the Bernardo property was ultimately sold after the Civil War, his and other family members' remains were removed to the city cemetery in Hempstead.

Family members and many acquaintances spoke highly of Jared Groce II. Biased and overtly displaying the paternalistic view toward their charges common among white slaveowners, these accounts do convincingly demonstrate that cruel treatment was not the norm at Bernardo. The bondsmen were provided food, clothing and shelter that likely exceeded that available to many poorer white settlers. Time off from work, and the ability to live in stable, nuclear family units is evident.

Sarah Groce Berlet said Jared was "the most devoted father in the world, unselfish, and always thoughtful of our comfort and welfare. He taught his children to be kind to the negroes, and all his servants loved him." Samuel H. Dixon in "Men Who Made Texas Free" said that Groce "was a man of towering intellect, but his failing health prevented him from taking an active part in the affairs of State. He had a most retentive mind, for it has been said of his that he often dictated a letter to his Secretary, and at the same time would carry on a conversation with someone else." [90]

David B. Edwards, a contemporary who personally knew Jared Groce II, wrote of his character: "It is a known fact that Colonel Groce treated his slaves with kindness, clothed, fed, and attended to them in sickness. Each family had a patch of land to cultivate. The products of these patches and of their labor for the Colonel were sent along to market with his and proceeds given to the slaves to expend as they pleased, except for liquor." Dudley G. Wooten wrote that "Some of the colonists owned slaves; no one had many except Jared Groce, who treated them very kindly". [91]

Further evidence of the high regard in which Jared II was held by most is given in a letter from David G. Burnet to L.W. Groce from San Jacinto, March 23, 1852 concerning an interrogatory on an unnamed subject. "... I have never forgotten the olden times in Texas or the three days of very pleasant frolic and amusement which I spent at your Father's hospitable residence [at Retreat]." This visit took place from March 19 - 21 as the newly elected Texian Government paused at Retreat on their way from Washington to Harrisburg. Not everyone held Jared Groce in such high regard. James Erwin, one of his business partners dating back to earlier residence in Georgia, wrote a scathing letter to Stephen Austin filled with derogatory remarks about Groce, who had suddenly moved to Texas owing Erwin $10,000 from the bankruptcy of their former business (see Appendix II). Others described Groce as being a vain opportunist. John Coles wrote to Stephen Austin: "You know Groce. If you were to give him Twenty Leagues he would want forty." [92]

Historical accounts record that Courtney Groce also treated her slaves with respect and dignity. "When the negroes were sick, Mrs. Groce attended to their comfort in person. Accompanied by a maid, carrying a basket filled with delicacies from her table, she saw that they had every attention. In fact, she was an angel of mercy to anyone in sorrow, and was loved by all who knew her. Years after her death, one of the old slaves came to the house of her son, Dr. L. W. Groce of Hempstead, and standing in front of her portrait, said: "old Miss was an angel if there ever was one, and I shore hope to meet her in Heaven.". Then looking at the portrait of the Colonel, she said, "old Mars was good too, but I ain't so shore about meeting him in Heaven." Clara Chappell, born a slave at Bernardo, indicated that they were well fed with the same food that the Groces ate, were properly clothed and provided cabins in which to live. She indicated that the overseer was "mean", and would "genteely whip" slaves who disobeyed orders, but that "marster was good and the niggers all loved him" (see Appendix V) [93]

Bernardo played a pivotal role in the Texas revolution. Sam Houston camped across the Brazos from Bernardo for the first two weeks of April, 1836, where he trained his volunteer army in preparation for their coming encounter with Santa Anna. Leonard Groce took his family to Louisiana for safety during the Runaway Scrape, but Jared III stayed and assisted the Texian army. Bernardo foods fed the army. Jared II came from Retreat to check on the activities and dine with Houston and his staff. Houston camped for two days at Bernardo after he crossed the Brazos on the steam boat "Yellow Stone", and he took delivery of the Twin Sisters cannons, the only artillery he had at San Jacinto, on the front lawn of Groce's house. Details of the activities at Bernardo during the revolutionary campaign are given in the chapter "Aiding the Texas Revolution".

Life at Bernardo plantation resumed its former activities after the war. Noted for its generous hospitality, many visitors coming from the United States were entertained in grand southern style by Leonard and Courtney Ann Groce. Family members noted that there were seldom less than twenty guests at the dinner table each night. Travelers from Houston to the new capital at Austin often stopped for a night or more. No wonder Bernardo was generally known in early Texas as "Dixie Land of Texas"! [94] Sam Houston was a frequent visitor and a favorite with the children and a close friend of Leonard Groce. On one of these trips Houston wore a vest which Groce admired. The General promptly gave the vest to his friend, and Leonard had himself photographed wearing the prized new vest.

Tragedy visited the Groce family three times within six months beginning in the fall of 1838. On September 2 of that year Sarah Wharton Groce, the three-year-old daughter of Leonard and Courtney, suddenly fell ill and died at Bernardo. Jared III died of "consumption" (tuberculosis) in February of 1839, and William Wharton died at Bernardo in March.

A prolonged illness plagued Jared Groce III in 1838, as indicated by the following newspaper offer from the July 9, 1838 issue of *The Telegraph and Texas Register*: "I am compelled on act. of bad health to travel and offer for sale any of my lands on the Brazos, Bernard & Colorado Rivers. Those on the Brazos are scattered on both sides of the river to the old Bexar Road; & I will also include my plantation where I now reside. Bargains can be had, but delay and all chance is lost. Jared E. Groce, Pleasant Hill, June 28."

Bad health did not keep Jared from conducting business. An invoice to his account was posted in New Orleans on August 20, 1838 for shipment of "sundries" to Harrisburg consigned to J. Bankston and by his agent Joseph House. The goods included one barrel of sugar at $26, one bbl. of "sugarhouse molasses" at $13, 1 bbl. whiskey at $14, 2 bbls. of superfine flour at $10 each, one bbl. rice at $19, 1 bag coffee at $22, and 1 bag fine salt at $6. On August 25 he signed a promissory note to pay his wife's uncle F. J. Calvit $330 in "Louisiana and US money". On October 28 he paid an invoice to Harrisburg County Spring Creek invoice for schooling and teacher's board for his son Jared IV. [95]

Jared Groce III died at Pleasant Hill on February 3 after a lingering illness of several months. Notice of his death was posted in the March 13 issue of the *Telegraph and Texas Register*. In January as his condition worsened, his sister Mary Ann and husband William Wharton came from Eagle Island to be with him.

After Jared's death the Whartons remained for a few days as William assisted Leonard in closing Jared's affairs. Then, on March 4, William mounted his horse to return to Eagle Island. When checking his pistol it accidentally discharged, striking him. He died from this wound ten days later at Pleasant Hill on March 14, 1839 and was buried at Eagle Island. The Telegraph and Texas Register covered the incident, saying "He was preparing to return to his residence at Eagle Island. While adjusting his holsters and attempting to draw out one pistol to examine it, the weapon went off, shot off two fingers, and the ball lodged in his abdomen. Symptoms of tetanus appeared on the third day after the accident and he died." Leonard Groce displayed his distraught emotions in an entry describing the accident in the Groce family bible. [96] Upon the request of William's widow Sarah Ann, Leonard and Courtney Groce changed the name of their then-youngest son from Edwin Waller Groce to William Wharton Groce to preserve the memory of their friend and brother-in-law.

This image, believed to be of Jared Groce III, is held by Mary Catherine Clarke Weatherford, one of his great-great-granddaughters. Based on apparent age of the subject and clothing style, it was probably painted in the late 1830's.

Efforts to probate Jared's will began in early 1839. On April 4, John Sharp, husband of Mary Ann Groce's sister and a lawyer in Brazoria, filed a copy of Jared III's will that he testified was "signed, sealed and witnessed in my presence and that Jared Groce did at that time acknowledge and declare to me that the same was his last will and testament." It was dated October 9, 1838. Jared signed this will, as did eight witnesses including Edwin Waller. The will contained a number of provisions, including gifts of $1,000 to Courtney and $500 each to his wife's sisters Sarah Jane Sharp and Mackall Calvit. His wife Mary Ann was to be given a lump sum of $8,000 in exchange for her renouncement of any community property interest in the estate, along with a $400 annual annuity until she remarried. Mary Ann was also allowed to continue living in the house at Pleasant Hill at no charge, given the continuing service of Jared's slaves for her household and kitchen work, and provided with a carriage, horses and attendants any time she wanted to travel. The partnership between Jared and Leonard regarding the operation of the plantation was to continue until Jared's son became age 21. He left the remainder of his estate to his two children, to be conveyed at the time of their 21st birthday. In the meantime, Leonard was appointed their guardian and was to assure "they be raised as good and moral children, and receive an education including the instruction of French and Spanish" Leonard, and Mary Ann's uncle Frederick J. Calvit, were appointed co-executors.

On April 15, 1839 Leonard filed a petition in the Austin County Probate Court reiterating Jared's will and their partnership agreements, asking that Jared's will be executed and he be granted Letters Testamentary and Guardianship of the children. These were granted by the court on April 29. As Executor and Guardian, Leonard was required to keep an accurate record of expenses related to these duties, and file a periodic status report of same with the Court. Many such expense records are present in the Austin County Probate Records for Jared Groce III and provide a fascinating view into the lives of Mary Ann and her children, and the affairs of the plantation for the next several years. Purchases were detailed in the running accounts at merchants such as McKinney & Williams in Galveston and David Ayres at Centre Hill, John Sharp in Brazoria, consigners in Houston, Galveston and New Orleans, or paid in cash specified on the receipt as "Texas Money", "U.S. Money", or gold. The currency issued by the Republic of Texas had quickly devaluated, prompting creditors to specify the type of money to be used to pay debts.

Leonard filed the inventory of his deceased brother's estate in the Austin County Court on February 29, 1840. It included a listing of the slaves and personal property owned by the Jared's estate and lands jointly owned by the two brothers. The 60 slaves are listed individually by name, gender, age, and value ($26,250 total). A detailed listing of this slave inventory is given in Appendix IV. Also listed in the inventory are 12 horses, 8 mules, 3 ponies, firearms (1 double barreled shotgun, one brace each of holster and belt pistols, $120 total), household and kitchen furniture ($1,000), 1 carriage and 2 horses ($400), 1 saddle horse ($200), plantation and farming utensils ($35,000) and two horses ($200). Then the inventory lists 21 parcels of land (60,000 acres, $55,900 total) and livestock (600 head cattle, 12 yoke oxen, 250 hogs and 30 sheep, $3,180 total) and a list of

30 notes and accounts to individuals and firms owned in common with Leonard in which the Jared's estate held an undivided half interest.

Leonard Groce built and staffed a school at Bernardo for his children and relatives. His nephew John A. Wharton attended this school, where he penned a letter to a cousin on November 1, 1839, which reads in part: "I am going to school to Mr. Dean. We have but ten scholars at school, we expect to have 15. Hiram and Edwin will be down soon, they are going to stay at Aunt Mary Ann's [at Pleasant Hill]. We have a very pretty school house, it is white out side and in side." Hiram and Edwin were sons of Edwin Waller, who lived between Bernardo and San Felipe. This school is shown in the sketches of Bernardo by Sarah Berlet as being north of the main house, toward Pleasant Hill.

Dr. Richard R. Peebles presented Leonard a bill for $400 dated December 29, 1839 for medical services during the final days of Jared II and Wm. Wharton. At that time Peebles was in a medical partnership named Peebles and Heard, located in Washington. Peebles came to Texas from Ohio in 1835 as a young medical doctor in the early days of Austin's Colony, where he soon moved to Washington and set up shop as a physician.

By 1840 Leonard began selling land from Jared's estate to pay for support of Jared's children. Mary Ann Groce apparently continued to live the affluent life of a planter's wife, both at Pleasant Hill and with her relatives in Brazoria County. One invoice from John Sharp of Brazoria lists a large quantity of items she purchased at his store between April and September, 1839, primarily clothing and dressmaking supplies.

Leonard received an invoice (next page) dated November 5, 1840, from David Ayres mercantile store in Centre Hill, a community some nine miles west of the Brazos from Bernardo. The Ayres store had a post office which was the one primarily used to receive Groce mail. This invoice is one of several that provides insight into the lifestyle of Mary Ann Groce during the period she was a widow from 1839 to 1843. Here she bought luxuries like an expensive fur hat and dressmaking supplies as well as utilitarian items necessary for operation of the plantation including shirts and weeding hoes for the slaves and bailing rope for the cotton crop. Several buried, well-used and worn out weeding hoe heads have been found at Bernardo since archaeological activities began in 2009. Perhaps some of these were the ones purchased in 1840! Mary Ann also often drew cash from the accounts with merchants, as indicated by a note from McKinney and Williams that $100 had been forwarded to her by Capt. Haviland in December of 1842.

Mrs. Mary A Groce
1839   In a/c with I Ayers & [?]

				Postage	
May	2	To	2 Pocket Books @ $1 - 10		2.00
"	"	"	Postage		.50
Oct'r	14	"	1# Tea		2.00
"	"	"	½# Spice @ 50¢		.25
"	"	"	1 Doz Nutmegs		.50
"	"	"	1 Fur Hat		2.50
1840			Am't last year's Acc't		$ 2.7.81
January	11	To	2 Negro Shirts 1.50		3.00
"	"	"	2 Hdk'fs .50		1.00
"	"	"	¼ Doz Screws		.12½
Feb'y	12	"	3 yds Ribband .50		1.50
"	20	"	6 " Calico @ 37½		2.25
"	"	"	2 Augers		1.50
"	"	"	1 Spade		2.00
Mch	6	"	2 pr Blk Hose 2.00		4.00
"	"	"	1 yd Muslin		1.00
May	2	"	Postage	.50	
"	14	"	"	.28	
Oct'r	7	"	1# Pepper 50 ½# Cloves 25		.75
1841					
Jan'y	6	"	2 Weeding Hoes @ 1.00		2.00
"	"	"	2 Coils 20.4 Baling Rope @ 16½		3.9.3
				$1.94	$13.81
			Postage since 1845		1.94
					$1.94

Two oil portraits of Leonard and Courtney Groce have survived. They are not dated nor signed by the artist. The facial features in this portrait of Leonard suggest a man in his early forties. Leonard was 40 years old in 1846; Courtney was 30 then, suggesting that these paintings were drawn in the 1840's. They hung on walls at both Bernardo and Liendo.

According to Groce family members, during the Mexican invasion of Texas in 1842, Leonard Groce sent all of his horses and even his gin mules for the use of the Texas army. The Galveston TT&R newspaper reported that on November 7, 1842 Leonard Groce and "a servant" departed Galveston on a steamer "Lady Byron". The destination was not given but presumed to be New Orleans. Fielding, Leonard's longstanding manservant, was likely his companion on this trip.

Dr. Peebles moved to Austin County in 1840, opened a mercantile business in partnership with John Shakelford and lived at Bernardo, presumably in the "Doctor's house" shown on the Berlet sketches near the main house. During this time he also provided medical services to the Groce family and their slaves. A three page invoice from Peebles to Leonard found in the probate records provides an itemized list by name of the Bernardo and Pleasant Hill residents, black and white alike, that he treated between May 12, 1842 and March 1, 1843. The usual treatment was to dispense "pills" and "powders". A typical house call was five dollars. Peebles' total bill for this period was $745.

During this time Peebles saw Mary Ann Groce frequently, and they married on March 8, 1843, in a ceremony at Pleasant Hill. After their marriage, the Peebles lived at Pleasant Hill raising her two children by Jared III and those who came later.

Mary Ann's status changed in several ways after her marriage to Richard Peebles. Prior to this time she continued to live the life of a wealthy planter's wife, purchasing luxury goods as well as living necessities and having full access to slaves to attend to her personal needs and operate the household. All of this was arranged and paid for by Leonard from her deceased husband's estate, as had been specified in Jared's will. Upon her marriage to Peebles, Leonard ceased to provide for her in this manner - again as specified in Jared's will. On March 13 Peebles acknowledged receipt from Leonard of a "Memorandum of Understanding" which stated that upon her marriage she could no longer charge household expenses against the Estate, that the household furniture and other assets would cease to be at her disposal. Leonard stated his desire to "pursue whatever course will be agreeable to Mary Ann and Dr. P." and that he was not disposed to do anything not provided by the Jared's will, wanted "matters to be arranged as soon as convenient". He said that he held the Peebles in highest esteem and wanted to advance their interests and promote their happiness. Leonard indicated that he would pay the $8,000 owed Mary Ann by Jared's will as soon as possible and that he would pay in land if they so chose. He offered to let Mary Ann continue to use the household and kitchen furniture and the carriage, and that this value not be deducted from the $8,000 but settled upon the children coming of age. Supplies on hand were to be left if wanted but must be purchased by Peebles, and that an arrangement could be made for occupying the house if desired by the Peebles. Leonard did offer to continue to provide for Jared's children, again as specified in Jared's will. Two receipts signed by both Peebles dated June 5 certified that Leonard had paid them $2,755 and $4,000 "in part payment of the legacy or bequest" from Jared's will.

A lease of the Pleasant Hill plantation was entered into on April 22 with Peebles by Groce as Executor of his deceased brother's estate. The lease included "all the negroes belonging thereto". Peebles was to treat the negroes "with humanity" and to feed and clothe the two children of Jared III and Mary Ann at the estate's expense but not to charge for board or any medical services he provided the two children. Household and kitchen furniture were included in the lease, which required an annual payment $2,000 for ten years, effective December 31, 1842. Peebles was granted rights to using timber on the plantation for building and repairing fences. Both parties agreed to each appoint an appraiser who would work together to produce a cash value inventory of the kitchen and household furniture and other perishables as of the date of commencement of the lease.

Courtney Ann Groce wrote a will on March 17, 1848, stating that Leonard owed her a large sum from the time of their marriage, and that if she died, Leonard was to give their children $40,000 to be divided equally - "half negroes and half land at cash valuation". This payment was to represent all that Leonard owed her from his earlier Deed of Trust. The remainder of the property was to belong to him.

The 1840's and 1850's were a time when the Groce children were growing from children to young adults. William Wharton Groce and his cousin Jared Groce III were about the same age, born September 12 and May 28, 1837, respectively. They lived one-half of a mile apart and were inseparable companions. Leonard Groce treated Jared as his own son, giving him the same things he gave his own children. Two of the young slaves on the plantation, Tom and Buggy, were constant companions of William and Jared. When they were six years old and at the Peebles' wedding, William and Jared committed the first of many mischievous deeds by stealing the wedding cake, taking it to the yard and sharing it with Tom and Buggy. At Christmas, the children would hang their stockings on the old rock fireplace. Again at age six, William sprang out of bed on Christmas morning to see what Santa Claus had left in his stocking. He was disappointed when he saw his sister Nettie's stocking full but his contained only one sweet potato. He promptly heard heavy steps in the hall and was greeted by "Uncle Fielding", Leonard's manservant, holding a beautiful Rocky Mountain pony complete with a saddle. Jared had received one also. William rushed over to his cousin's house to find him already saddled up and ready to ride. The Groce boys rode frequently thereafter, with Tom and Buggy behind them. A few weeks after Christmas, Courtney drove to Houston in her carriage. William accompanied her, riding his pony the entire trip despite his mother's pleas to join her in the carriage.

In 1844 at age seven William was schooled at home. His father employed a governess, Miss Mary Ann Roan, who at first taught only William, his sister Nettie, and cousins Jared and Barbara Groce on the second floor hall of the Bernardo house. They were soon joined by two daughters of a widow from Georgia, Mrs. Bass. Clara became William's "sweetheart", and her sister Helen, Jared's. They stayed at Bernardo for several years. Miss Roan, a timid woman, sat at the edge of the stairs as she taught her pupils. She had very long hair, worn in two long plaits or pigtails. One day when she was distracted William tied her pigtails to a chair and ran down the stairs crying "fire !!!". Miss Roan jumped up and ran down the stairs with the chair tumbling behind, fainting when she reached the ground floor. Frightened at the outcome of his prank, William fled to his aunt Mary Ann's house, fearing punishment from his mother. Miss Roan convinced Courtney not to punish William for his misdeed.

One day William took Clara riding in a cart pulled by a pair of yearlings. He wanted a kiss from Clara but she refused. He told her that if she would not comply he would drive the cart into a pool of water in the road ahead of them and drown them both. Clara changed her mind and promptly kissed William, which caused him to lose control of his team, who proceeded to drive into the foot-deep water. Once Clara perceived William's deception, she hit him with both fists. Now completely out of control of the cart, it overturned and both went home covered with mud and water. After that experience, William reported that he was frequently kissed by Clara.

Mack Mott was a Galveston cousin of William's who came to visit. Accompanied by one of the plantation slaves, they set out one day in an ox cart to go fishing, stopping to pick some blackberries on a fence row. William was barefooted, and a rattlesnake bit him on his foot. The negro tied his handkerchief around William's leg and carried him home on his shoulders. By the time they arrived his leg was swollen to the hip; it took several weeks before he could walk again.

Another story recounted by William Groce occurred about 1842, when he was five years old. Joseph Calvit of Brazoria was living at Pleasant Hill with his niece Mary Ann Groce. Unknown to William, Cavlit was bald and wore a wig. Cavlit challenged William to a hair-pulling contest. Both grabbed the other's hair and pulled. William tumbled backward, carrying Calvit's hair with him. William screamed, thinking he had scalped him as he had heard described done by Indians. His mother explained what had happened, but not before he had received the scare of his life!

Leonard took his son to Houston in 1842. William slipped away while his father was transacting business at T.W. House's bank. Walking down to Buffalo Bayou, he encountered some boys who offered to take him for a ride in a skiff. They were gone several hours, by which time Leonard had the whole town out looking for him.

One afternoon William's cousin John Wharton and several men were sitting in the parlor at Bernardo. The subject of ghosts came up. William's brother Jack, then about six, was present and remarked that HE was not afraid of ghosts. Wharton had a beautiful pacer saddle mule named Nellie. Wharton told Jack that if he would go into the negro graveyard, located a quarter mile from the house, at midnight an bring back a headboard from one of the graves, Nellie would be his. Leonard told John that he would likely lose the mule because Jack was fearless. The night was dark and stormy. Wharton, fearing he might lose the mule, went first to the graveyard where he hid behind a large tree. John arrived at the appointed hour and began tugging on one of the headboards. Wharton made loud noises in an attempt to mimic a ghost and scare Jack. The boy, recognizing his cousin, announced "You can Mourn and Groan all you want, but Nellie will be mine in the morning.". And she was. [97]

Leonard Groce and Richard Peebles both worked actively to entice the emerging railroads out of Houston to route across their lands. The economic advantages of having a railroad cross your land was immense, and was actively sought. In October of 1856 Leonard gave the Galveston and Red River Railway Company a right-of-way for a railroad on any of his land in Austin County. In November of that year Leonard joined with his cousin J.E. Kirby to give the same railroad a right-of-way over any land they owned east of Clear Creek. Richard Peebles helped persuade the organizers of the Houston and Central Texas Railway to route the line through the northern portion of his Pleasant Hill lands. He was elected a director of this railroad in 1858, and helped organize the Hempstead Town company in that year to lay out a new town on that line. He named the new town Hempstead, after his brother-in-law in Ohio, Dr. G.S.B. Hempstead. By 1860 Richard Peebles, Leonard Groce and Jared Kirby were among the wealthiest men in Texas.

The 1850 U.S. Census contains the following entries for Free Inhabitants: L.W. Groce (age 45) wife + 7 children; farmer, $70,000 real estate value; and R.R. Peebles (age 40) wife + 7 children, farmer, $14,025 land value. By this date Peebles was no longer considered a doctor. The 1850 Census Slave Schedule is very faded and difficult to read. Individuals are listed by age, sex and color (B or M). No names or initials are given. Leonard Groce is shown with >113 individuals, and R.R. Peebles with 85 individuals.

Following the birth of their tenth child, Leonard and Courtney decided that they had outgrown the main house at Bernardo and in 1853 built a new residence at Liendo, the large plantation some five miles north of Bernardo on the head of Clear Creek. The plantation was named after the original owner, José Justo Liendo, and had been purchased by Groce in two transactions. The first, in 1841 was 3,000 acres for $2,500 to Liendo; the remainder in 1849 was at an auction for taxes due. In this second transaction Groce paid the county $16.45 for the taxes due, and $2,000 to Liendo.

According to Sarah Berlet, from 1853 to 1858 the main house at Bernardo was occupied by several relatives of Leonard Groce, including Mrs. Richardson Scurry (Evantha Foster, Leonard's cousin) and a Mrs. Tippet. William Wharton

Groce, son of Leonard and Courtney, lived at Bernardo and had charge of the plantation from 1858 until 1861, when he joined the Confederate army. After his marriage in 1864 he received permission from his father to dismantle the main house at Bernardo and to remove the chimney stones and best logs for use in building his home at Bonny Nook plantation, some four miles below Bernardo on property deeded to him by his father. This occurred in 1865.

The following image from the archives of the Brazoria County Historical Museum is of Wm. Whaton Groce and his bride Kate Wyatt.

The 1860 U.S. Census lists the following Free Inhabitants:

Name	age	sex	occupation	$ real estate	$ pers.prop.
L.W. Groce	54	M	planter	100,000	225,000
C.A. Groce + 8 children	44	F	farmer		
J.E. Groce	23	M	farmer	$50,000	25,000
J.F. Groce with wife + 2 children	27	M	farmer	58,500	45,000
R.R. Peebles with wife M.A. + 7 children	50	M	planter	200,000	30,000

Leonard and his wife Courtney Ann are listed separately, which was unusual for a man and a wife. Based on other listings near theirs it appears that at the time of the census Leonard was at Liendo and Courtney Ann and the children were at Bernardo. Richard and Mary Ann Peebles were at Pleasant Hill. The 1860 U.S. Census Slave Schedules show Leonard Groce with 119 individuals and Richard Peebles with 50 individuals. Peebles had transferred title of several Pleasant Hill slaves to Jared and Barbara Groce a few years before 1860.

The following photos of Leonard and Courtney Ann Groce were taken around 1860. [98]

Civil War Period

When the Civil War began in 1861, four of Leonard and Courtney's sons joined the Confederate army. Jared Fulton, William Wharton and Leonard Waller Jr. served in Company B, 8th Texas Cavalry (Terry's Texas Rangers) under their cousin John A. Wharton. John Harris (Jack) was fifteen and wanted to go but was refused by his parents. He ran away from home and joined Gen. Magruder's regiment at Galveston. Jared E. IV was also in Wharton's command, as was another cousin Jared Kirby White, who was killed the last days of the war.

Neither Bernardo nor Pleasant Hill plantations hosted any official military activities during the Civil War. However, nearby Hempstead held one of the largest concentrations of Confederate forces in Texas and was home to a prisoner of war camp for Union soldiers during the war and to the Union occupying army for three months after the war ended. Military visitors to Pleasant Hill and Bernardo were probably very common; at least some of the thousands of troops in the immediate area surely camped temporarily on these plantations as they traveled to and from the permanent camps at Hempstead. By November 6, 1861, Austin County had nearly 400 men in the military service. The local newspaper reported that four companies of men had been raised for the war from the county before the end of 1861 and all the men who could be spared were already enlisted. However, the increasing needs for manpower to support the Confederate effort continued to glean the countryside of eligible men, with the focus shifting from volunteerism to forced conscription as the war years progressed.

An examination of the area's only newspaper during this time, the *Bellville Countryman,* contains several references to near-by Civil War activities or people connected to Bernardo. Major Edwin Waller, Jr. was promoted to Colonel and assigned command of the forces near Hempstead (February 8, 1862). Also on this date it was reported that William W. Groce had been promoted to 1st Lieutenant of the "Archer's Grays" division of Terry's Regiment commanded by his cousin Col. John A. Wharton. On June 19, 1863, a group of men from the area including Leonard Groce and Jared Kirby invited Waller to a public dinner in his honor in Hempstead. The event was held on June 27: "The Barbeque was a decided success, and the oration by Gen. Portis a noble and just and eloquent tribute to Maj. Waller and his Battalion. ... There was general attendance from different portions of the county. Our neighbors from Washington County also graced the occasion, and added largely to the interest of the day. The morning was occupied by Col. Holland, Col. Kirby and N.W. Bush, the first and last named gentlemen offering themselves to represent us, one in the Senate and the other in the lower house of the coming legislature. The events of the day were concluded by adjournment to the ball room, where Terpischore [a Greek goddess of music, song and dance] was zealously worshipped."

Leonard Groce supported local troops in their war campaigns. He received a letter dated August 15, 1862 at a Ranger's camp near Athens, Tennessee, from R.F. Bunting, Chaplain of Terry's Texas Rangers, acknowledging receipt of $420 to assist ill soldiers in the Ranger's unit, and for a subscription of cotton by Courtney for the same purpose. Apparently Courtney had convinced several neighbors to pledge some of their cotton crop to be sold for this purpose.

Leonard paid his federal taxes during the war primarily by presenting Confederate treasury notes. On March 10, 1864 he paid $625 for his 1863 Confederate Tax plus another $558 for the County War Tax; on November 23 of that year he paid $200 for 1864 taxes and another $8,511.25 for the "Confederate Tax". Receipts for these tax payments are among the Groce Papers archives. He also bought several Confederate bonds during the war, including four bonds totaling $3,700 in May and June of 1864, by which time it was becoming apparent the Confederacy was likely to lose the war. He paid his local Austin County taxes "in-kind". On November 20th, 1863 he delivered 1,384 pounds of sweet potatoes and another 603 pounds on December 10 for his taxes that year. Likewise he paid his 1864 local taxes with 79 bushels of corn and 1,000 pounds of fodder. On May 30, 1864 he submitted an estimate of his Cotton, Sugar, Molassas, Tobacco and Bacon Tithes Due for 1863, including Cotton valued at $5,150 and Bacon at $5,925. On July 30, 1864, the agent for the Confederate government in Hempstead issued a receipt to Groce for fifty bales of cotton after harvest, representing half of his cotton crop for that year. Ending the war did not stop the taxes! On August 6, 1866, the U.S. Internal Revenue Service issued an invoice for $1,199,83 in federal income tax due for 1865. Sara Berlet mentioned that she had receipts for more than $40,000 that Leonard paid in 1863 for Confederate war taxes, bonds and army supplies.

Soldiers were seldom paid on time, and supplies were often lacking. By the middle of 1862 the state government's supply of arms was running out. Foundries in Bellville and Hempstead produced canteens, skillets, and camp kettles under contract with the state of Texas; the Hempstead Manufacturing Company made woolen blankets, cotton cloth, spinning jennies, looms, and spinning wheels. Many who enlisted in 1862 left home well mounted but without arms or uniforms. While approximately three-fourths of Austin County's men were between the ages of 18 and 49 and thus eligible for duty, only one-third of those eligible actually served. Some enlisted at age 16. In the western part of the county predominately populated with German and Czech immigrants, indifference to the issues and resistance to conscription was stronger, only one-eighth of the adult men served.

Early in the war Camps Groce, Carter and Hébert were formed near Hempstead. Camp Groce became one of two camps in Texas where Union prisoners of war were held. The first group of 450 prisoners was transferred to Camp Groce from the state penitentiary in Huntsville in June 1863. Other Union soldiers captured in Louisiana soon joined them. All of these were paroled by December of 1863, but another group of 650 Union prisoners occupied Camp Groce from May through December 1864, when they were paroled and the camp was abandoned as a prison. There was a Confederate military hospital in Hempstead.

During the Civil War cotton production continued at Bernardo and Liendo. Half of the crop was taken by the Confederate government and sent to the prison at Huntsville where it was spun and woven into cloth for use in clothing the soldiers. The fact that Hempstead was the western-most terminus of the railroad at that time was the reason for this very large concentration of Confederate forces here during the war. Most of the activity during the war and initial Union occupation was in the Hempstead - Liendo area. Several Civil War era military artifacts have been found at Bernardo.

The war was clearly coming to a close in early 1865. Many Texas soldiers in the Confederate Army in Louisiana began to return home, and by March Hempstead became a congregation point for these men, estimated at 20,000, where they stayed at Camp Groce. A month later they received a rumor and then confirmation that Robert E. Lee had surrendered at Appomattox. Confederate president Jefferson Davis had fled to Louisiana where he advocated continuing the war despite Lee's surrender. He was captured there on May 10 as he was heading to Texas to join the remaining loyal units of the Confederate army. Generals Kirby Smith, Magruder and Forney were staying at the Alta Vista plantation, home of Leonard Groce's cousin Jared Kirby. They appealed to the soldiers in Hempstead to continue their active service, promising reinforcements from the east if they would fight on. The disenchanted officers and men politely listened to their superiors and decided that further resistance was hopeless. They were Texans first, and their families needed them now more than ever. They began to disband in the open daylight, gathering their belongings and walking away toward home, their actions in effect a non-violent mutiny directly disobeying their General's orders. The war was over.

The Bellville Countryman reported on June 6, 1865: "We are now a conquered people and must submit to such terms as the conquerors may choose to impose. Our army has disbanded. There is no longer any effort to defend our liberties or our homes".

Brevet Major General George Armstrong Custer (of later Little Bighorn fame) organized his Union army troops in Alexandria, Louisiana, in preparation for the occupation of Texas. His was one of two units so engaged in the immediate aftermath of the war's ending. Custer left Louisiana on August 8, 1865, crossed the Sabine River and marched eastward. As he approached Houston he diverted his troops to Hempstead because he believed the grass and forage for his animals, and food supplies for his men, would be more plentiful at that location. His weary troops dismounted in Hempstead on August 25, where they stayed until the end of October before moving on to occupy the state capitol at Austin. Custer was accompanied by his wife Elisabeth. They camped at the Liendo plantation of Leonard Groce and enjoyed warm relations with the Groces, Peebles and other local Texans. The march from Alexandria had been very difficult, characterized by severe shortages of food and other supplies. Shortly after arrival in Hempstead local food (hog jowls and hard bread) was procured, probably from the Groces. According to one of the soldiers, "the jowls had about one-fifth of the hair still on, and out of them which tusks were taken measuring seven and one-half inches in length …". Given these dire conditions, some of the soldiers took matters into their own hands - "Some beef cattle running at large on the prairie were killed in disobedience of orders to obtain food to appease the cravings of hunger of the half-starved men." It turned out that these cattle belonged to Richard Peebles of Pleasant Hill Plantation and he immediately complained to Custer. Tents of the troops were inspected throughout the camp and portions of the beef were found in the camp of the Twelfth Illinois and Second Indiana regiments. Custer issued a memorandum summarizing the situation on September 5, in which he specifically mentioned Peebles and his Union sentiments.

Two men, Horace C. Cure of the First Iowa regiment, and G. Darr of the Twelfth Illinois Cavalry were judged guilty without trial and summarily punished for the incident by having their head shaved and given 25 lashes. This acton outraged most of Custer's troops and nearly led to mutiny. Letters complaining of Custer's "barbarous" treatment were sent to the governors of Iowa, Wisconsin, Indiana and Illinois who in turn notified the War Department of their displeasure

"Headquarters Second Division Cavalry
Mil. Div. of the Gulf, September 4th, 1865

"Col. Wm. Thompson, *Comdg. Second Brigade:*

"For the past few days parties from this command have been committing depredations upon the persons and property of citizens of this neighborhood. Yesterday, without even the excuse of want, a party of soldiers belonging to this division butchered a number of cattle belonging to Dr. Peebles, who is probably the most thorough Union man in the State, having been incarcerated in prison for nearly a year by the rebel authorities, owing to his strong Union sentiments, and afterward forced to leave the State to save his life from rebel mobs. The party referred to as having committed the depredations yesterday, beyond appropriating a portion to their own use, wantonly destroyed the greater portion of what they had stolen. To arrest and bring to punishment the guilty parties, a staff officer was sent from these headquarters this morning, one to each regiment in the command, with orders to make a thorough search for the stolen property. The search and investigations have been completed, and while two regiments of the First Brigade (the Second Illinois and Seventh Indiana) were found in possession of large quantities of the stolen property, the regiments of your brigade are reported as being not only fully exonerated, but above the suspicion even of participating in the outrages referred to above, and I take pleasure in congratulating you upon having a command the officers and men of which are so strictly honest and upright as to afford a shining example to other portions of this command.

"I am, Colonel, very respectfully yours, &c.,

"G. A. Custer, *Major General Comdg.*"

at this action involving their native sons. The governor of Iowa specifically requested the War Department that their regiments be mustered out of Custer's command. [99] The War Department referred the request to Gen. Phil Sheridan, commander of the Military Division of the Gulf, ordering him to investigate and take appropriate action. Sheridan referred it back to Custer, who ignored it. Custer's troop discipline and insistence they not to forage without permission or to harm any citizens or their property did however somewhat relieve local concerns about the large army in their midst.

Elizabeth Custer later wrote a book vividly describing her surroundings and experiences while at Camp Groce in Hempstead. [100] Many modern historians discredit Mrs. Custer's writings because they are very self-serving and seem only written to present positive propaganda about her husband. Despite these shortcomings, her description of her time in the Hempstead camp records pertinent information about Liendo, Pleasant Hill and the area's plantations. She commented that when marching into Austin County from the southeast Texas pine forests, she and the General would ride in front of the troops and attempt to buy butter and eggs from farm-houses. Often the Texas women were wary of these newcomers but one in particular "found that we neither wore horns nor were cloven-footed", and apologized for not having extra butter as she was milking only seven cows at that time. Elizabeth derided the Texas cattle, saying "what makes a respectable dairy at home, was nothing in a country where all the cows give a cupful of milk and all run to horns." At Liendo they were joined by General Sheridan who had come by way of Galveston, bringing Gen. Custer's father to visit. Some four thousand troops were in this camp.

The Custers were hospitably received by the local residents. Mrs. Custer indicated that Leonard Groce, "one of the oldest residents of Texas", welcomed them and offered for them to stay in his house, which they declined. Courtney sent a chair to make their tent more comfortable, and supplies of milk, vegetables, roast of mutton, and jellies. Groce also provided dogs for use in hunting, and Custer reciprocated by sending the Groces' wild game that he and his men bagged on hunts, and made certain that his estate was protected from damage by his men.

Mrs. Custer was also impressed with the customs she witnessed at the nearby Pleasant Hill plantation. Approached by one of the Peebles daughters, they quickly became friends with the family, taking long rides together over the countryside and attending many social events at Pleasant Hill. Custer never mentioned the Peebles name in her writings, but her description of the plantation owner as being "the newly appointed collector of the port … a Union man during the war (who) was hopelessly invalidated by a long political imprisonment." leaves no doubt that their benefactor was Richard Peebles, at Pleasant Hill. Custer wrote that "The house was always full of guests. The large dining-table was not long enough, however, unless placed diagonally across the dining-room, and it was sometimes laid three times before all had dined. The upper part of the house was divided by a hall running the length of the house. On one side the women and their guests, usually a lot of rollicking girls, were quartered, while the men visitors had the rooms opposite; and then I first saw the manner in which a southern gallant comes courting or flirting. He rode up to the house, with his servant, on another horse, carrying a portmanteau. They came to stay several weeks. I wondered that there was ever an uncongenial marriage at the South, when a man had a chance to see his sweetheart. This was one of the usages of the country that our Northern men adopted when they could get leave to be absent from camp, and delightful visits we all had." Elizabeth Custer also reported that her maidservant Eliza was quite an attraction for the local African-Americans. She wrote: "At that time Eliza was a famous belle. Our colored coachman, Henry, was a permanent fixture at the foot of her throne, while the darkies on the neighboring plantations came nightly to worship. She bore her honors becomingly, as well as the fact that she was the proud possessor of a showy outfit, including silk dresses. The soldiers to whom Eliza had been kind in Virginia, had given her clothes that they had found in the caches where the farmers endeavored to hide their valuables during the war."

Although Peebles had helped organize and presided at a public meeting to voice Southern grievances in Bellville, the county seat of Austin County, he opposed secession and was arrested in 1863 and charged with treason with four other Unionists for distributing a pamphlet advocating the end of the war. He was held in the jail at Anderson [north of Retreat], where he almost died of typhus and lost the sight in his left eye. He was deported to Mexico in 1864 and from there returned to Ohio and New Orleans until the war ended. After the war he was appointed customs collector in Galveston and returned to Texas in 1865. [101]

Perhaps sensing that with the end of the war his future as a wealthy planter was in jeopardy, Leonard again placed Bernardo in trust for Courtney on October 1, 1865. On this date he conveyed Bernardo and other lands and property (for the first time not including slaves because he no longer owned any) to his nephew Jared Groce IV. In the deed of trust Bernardo was to serve as collateral to cover the principle and interest on the $10,000 dowry to Courtney on their wedding day plus the $5,356 given her on February 9, 1834 by her guardian Thomas Hooper as her part of her father Alexander Fulton's estate. Included were the 1,100 and 900 acre tracts immediately south of Pond Creek that were in the original Bernardo grant. Bernardo boundaries as given in this document read as follows: "East of and fronts upon the Brazos River and is south of and adjoins the lands of Mrs. Mary Ann Peebles and is bounded on its south by Pond Creek (it being the same tract of land on which I formerly resided and contains two thousand acres, more or less." When requested by Courtney or her heirs, Jared was required to sell the land at public auction and convey to her the proceeds. [102]

The end of the Civil War forever changed the lives of all the people who had lived at Bernardo. Leonard and Courtney Groce struggled financially, with Leonard being declared bankrupt in 1868. Richard Peebles and his family apparently fared much better, continuing to live at Pleasant Hill. Descendants of the white plantation owners lived nearby as farmers for another generation, then dispersed. Many black residents of Bernardo and Pleasant Hill continued to live on the plantations as they had before the war, either as hired farm labor or as sharecroppers. In the latter 1800's many moved to the community of Lewisville near Hempstead, where descendants still own land today.

Enslaved African Americans

The agricultural empire created by Jared Groce at Bernardo was made possible through the efforts of his slaves. Jared grew up in a slaveholding family and as he reached adulthood and began his own life's work, slave ownership was a natural component of his endeavors. Jared's father farmed and owned slaves in Virginia and Georgia. Several were willed to Jared when his father died in 1804. The circumstances of Jared's ownership of slaves, beginning with his acquisition of some 47 newly-imported African-Americans in 1818 and continuing throughout his dynasty in antebellum Texas, have left extensive records about the individual bondsmen. Such records, especially on a large group of related individuals, are very rare and provide an opportunity today for historians and descendants to know several generations of family history, in some cases extending back to Africa. By the time you, the reader, reach the end of this chapter you will not only know these people as individuals, but how they lived and expressed their culture. We know them only by their first names when they were bondsmen. Only after they became free do we learn the last names they chose.

Groce likely acquired his first slaves around 1804, when three individuals were inherited from his father early that year. During the next few years he expanded his holdings in land and slaves in Georgia, and again after he moved to Alabama in 1814. Only one bill of sale from that period is known to exist; in April, 1817 he purchased six adults with three children.

During the winter of 1817 - 1818 Jared Groce II acquired 47 enslaved Africans who had just been illegally imported to the United States, landing at the port of St. Mary's on the river of that name which is the boundary between Georgia and Florida, which was Spanish territory at that time. Importation of new slaves had been banned by the United States in 1808 but a large illicit trade continued to exist. The St. Mary's port was a popular place to land newly enslaved Africans because of its remoteness from United States authorities and proximity to Spanish Florida where slave trade was illegal but openly tolerated. Several letters (detailed in Appendix II) indicate that 88 Africans were landed at St. Mary's in late 1817 and purchased there by a Captain Bowen who was an employee of Erwin, Groce and Co. Bowen took the Africans to the Creek Indian Agency in Georgia where they were held, with the sanction of and likely for a fee, by General David B. Mitchell, the U.S. official in charge of the agency. Soon Col. Gideon Morgan, another agent of Groce, Erwin and Co., called at the agency asking if Mitchell was holding any negroes. Morgan was carrying a letter of credit from Andrew Erwin which indicated that the company would cover any charges agreed to by Morgan for anything he might decide to acquire - worded in this obtuse fashion to avoid direct written instructions regarding fees related to illegal acquisition of slaves. Morgan apparently became concerned about the illegal activity in which he was about to engage, and left without the slaves. Soon after this, Jared Groce arrived at the agency and took delivery of 47 of the slaves, then departed for his home in Alabama. Before he arrived he was apprehended by Wm. McIntosh, Collector of the Port of Darien near Brunswick, Georgia. McIntosh confiscated the 47 Africans from Groce as well as the 41 who remained at the Creek agency and escorted them all back to Darien. In a letter to his superiors, he lamented that agents of the governor had immediately placed demands on the slaves, and that he fully expected that "the very aggressors may, by a forfeiture of the mock bond, be again placed in possession of the smuggled property, at but little additional expense to him, but at the entire ruin of the officers who had executed, with fidelity, the laws they felt bound to observe." This apparently occurred. Although definitive proof is lacking, it seems likely that Jared Groce did regain possession of at lease some of these newly-imported slaves, whose efforts in harvesting timber and cotton at his home on the Mobile River no doubt rapidly increased his fortunes.

Some of the people that play a prominent role in the story of Bernardo came with Jared when he moved from Alabama to Texas in 1822. Elbert, Delphy and Rachal were inherited from his father in 1804. [103] His housekeeper Myra was in this group, as was Sally, his nurse. Among this group was Thamer, a woman who was born in 1782 and lived past 1870. Thamer is an Arabic name meaning "the productive one". She probably acquired this name from her black Muslim parents as a young girl, or was given it by northern African traders speaking Arabic who obtained her as a captured slave from inland tribes and sold her to slavers on the African west coast. Chincanaba also appears in the records at Bernardo. This sounds like an African name although he was born in Texas. Most of bondsmen at Bernardo had typical southern African-American first names.

We know a lot about the slaves at Bernardo from William Wharton Groce, who was born in 1837 and spent his early life at Bernardo. His daughter Sarah Groce Berlet interviewed him in the early 1900's and records of these interviews have provided outstanding insight into everyday life on the plantation in the 1840's and 1850's. Many of the slaves named by Groce in his recollections are found in the several inventories from 1831 to 1859. Over at least a decade Berlet produced several documents containing these family stories; some remained unchanged and some were modified as she gained additional information. The following paragraphs present information given in her manuscripts. [104]

The "negro quarters" at Bernardo were located about 3/4 mile southeast of the main house on Bernardo Lake. The quarters consisted of a log cabin for each family, the overseer's house, a blacksmith shop and cotton gin, a large communal kitchen and dining hall which also served as a day nursery. Bernardo Lake was an ancient loop of the Brazos River, long ago cut off to become an "ox-bow" lake. During the early years of Bernardo it was maintained full by the spring-fed creek that rises northwest of the main house. This creek ran into the upper arm of the lake, and drained to the river from the lower arm of the lake. A sketch of the quarters by Sarah Berlet follows: [105]

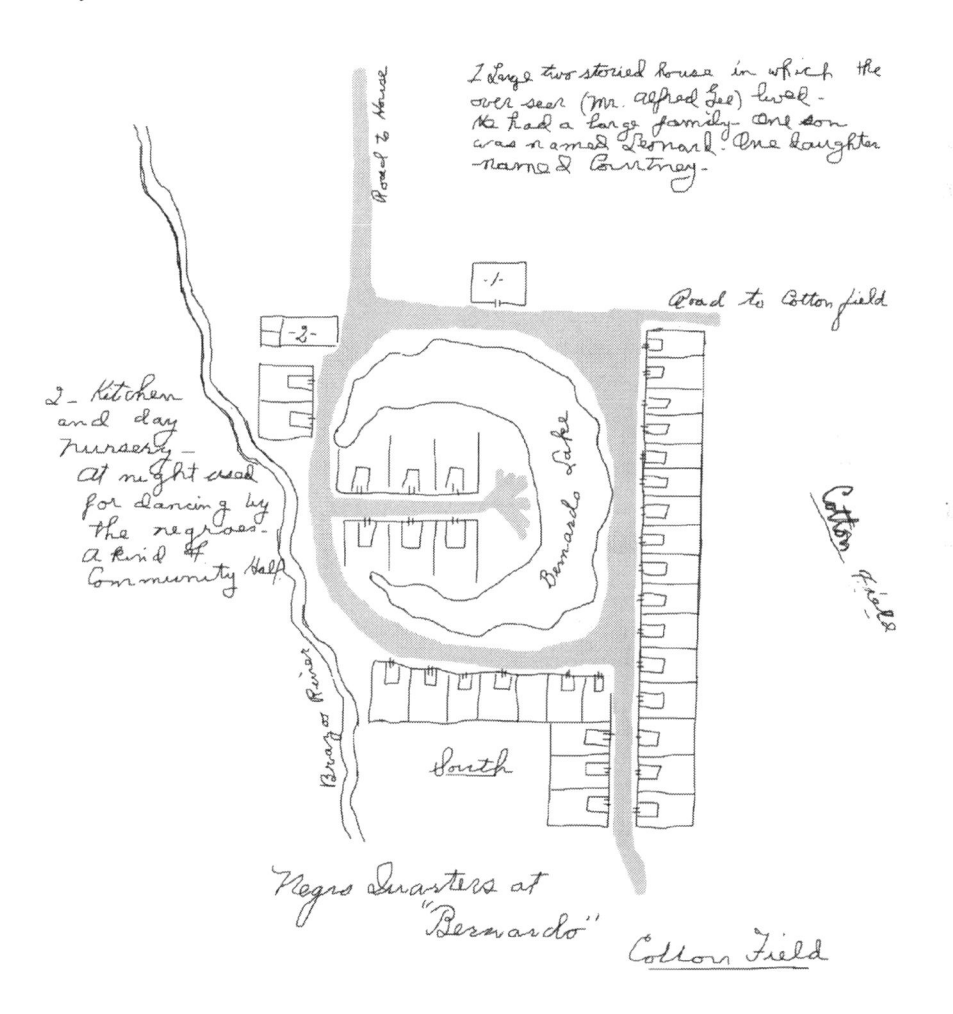

The quarters were like a small village, entirely separate and distinct from the Groce dwelling complex. Other sketches of Bernardo (shown earlier in "The Place") indicate several cabins near the main house that were probably used by the cooks, housekeepers and other servants who worked daily at the "Big House". Myra and Sally would have lived here.

Each family at the Quarters had their own chickens, hogs and a cow. A large communal garden was worked by all, and the overseer divided the vegetables. Milk was supplied them from the dairy; clothes were woven and made in-house by skilled seamstresses. The kindest and most tender-hearted women were made the day nurses, while the strongest were chosen for field hands. Most of the men worked as field hands. The servants at the Big House felt themselves superior to those at the Quarters, and would mimic the "refinement" they had observed among the master's family.

The blacksmith shop was another hub of activity. Horses and mules were shod, wagons and buggies were mended, and all tools and implements kept in good condition.

A large plow share or blade was hung at the overseer's house, used to send notice of key daily events. When struck with a piece of iron, it could be heard for a mile or more. This was the signal for all hands to get up, and was usually sounded about two hours before daylight. The mules were fed before breakfast. Several cooks were needed to prepare food for the large number of people in the quarters - usually over one hundred. The first task was to brew steaming pots of strong coffee. At daybreak the gong was sounded and all hands came to the "hall", which joined the kitchen. Young boys and girls served coffee, after which the hands went to the field; men with plows and women with hoes. The children and babies were left in a nursery in the hall under the care of older women. Breakfast typically consisted of ham or bacon, hot biscuits and fresh steak. It was cooked in the kitchen, packed in buckets and sent to the field in carts to be distributed among the workers around 7:00 a.m. At 12 o'clock dinner was cooked and served in the same manner. At 6 p.m. work was finished and all gathered at the "hall" for hot supper.

After supper the babies were taken home and the young folks stayed at the nursery to play, dance and sing. There were always musicians among the slaves who could play the fiddle, and others would "cut the pigeon" (tap dance). Their voices could be heard at the Big House any night in laughter and song. Many of the old melodies are still with us today.

A myriad of other activities filled the work day during periods of inclement weather when plowing and hoeing were not pursued. Saturday afternoons and Sundays were holidays, free time to be spent "mostly in fishing and frolicking."

Traveling preachers often came to Bernardo and held services for on Sunday afternoons, under trees or at the hall. Camp meetings were occasionally held, during which "all got religion which lasted for awhile". Baptizing took place in the lake, attended by blacks and whites alike.

Groce recounted a happy time among the lives of the slaves: "While the younger people danced and sang, the older folks would sit in front of their cabins, or in the house by the fire, and talk of the old days back in Georgia and Alabama. They had not a care in the world. They were well fed and clothed, and were a happy, contented people. Several beeves were killed each week to supply the table with fresh meat, and the slaves of Jared Groce never lacked any good thing." Viewed from today's perspective, this statement appears as a typical slaveowner's paternalistic view of the people under his ownership. It fails to recognize the stark fact that these people were not free to exercise their own will, although at Bernardo treatment of the slaves does appear to have been reasonable. Life there probably represented the best choice available to the residents of Bernardo's Quarters.

Many superstitions harking back to life in Africa were held by Bernardo residents. Sickness, injuries or just a streak of bad luck were often interpreted by the victim as a result of having been "hoo dooed" involving a "conjure doctor". Witchcraft was commonly practiced but in secret; the identity of the witch was withheld from the master. Older women made money practicing witchcraft, and most of the negroes believed that witches had special powers which could be used for good and evil. A person seeking revenge from another would visit the witch and receive a small "conjure bag" containing items such as horse hair, wool, nail parings, an old tooth and the claws of some animal. The bag was taken to the home of the enemy and hidden, sometimes sewn inside the mattress or feather bed. Lingering illness or bad luck were a sure sign that a conjure bag was on the premises, prompting an exhaustive search to find it. Once discovered, it and its contents were burned, destroying the spell that had been cast by the "Conjurer", or witch.

One incident at Bernado involved an elderly woman who had been ill and under the resident doctor's care for several months. No cause for the illness could be determined, and all efforts to treat it failed. A visiting physician was asked to examine the woman. He found her thin, weak and unable to walk across the room. She reported that she had been "hoo dooed". The new doctor reported that no amount of medicine would cure this woman as long as she believed that she was under the spell of a witch. He indicated that he could break the spell, and was told to proceed. William Groce accompanied the doctor back to the woman's cabin, who told her "Well Aunty, I've discovered how to cure you." He lifted her into a sitting position and pointed to a crack near the rock chimney, telling her that that was where the evil spirit had entered. Telling her to remain motionless and pay close attention, he mumbled some words in Latin which sounded very mysterious to her, and proclaimed that the evil spirit was leaving back through the crack from which it came, never to return. Placing her feet on the floor, a happy expression came over her face and she began to thank the Doctor, laughing and crying in turn. In less than a week, she was perfectly well. Upon hearing of the cure, Jared Groce said, " 'by guar' what I need on this plantation is a Conjure Doctor!", and from that time on if the resident doctor's medicine failed, the "hoo doo" remedy was employed and generally succeeded.

Christmas was a special holiday anticipated by all the people at Bernardo. Leonard Groce would prepare for the holiday by making a trip to Houston in late November, sometimes being gone for several days. He returned with his wagon loaded with fruit, candy, raisins, flour, sugar, spices and presents for every one on the plantation. He would be greeted by scores of children who would wave, shout, and follow the wagon right up to the back gate. Provisions were handed out to the head of each family, and for days there was baking in the cabins at the Quarters.

Everyone gathered in the yard of the Big House on Christmas morning. When Leonard and Courtney came to the door, shouts of "Christmas gift! Christmas gift!" would be responded to with a present, delivered by the Groce children. Groce reported that the white children copied this custom of shouting "Christmas gift!". Among the gifts were always new bandanas for the women, and a good Sunday dress. A supply of tobacco was among the gifts for the men. When the presents were all distributed, and the children had all the apples and candy they could carry, the slaves returned to the Quarters to cook their own dinners consisting of turkey and a full range of other foods available on the plantation. The week between Christmas and New Year's day was a holiday, enjoyed to the limit by young and old alike.

Now let's get acquainted with the Bernardo slaves, starting with Myra. She was Groce's housekeeper and was nanny for his children. She was an early acquisition in Georgia, and with her son Nelson accompanied Groce to Bernardo in 1822, to Retreat in 1833, then came back to Bernardo when he died in 1836. Family lore indicates that Jared provided for his older slaves who were no longer able to work while they remained his property. Accounts of family and acquaintances indicate that Jared "freed" his slaves in their old age. More likely, there was no manumission involved but the elderly slaves were supported with food and shelter on the plantation. In the case of Myra, as he approached his final days, Jared was said to have "set her free" and made his sons promise to assure she had a comfortable rest of her life. Something akin to manumission did occur in this one case; an 1850 inventory of slaves states that Myra was valued at only $1 because she was "nominally free". [106] Other adult slave women were valued around $75 in this same inventory. The law in Texas at that time required all freedmen to leave the state, so to list Myra as being totally free would have exposed her to deportation by the authorities, something that the Groces (and probably Myra) did not want to happen. In 1831 Harry, a servant of Retreat neighbor Joshua Hadley, was sold to Groce. Jared "purchased Harry for $1000, though Harry was crippled and could not have been sold to any one else for more than $400." [107] Harry is listed in an 1831 inventory of Bernardo slaves, but living with another family. The first inventory in which he is listed as living with Myra was in 1850. Family lore and the Zuber account mentioned above indicates that Harry was crippled, but nothing in the archival records indicate that this was the case. His value in several slave inventories was always that of a healthy man in his prime. There was one slave named Jacob who was called "Lame Jake" and may have been confused with Harry by family member William Groce in his recollections. Lame Jake looked after the cattle herd at Bernardo; his physical disability yielded him a lower valuation in the slave inventories.

Edom was Jared's manservant and "came with the family from Virginia". He must have been well respected in his community as his unusual first name was passed down several generations. We first learn of Edom in 1824, when Jonathon P. Coles wrote to Stephen Austin indicating that he had recently visited Groce and found him in ill health, and his servant "Edmon" near death. Other records suggest that Edom died at this time and was replaced by Kelly as Jared's manservant. Another source indicates that Edom was freed by Jared and provided care for the rest of his life, but this does not appear to have been factual. Edom likely died in 1824 as Cole predicted, as his name does not appear in an 1831 inventory of Groce's slaves. [108] The name Edom appears to have been a contraction of Edmond.

Moses ('Uncle Mose') was the plantation's hunter and with his gun and hounds kept the table supplied with deer and turkey, often accompanied on his hunts by a young Wm. Groce on his pony. Lydia ('Aunt Liddie'), Moses' wife, oversaw the operations of the dairy behind the Big House. Inside the cedar dairy were shelves on two walls with troughs hollowed out of the logs and filled with water in which pans of milk were placed. A cover of thin muslin tacked to a frame covered the pans. William Groce described the dairy as pleasant, sweet-smelling and spotless, and to "watch Aunt Liddy churn, keeping time to the old tune, 'Come, Butter, Come'. When she had 'gathered' the butter she would insist on your drinking a glass of fresh buttermilk." The words to this song are: "Come, butter, come. Peter stands at the gate, Waiting for a butter cake. Come, butter, come." [109] This drawing by French artist Jean-François Millet from 1855 is titled "La Baratteuse" [Woman Churning Butter]. One can easily image this is Aunt Liddy, in the dairy at Bernardo, hard at work.

Sally had been purchased in South Carolina on January 1, 1817. [110] She was Jared's nurse during the early days in Texas, and helped look after the Groce children. She was "a privileged character, four and a half feet high and almost as broad." Her room was among those of the other house servants in the back yard of the Big House. By 1847 she had become feeble with age and kept to her room most of the time. The Groce children would often visit her, be greeted with a smile and at times a story about "bro Rabbit and de Bar, or the Elephant who crossed the frozen stream, etc. Her bed was the customary four poster, and in the winter she used two feather beds, and she would sink out of sight, except for her white wooly head which was propped up on several pillows."

Sally participated in the foundation of Stephen Austin's capital of San Felipe. On October 2, 1823, land commissioner Baron de Bastrop wrote to Governor Garcia that he and Austin had selected a site for the new capital on the west bank of the Brazos at the crossing of the Atascosito road. Austin had decided on the location of the capital of his new colony in September, 1823. Austin immediately began to build his house and begin government operations. Town lots were surveyed in November. On October 19, 1823, Austin penned an agreement with Jared Groce in which Sally, two of her children, Lame Jake and Kelly were leased for several months, apparently to help him build and operate his new home. [111] It seems likely that cloth and tailoring supplies purchased by Austin from Groce the day before the rental agreement was signed were to be used by Sally to make clothing for the Empresario, and that Lame Jake and Kelly would help build his log cabin residence at San Felipe. The leasing of the Groce slaves to Austin was likely the first such agreement made in Texas. The practice became common later and provided slaveholders with an alternate source of income. One study revealed that 396 slaves were leased in Texas between 1853 and 1857. [112]

Matt, Sally's son, managed the dairy herd. It was his job to drive the cows in from the pasture, and while others milked he would hold off the calves, which had been allowed to take just enough milk to 'draw it down'. Fielding was Leonard's manservant and occasional carriage driver. He and Pickins were also Sally's sons. Mack was the gardner, remembered for his wonderful vegetables and ripe strawberries in season.

The cook at Bernardo during this period was Davie. He had been the cook at the St. Charles Hotel in New Orleans when, on a visit to that town, Leonard Groce bought him for $2,500.00. Cooking was done in the kitchen behind the Big House on an open fireplace. Large quantities were the norm as there were usually fifteen to eighteen people at the table, plus house servants, to feed. Davie had several helpers in the kitchen in addition to the boys who carried the cooked food from the kitchen to the dining room. Leonard Groce bought a cast iron cook stove and had it delivered as a surprise for Davie. A flue was built and the stove connected, but after a few days Davie was again using the old fireplace and continued to do so for a long time. Finally he became used to the stove, but if he wanted something cooked especially well, he used the open fire and hearth. Fragments of a large cast iron stove found during archaeological activities in 2010 near the Big House may well have once been Davie's stove.

Jerry was the butler. He had been a Fulton slave in Alexandria and as a young man was given to Courtney when she married in 1831. Courtney taught him how to be a butler; he presided in the dining room, receiving hot dishes from the boys at the door, and distributed them among the waiters. He then took his stand behind Leonard's chair and watched the table, seeing that all were served and had the dishes replenished when empty. Jerry and his wife were hired by Leonard and Courtney Groce to continue their services to the family during 1867. They were paid $40 per month, plus board for them and their two children. [113]

Harriet was Courtney's maid. Like Jerry, she had also been a Fulton slave and accompanied Courtney to Texas. Courtney had auburn hair that shone after Harriet would brush it using one hundred strokes at a setting. Harriet helped her daughter Frances, who was the seamstress, to do the fine sewing. Most of the sewing was done by hand until 1847, when Courtney bought a sewing machine. It was screwed to a table and turned by hand. Frances was married to Lewis

Baker; they both contracted with Leonard Groce to work at Bernardo during 1866.

Caroline was the head house maid, and she and her staff of girls kept the house spotless. These servants were so well trained that even when the house was full of company, there was no confusion. After the guests and family had retired, the rooms were cleaned and dusted, ready to be used in the morning.

Arimenta was the laundress, called the "wash woman". She gathered up the clothes each morning from all bedrooms. They were taken out to the wash room where they were washed daily to keep up with the volume of dirty clothes from the large family and their guests. She took pride in her work, especially the dressed and fluted skirts for Courtney and her daughters which were hung on long wooden pegs in the closets. Several "sad" or flat irons used to iron clothes were found about two hundred yards behind the Big House near the stables and a buried brick floor. These likely represent remnants of the wash room and Arimenta's work tools.

Minerva ("Aunt Minervy") was William Groce's nurse until he was six years old, and "another privileged character". Groce recounted that "She used to put me to sleep with her favorite song, 'Old Grimes is dead, that good old man, we'll never see him more. He wore brass buttons behind his coat, and likewise down before.'" When Wm. returned from college, after greeting his family he went to see Minerva. He recalled "I thought at first she was going to kiss me, she seemed so delighted at my return. She said, 'well Buddy you sure have growed up', to which I replied 'since you recognize that fact Mammy, don't you think you should call me Mars William?' She was indignant, and said, 'Look here Buddy, whose you talking to? I is forgot the times I held you in dese arms, undressed you, and rocked and sung you to sleep. Just go along now, and de next time you meet your old Mammy on the road, you just remember who you am talking to.' And I was 'Buddy' to Aunt Minervy as long as she lived."

Buggy was Wm. Groce's " own boy". He was a few months older than William, and given to him by his father when he was born. The two were inseparable companions. When William rode his pony, Buggy jumped on behind. The two boys were together all day long, separated only at night and during meal times, until William left for school.

Lorenza Dow was William Groce's first real valet (or body servant), assigned on his seventeenth birthday. He was a young French mulatto from New Orleans, whom his uncle Marcus Fulton had given to Courtney. William remembered him as "respectful and efficient in every way", but knew that he was not happy in the country, and often longed to return to New Orleans. In 1856,

Elisha Pease (Leonard's lawyer) was moving to Austin from Brazoria County to serve his second term as governor of Texas. He stopped at Liendo for a few days; with him was his body servant Sam, "a tall negro, black as the ace of spades". William overheard a conversation between Sam and Lorenzo, in which Sam said he hated to go to Austin, and Lorenza said he wished he could take his place. William appealed to his father and Governor Pease, proposing a trade, which was agreed upon. Lorenzo accompanied the Governor to Austin, and Sam Pease, remained at Liendo with William, "as faithful a servant as ever lived." Lorenzo Dow was living in 1870 in Danville, Montgomery County, with his wife Louisa.[114]

Whereas personal servants of both Leonard and Courtney Groce often accompanied their masters on trips, it was a rare occasion when other slaves left the plantation vicinity. One Groce family story told of a visitor who enjoyed Leonard Groce's hospitality for several weeks before departing, during which time he was afforded the services of a young slave named Joe. His offer to reimburse Groce for his stay being refused, the visitor gave $50 to Joe, telling him it was for him alone in thanks for his services. Joe turned the money over to Groce, who decided that Joe should accompany him to Houston to see for the first time the sights of this big "city". In Houston they found a steamboat readying to depart for Galveston. Groce bought a ticket for Joe, gave him the rest of the $50, and told him have a good time and then return to Bernardo. Not knowing if he would ever see Joe again, Groce returned home. So did Joe after a few days, telling all that it was too lonesome for him in Galveston and that he was glad to be home among friends.

When a bondsman was sold from one owner to another, a bill of sale was commonly drawn up, given to the new owner, and sometimes filed in the county courthouse as a proof of ownership. During the entire antebellum period Bernardo was part of Austin County. The record of bills of sale in that county appear incomplete before 1868. They are non-existent before 1848, and a single record book contains some entries between 1848 and 1865. [115] There are dozens of bills of sale for slaves in this record, but only three involving Leonard Groce.

One appears to be an outright purchase of eight individuals, all "of dark complexion", from Louis Dufour on February 22, 1851, in which Leonard paid $1,000 for Ellick (27 yers old), Sarah (18) and her child Charles (3), Martha (16), Peter (15), Isaac (15), Flora (13) and Frank (11). In a second purchase dated January 26, 1852, William Stubblefield sold three slaves to Leonard Groce for $1,700: Jeffords (22), Lishey (22) and her child Caroline (3).

The third record is a trust arrangement and not a direct sale. On December 6, 1858, Harriet Simmons conveyed in trust Charlotte (22) and Caroline (15) to Leonard Groce. Simmons had borrowed $300 from Frank Lipscomb. In the event that Simmons was unable to repay the note, Groce was instructed to sell the slaves at public auction and use the proceeds to repay the note to Lipscomb. These two women probably remained the property of Simmons or Lipscomb and never resided at Bernardo.

Nowhere in the Austin County records, family accounts or the accounts of others is their any mention of any Groce selling slaves. While this seems very unlikely over such a long period, if it happened it must have been a rare occurrence. The various slave inventories from Bernardo and Pleasant Hill from 1831 to 1858 indicate that family units remained stable. Groups of slaves were transferred to other family members, as happened with William Wharton in 1831, and Jared Groce III in 1835, and later to his widow and two children. On more than one occasion Leonard placed his slaves in trust to assure sufficient money was available to repay the money Courtney had given to him from her marriage dowry and gifts; ownership always reverted back to Leonard. Even the hard times of the Civil War did not force Leonard to sell his slaves, as evidenced by the county tax assessor stating that he owned 135 slaves in April of 1865, up from the 119 shown in the 1860 census.

Many of the former slaves at Bernardo and Pleasant Hill continued to live and work after the Civil War ended as they had before. The 1870 United States census is the first such record in which African Americans are enumerated with last names. The previous two census (1850 and 1860) contain slave schedules in which slaveowners are shown with their chattel listed only by gender and age. Antebellum deeds, probate records and bills of sale dealing with slave ownership typically described the individuals by first name and age, and at times indicated family relationships. Last names were virtually never recorded, and may well never had existed in many cases. At Bernardo, however, it appears that at least several of the families had last names they understood, even if they were never mentioned in the records before 1870. An examination of the 1870 census shows a number of people living near Bernardo and Pleasant Hill with Collins, Livingston, Sprigs and Lilley surnames. These people can be directly connected to former bondsmen at the two plantations using the first names, ages and family relationships provided in several inventories of slaves from 1831 to 1859. Elsewhere, newly freed slaves took the surname of their former master if the relationship had been satisfactory, or the name of the place they lived (eg: Bellville for some Austin County residents), or the name of a famous person (eg;

Washington, Jefferson). At Bernardo, individuals who had resided there and been owned by Groces for over fifty years did not take that last name when freed. Instead, they maintained a family name that must have been carried forward for several generations. Perhaps these names were those of the original owner of the family patriarch, acquired before Groce ownership. There are a few instances where freedmen took the name Peebles and Clark from their Pleasant Hill owners.

Several black individuals in the 1870 census have the last name Groce in Harris and Grimes counties, including a man named Jared who was born about 1830. None of these individuals appeared in the various inventories. They may have been owned by Leonard Groce, or his sons Jared F. or William, or his nephew Jared IV.

The chapter "Descendants of Bernardo Residents" expands on the efforts to tie specific individuals listed in the 1870 census to those known to live at Bernardo and Pleasant Hill before the Civil War.

Notable Visitors and Events; Groce Texans

Bernardo was a well known social center and the Groces were the richest family in Texas for many years. Historical accounts repeatedly mention that the plantation house was full of visitors nearly every day. People who were traveling through stopped there for a night or two. Family and friends were frequently present. Others came to do business, or access the extensive resources that were available. Because of their powerful status and leadership among the plantation owners, Jared and Leonard Groce counted many notable Texans among their friends and associates.

Stephen F. Austin was a frequent visitor at Bernardo. He bought supplies and leased three slaves from Groce as he was establishing San Felipe as his new capital. Austin granted Groce ten leagues of land, the largest granted to any settler, in recognition of the large number of slaves he owned. Austin briefly courted Jared Groce's daughter Sarah Ann. He recognized the importance of Groce's resources to his nascent colony, and utilized these resources on several occasions.

One of the earliest examples of Groce's assistance to Austin came in 1824 in response to repeated raids on the colonists from Karankawa Indians. The traditional homelands of these Texas natives extended from the western margins of Galveston Bay down the Gulf Coast to Corpus Christi Bay. The Karankawa subtribe known as Cocos or Capoques lived initially along the lower Brazos, Colorado and Lavaca rivers. In the wintertime they would leave the coastal margins and travel up to a hundred mies inland in search of food and shelter. Raids on settler's cabins in the first years of Austin's colony were common and resulted in both loss of life and theft of horses, cattle and other goods. Most of these raids occurred along the lower Brazos and Colorado Rivers. Stephen F. Austin led a group of 40 to 50 volunteers to the Lavaca River in July, 1824, to punish marauding Karankawas. They were not successful in engaging the Indians in this venture and another expedition was promptly planned to proceed further west. A force of fifty settlers was raised and left in August, augmented this time by thirty armed and mounted slaves provided by Jared Groce. Jared went with the group as commander of his slaves but was not able to personally engage in combat as he was crippled in both arms and thus exempt from military service. The Texian militia proceeded along the Atascosito road to Manahuilla Creek just east of Goliad where they stopped and parlayed with local townsmen and priests who represented the Karankawas. An agreement was reached by which Austin would cease his military offensive and the Indians would not travel eastward beyond the San Antonio River. Austin's troops returned home but the Karankawas soon broke their promise and resumed raiding in Austin's Colony. This was the first of several instances in which the Groce family significantly assisted Texian military campaigns. Although never personally participating directly in military actions, Groces provided supplies and funded others to participate. [116]

Upon returning to his colony from Mexico in August of 1823, Austin soon selected a site for his new capital of San Felipe de Austin some twenty miles down the Brazos from Bernardo, at the Atascosito road crossing. Groce's operation at Bernardo was a nearby source of labor and supplies. On October 18, Austin purchased supplies from Groce that he needed as he built his new home in San Felipe. [117] In this transaction he also borrowed money from Groce to pay other creditors. The amount due Groce from this transaction was applied against Groce's fees from Austin for obtaining his land grants.

In a separate document on the same day Austin indicated that he would pay the $326.49 debt to Groce in land at eight acres for each dollar owed, and that this covered partial payment for two of the seven leagues offered by Austin. Groce had already settled on the other five leagues. The next day Austin leased three of Jared Groce's slaves to help him in his new endeavor at San Felipe. It seems likely that the cloth and tailoring supplies purchased by Austin from Groce the day before were to be used by Sally to make clothing for the empresario, and that Jack and Kelly would help build his log cabin residence at San Felipe.

Stephen Austin was occasionally perturbed with Jared Groce's actions, as when Groce complained directly to Mexican officials about surveys of his land grants. This action, bypassing Austin, was an obvious political affront to the empresario. Austin also became aware of troubling questions about Groce's past including the possibility that he had obtained slaves illegally and had fled the United States to escape payment of a business debt to Andrew and James Erwin. Austin knew that he needed access to Groce's assets as he built his new colony in Texas, and astutely decided to ignore Groce's shortcomings. [118]

A candid view of the Groce family and their operations at Bernardo was chronicled by a French military commander named Maurice Persat, who traveled through Texas in 1826. He stopped at Bernardo on October 15, where he was greeted by Sarah Ann Groce; her father Jared was away from home at the time. They arrived soaked from a rainstorm and were given some of Jared's dry clothes to wear. They planned to depart the next day but were persuaded by Sarah Ann to remain another day. Persat commented that Groce owned a hundred slaves and had two houses (Bernardo and Retreat) "that were not inferior in any way compared to the most beautiful I have seen on the banks of the Red River and the Mississippi. Cotton was harvested there in large quantities [with yields] higher than those of Louisiana." He predicted a strong future for Texas, saying: "I believe that twenty years will be enough time for Americans to make Texas one of the richest countries of the North and South; while remaining in the hands of vandalous Mexicans, the vast province shall never flourish." Sarah Ann provided a guide to take Persat's party to Retreat, where they met Jared and stayed for two days. During this visit Jared described his past life in the United States. Persat opined that Jared, "being a libertine, gambler, and even a bankrupt in the United States, had become among the forests of Texas, a gentleman, a good father, and peaceful farmer. I must say again, in praise of Mr. Groce, that he was very humane to his blacks, who in their turn, were very dedicated to him." [119]

Another incident in which Groce aided Austin involved Benjamin Edwards, a would-be empresario and filibustier. When his colonization grant in east Texas was cancelled by the Mexican Government because of his suspicious activities, Edwards plotted with the Cherokee Indians to rise up against the Mexicans and remove a portion of Texas from their control. On November 22, 1826, some forty men under Edwards captured Nacogdoches, arrested the alcalde and seized the archives. There he proclaimed the Republic of Fredonia and instituted the minor revolt known as the Fredonian Rebellion. Stephen Austin and other colonists sided with the Mexican authorities in opposition to Edwards. Austin led a military force to Nacogdoches to suppress the rebellion, stopping at Bernardo on January 29 & 30, 1827, where they obtained all of the supplies for the expedition. Jared Groce provided food, wagons, teams and slaves for the expedition. Austin provided to Groce a list of these items and promissory note to pay Groce at a later date: "Recd. the above articles amounting to ninety nine dollars and sixty seven and a half cents for the use of the expedition to Nacogdoches and for the payment of which to J.E. Groce, I am responsible. Jany. 30, 1827. Stephen F. Austin". As Austin's troops approached Nacogdoches, Edwards chose not to fight and retreated to Louisiana. Another document from Austin's records is dated June 27, 1827 and shows a debt to Groce of eight dollars for beef, meal and corn. One year later, in June 1828, Austin's notes show that he had paid only part of the debt owed to Groce for quashing the Fredonian Rebellion. Austin had given Groce a wagon that they agreed as an eighty dollar credit against Austin's debt. In addition, Austin had paid $25 in cash and still owed Groce $2.57. [120] The Mexican government sent more troops to Texas after the rebellion. On September 2, 1827, the 12th Permanent Battalion of the Mexican army bivouacked at Bernardo and obtained food and supplies. On that day they conducted a full muster and made lists of every one of the some 120 soldiers and officers by name who were present. [121]

In 1831 the political chief of San Felipe wrote Manuel De Los Santos of Nacogdoches advising that Solomon Bowlin and companions were fomenting rebellion and were to be driven out and turned over to authorities. J. Franciso Madero apprehended the rebels and stayed at the residence of "Mr. Gros" on January 19, 1831. Groce was given custody of the prisoners until Feb. 15, 1831, when he turned them over to Mexican guards. [122]

Samuel May Williams, a major player in the government of Austin's Colony and later a successful businessman, owed his start in the new colony to Jared Groce. During part of the winter of 1822/23 Williams stayed at Bernardo doing legal clerking work for Groce, probably living in the Bachelor's Hall. He had arrived in Texas from New Orleans in June, 1822, under the pseudonym E. Eccleston (the last name was that of his woman companion). He first settled at Hawkin's Landing at the mouth of the Colorado River. After leaving Bernardo, Williams was employed as a tutor at the home of Robert Kuykendall on the lower Colorado. By the end of 1823 he had joined Stephen Austin at San Felipe as secretary of Austin's Colony, marking the beginning of a prosperous and influential career in Texas. [123] On April 17, 1824, Bautista de Arispe of Monterrey wrote a letter to Austin ask about their mutual friend Jared Groce. This letter mentions that in 1822 Groce had met Samuel Williams and invited him to Texas. [124] Texas historian Homer Thrall indicated that Groce met Williams in Mexico and invited him to come to Texas. If in fact Groce invited Williams to Texas, it probably happened in New Orleans in November or December of 1821, when Groce was visiting that city in which Williams had resided since 1819. Williams likely knew Stephen Austin before Texas as both resided in New Orleans where they worked and lived near each other in 1821. Groce's first known trip to Mexico was in late 1822 to sell his first cotton crop. At that time Williams was already in Texas.

Williams wrote a letter to Stephen Austin dated October 18, 1823 in which he indicated that he had been employed by Mr. Hanna in La Bahia in August of 1822, and described his stay at Bernardo the previous February. He related an incident during this visit when a Mr. Massey visited Bernardo and asked Jared Groce to buy a note that he held from William Pettus, and offered to include a slave in the transaction. Groce refused on the grounds that he and Massey had had a dispute with Pettus' brother. [125]

In late 1823 Stephen F. Austin employed Williams as translator and clerk at San Felipe. For the next thirteen years Williams was Austin's lieutenant; he wrote deeds, kept records, and directed colonial activities during the empresario's absences. In 1826 he was named postmaster of San Felipe and was appointed revenue collector and dispenser of stamped paper by the state of Coahuila and Texas the following year. He became secretary to the *ayuntamiento* of San Felipe when it was created in 1828. For these services he received eleven leagues (49,000 acres) of land which he selected on strategic waterways including Oyster Creek and Buffalo Bayou. [126]

Jane Long, known as "The Mother of Texas", spent the summer of 1824 with her daughter Ann and maidservant Kian as guests of Jared Groce at Bernardo. Jane's older sister had married Alexander Calvit of Alexandria, and Jane often relied on her sister for support as she pioneered Texas with her husband James Long in 1819. The Calvit's and Groce's were acquainted in Louisiana, and this connection was likely responsible for Groce's hospitality to her in 1824. [127]

William and John Wharton, brothers and both prominent in the affairs of Austin's Colony and the Republic, were also closely associated with Jared Groce and Bernardo. The Wharton's were from Nashville where they were associated with Sam Houston in the Texas Association, a group competing with Moses Austin to be the first to colonize Texas in 1821. William and John moved to Texas in early 1827, where they promptly visited Jared Groce at Bernardo. By the end of that year William had married Groce's daughter Sarah Ann.

Some accounts suggest that Stephen F. Austin briefly courted Sarah Ann Groce when she arrived in Texas, leading to animosity between Austin and Wharton. If this courtship by Austin actually occurred, it must have been in early - mid 1827. [128] One example of the strained relations between these two men is seen in a letter Austin wrote to his brother-in-law James F. Perry on August 25, 1834, during his imprisonment in Mexico City. In this lengthy letter, Austin specifically named William Wharton and Thomas Jefferson Chambers as opposing his (Austin's) being selected as the delegate to take the resolutions from the 1833 Convention at San Felipe to Mexico and to advocate for their acceptance by the Mexican government. He wrote: "*these same men* should now try to ruin me and perpetuate my imprisonment, and should rejoice and exult at my sufferings ..." [129]

Leonard Groce was a close personal friend of Stephen F. Austin, as was his father. In a letter to Thomas F. McKinney written during the period he was in prison in Mexico City, Austin specifically mentioned two individuals by name to whom he extended his greetings - Mrs. McKinney and Leonard Groce:

"Mexico October 18, 1834 - in the city prison. … Remember me to Mrs. McKinney and to Col. Groce and all his children and to my friends in genl. …. S.F. Austin".   Mckinney, Leonard and Jared Groce III had been business partners around this time. [130]

Wm. Wharton revisited Texas in early 1829. During this visit he met Stephen Austin at Cumming's mill. Wharton promised to visit Austin before he returned to Tennessee, but did not do so. Austin then wrote Wharton a long letter dated April 29, 1829, urging Wharton to move to Texas. This letter begins: "You and myself are almost strangers, our personal intercourse has scarcely been sufficient to enable us mutually to estimate each other properly. I have a very decided friendship for all Col. G (Jared Groce) I have full confidence in League [a Brazoria settler] and he assures me that W.H.W. is all that a man of honor and a firm and steadfast friend ought to be. …" [131]

Sam Houston was another notable Texan with a strong relationship with Jared Groce, who was instrumental in Houston's decision to move to Texas. Texas historian Louis Wortham wrote: "It was through a personal letter from Wm. H. Wharton, at Groce's suggestion, that Sam Houston came to Texas." Wortham indicated that Wm. H. Wharton, who had known Houston in Tennessee, related some anecdotes about Houston to Groce, who exclaimed, 'That's the kind of a man we need in Texas! Write to him and urge him to come!'". [132] Groce family lore indicates that this letter was written from Bernardo. Archival evidence shows that there were two Wharton letters to Houston, but they were from William's brother John and not written from Bernardo. One, dated October 25, 1829, was sent to Houston while he was living with the Cherokees in Indian Territory, having fled Tennessee after his aborted marriage earlier that year. John Wharton wrote: "I therefore request you once more to visit Texas. It is a fine field for enterprise. You can get a grant of land, and yet be surrounded by your friends." [133] When he wrote this letter he was on his way from Nashville to Texas in company with Leonard Groce and his brother William and Sarah Ann Groce Wharton, who were moving back to Texas to stay.   Perhaps Leonard and William told John about Jared Groce's interest in Houston moving to Texas.

The second letter from John Wharton to Houston was from New Orleans, dated June 2, 1832, in which he said he had given a Letter of Introduction to Branch Archer who had moved to Texas a year earlier. Archer was instrumental in the events leading up to the Texas revolution and served as Secretary of War in the Republic of Texas. Wharton mentioned that Archer was well connected, and "is of the opinion that there will be some fighting there next fall, and that a fine country will be gained without much bloodshed, he is very desirous that you should go there, and believes that you can be of more service than any other man. ... Texas does undoubtedly present a fine field for fame, enterprise, and usefulness, and whenever they are ready for action, I will be with them." Houston forwarded this letter to a Mr. Prentiss, writing: "Mr. Wharton is a lawyer of New Orleans of genius -- a young man, and is the brother of William Wharton, son-in-law of Grose of Texas. He can be relied upon and you know Dr. Archer. You can let Mr. Jackson [President Andrew] and our friends (such as you wish) see this letter [Whartons], and send it back to me enclosed to the postmaster here, or Mr. Blair, with any communications to me. If they come to the bar, they are often overlooked. It is important that I should be off to Texas! Write soon." Houston clearly knew of Jared Groce in 1832, as he introduced the Whartons by their connection to him; he had yet to meet Groce in person. [134]

Houston was in Washington at this time, where he had probably visited Andrew Jackson. Houston had an early tie to Texas in that he was a member of the Texas Association, a group of Texas colonization advocates from Tennessee that competed with Steven F. Austin in 1822 in Mexico for the rights to the first Anglo colony in Mexican Texas. He knew Andrew Erwin and the Whartons from this association and perhaps had heard of Jared Groce from Erwin prior to 1822. Houston crossed the Red River into Mexican Texas on December 2, 1832, to begin a new phase of his career. His motives for moving to Texas have been the source of much speculation, including a desire to profit from land speculation, as an agent of Andrew Jackson to determine when the time was ripe for annexation, or to participate in establishing an independent nation. Whatever his motives, Houston saw Texas as his 'land of promise', and so it was!

Richard Rogers Peebles was another influential early Texan who became intimately involved with the Groce family and Bernardo. Peebles had arrived in 1835 from Cincinnati, Ohio. Peebles established a medical practice in 1835 in Washington that covered several counties. In 1836 he served in the Texian army and cared for the ill and injured near Harrisburg during the Battle of San Jacinto. His involvement with Bernardo would begin in 1840 and is continued in the chapter on Three Generations of Groces at Bernardo. He would later wed the widow of Jared E. Groce III and inherit Pleasant Hill plantation, a portion of the original Bernardo grant.

Jim Bowie knew Jared Groce through mutual friends in Louisiana. Bowie had been a slave trader and land speculator in Louisiana for several years. He owned Acadia Plantation in Rapides Parish, Louisiana, where he became friends with his neighbors the Wells, Fulton and Cuny families. All three families were prominent planters and related; Cuny and Fulton had married Wells daughters. It was a result of these friendships that Bowie accepted an invitation to be an aide for Samuel Wells in a 1827 duel with a political rival. After the two dualists fired shots and missed, a deadly melee broke out among all the participants in which Samuel Cuny, brother of Philip Cuny who later moved to Texas creating Sunny Side plantation by Bernardo, was shot and killed. Bowie was seriously wounded in the fight but managed to use his large, uniquely designed hunting knife to disembowel and kill the rival duelist's second, Norris Wright. The media frenzy describing this "Mississippi Sand-Bar Fight" began the legend of the famous Bowie Knife. Bowie had prior experience in Texas as many of his slaves were purchased from Jean Lafitte on Galveston Island, with whom he conducted an extensive slave trading enterprise. Some historians believe that Bowie participated in the ill-farted Long Expedition in 1819, although he was not among those captured. Bowie had become engaged marry to Cecelia Wells (Courtney Groce's cousin) in September, 1829. Two weeks before their wedding date Cecelia died in Alexandria. This tragic event caused Bowie to leave Louisiana, and on January 1, 1830, he and a friend named Isaac Donoho left Thibodeaux, Louisiana, to come to Texas. They traveled through Nacogdoches and down the La Bahia road to Washington, then to Bernardo where he stopped briefly to visit his friends Jared and Leonard Groce before proceeding to San Felipe. There he presented a letter of introduction to Stephen F. Austin from Thomas McKinney. On February 20 he and Donoho (who would settle on the adjacent league northeast of Bernado) took the oath of allegiance to Mexico. Bowie, accompanied by Donoho, Wm. Wharton and his wife Sara Ann Groce Wharton, who had by then moved back to Texas from Tennessee, and several slaves traveled to San Antonio with letters of introduction to prominent citizens Juan Martín de Veramendi and Juan N. Seguín.[135] Then the group went to Saltillo where Bowie wrote a letter to Samuel Williams that he and Donoho were developing plans for a "cotton factory", likely encouraged by Wharton to serve as a market for Groce cotton. Bowie became a Mexican citizen on September 30, 1830, contingent upon establishing textile mills in the province of Coahuila y Tejas. He entered into partnership with his future father-in-law Veramendi to build cotton and wool mills in Saltillo, but these never materialized.

Henry Wax Karnes, a captain in the Texas army in the 1836 Revolution and later Texas Ranger, was employed at Bernado as an overseer for several months during 1835. He arrived in Texas from Arkansas earlier that year and joined the Texian army in late 1835 to participate in the taking of Bexar. A document from the probate records of Jared III's estate mentions a "Karnes

Bridge" across a ravine on the road leading east from the Bernardo main house. This was likely built by the slaves with Karnes as overseer in 1835. [136]

Warren D. C. Hall was a young man living in Natchitoches in 1819, and participated in the Magee / Guiterrez Expedition. He was an early settler in the Liberty area and participated in the skirmishes at Anahuac in 1832. He served as Adjutant General under Burnet in 1835, and as Secretary of War after the Battle of San Jacinto. [137] On August 3 and 4, 1823, Hall and a friend stayed at Bernardo with three slaves and five horses. Upon his departure he was presented with an invoice from Groce for services rendered during Hall's visit. [138] This invoice provides interesting perspectives: 1. lunch ("DInner") was the biggest meal of the day at 4 bits a person. Breakfasts and suppers were 3 bits each. 2. Horses cost three times as much as a human to put up for the night. That included food for the horses. 3. Three negroes were fed for the same price as two whites. 4. The ferry was in operation by this early date, and not cheap! It appears that Dr. Hall asked for and was given a loan of $11 cash, then was surprised with the bill and only had $20 (including the loan) to pay it partially. His brother John Hall, a Retreat neighbor who later founded Washington-on-the-Brazos at the La Bahia road crossing, later paid the rest of the bill.

Jesse Burnham was among the first Americans to bring his family to Texas, in 1821 before Stephen Austin received his colonization grant. After a brief stay on the Red River and at Independence in 1822, he settled on the Colorado River between LaGrange and Columbus. For around ten years this was the northernmost settlement on the Colorado. Burnam operated a ferry at his home, which was used by Sam Houston to move his army across the river in 1836 as he retreated from Gonzales and the approaching Mexican army. He visited Bernardo in late 1822 or early 1823 and was asked by Jared Groce to sell some dried buffalo meat for the support of Groce and his slaves in the year they were establishing their new homes in Texas. Burnam declined to sell the meat but offered it for free instead. Groce accepted, and gave one of Burnam's children a Mexican silver dollar for their father's generosity. Burnam later traded the dollar to a traveller for 2/3 cup of hard-to-acquire gunpowder at a time when he was down to six rounds and needed to hunt for more meat. [139]

Another of the many notables to visit Bernardo was Anson Jones. When he was a Senator from Brazoria in 1839, he departed Houston on October 20 in the company of Col. H.D. McLeon and Teddy O. Rourke. They stopped at Bernardo for a visit during their leisurely eleven-day trip to the newly created town of Austin. Jones later became the last President of the Republic of Texas. [140]

Several Groce neighbors in Virginia and Georgia over the years became relatives through intermarriage: Waller, White, Lipscomb, Chiles, Sheppard. Jared Groce II was instrumental in attracting several of these family members to move to Texas. One, Judge Edwin Waller, was born in 1800 in Spottsylvania County, Virginia, the cousin of Jared's first two wives. Waller arrived in 1831 and signed both the Texas Declaration of Independence in 1836 and the state Constitution in 1846. He and William Wharton were the leaders in the insurrection against the Mexican garrison at Velasco in 1832, often considered the first act of the Texas Revolution. In his later years he was a judge in Austin County and operated a mercantile store on the road east of San Felipe in the vicinity of today's Pattison. He surveyed the town lots of the new capital at Austin, and was that town's first mayor. [141]

Another relative was Pamelia (Mrs. James) Foster, a sister of Jared's wives. Jared wrote her in 1832 to come join him in Texas. Groce gave 1/4 league of land across the river from Bernardo to Mrs. Foster. This land was where Houston pastured his army's horses during his stay at the Texian training camp in April, 1836. Groce also gave his niece Julia Bracey 400 acres of land. Julia and her husband McLinn Bracey operated a commercial ferry near Bernardo from 1836 to about 1860.

Judge Abner Smith Lipscomb was Jared II's wives' double first cousin. Lipscomb was a lawyer, justice, and secretary of state during the Lamar administration. Born on February 10, 1789, in Abbeville District, South Carolina, he studied law in the office of John C. Calhoun, was a circuit judge of Alabama and from 1823 to 1835 was chief justice of the Alabama Supreme Court and a state legislator in 1838. He moved to Texas in 1839 and established a law practice. He was an associate justice of the Texas Supreme Court from 1851 and 1856. Lipscomb County, established in 1876, was named in his honor.

Phillip Minor Cuny was a cousin of Leonard Groce's wife Courtney Ann. He moved from Alexandria to Texas around 1840 and bought land adjacent to Bernardo with financial assistance from Leonard. [142] His plantation was named Sunny Side. Cuny was a three-term member of the Texas House of Representatives and a state senator. By 1850 he had accumulated 2,000 acres and 105 slaves. He had several children by three successive legal wives, and also several with his slave housekeeper Adeline Stuart. Cuny sent his mulatto children back east to obtain an education, and freed them and their mother in 1859. One of these children was Norris Wright Cuny, who became a lawyer and very prominent Galveston businessman in the late 1800's. [143] Norris was named after Norris Wright who was killed by Jim Bowie in the famous 1827 "Mississippi

Sandbar Fight" that spawned the legend of the Bowie Knife. Philip's brother Samuel Cuny was killed in that same fight.

Jared Ellison Kirby was another Groce relative who moved to Texas. His mother Sarah Harper Kirby was the eldest child of Jared II's sister Lucy, who had married Robert Harper. Sarah married Henry Kirby of Georgia and came to Texas after Henry died. Her son Jared moved to Texas in 1848, buying a quarter-league of land a few miles east of Bernardo, likely with his cousin Leonard's help. He became a prominent Texan, serving in the Civil War and developing Alta Vista, a plantation which at its zenith consisted of several tracts along Best and Iron's Creeks and had a population of over 150 slaves. Jared Ellison Kirby died in 1865; his widow Helen Marr Swearingen Kirby, Dean of Women at the University of Texas at Austin for 35 years, sold Alta Vista to the state in 1876 to become today's Prairie View A&M University. The name Prairie View is derived from Alta Vista which means "elevated view" in Spanish. [144]

John H. Sheppard was Jared's cousin. He moved to Texas in 1831, making his first stop at Bernardo. Sheppard later wrote that he did not participate in the Battle of San Jacinto because he had been sent from Bernardo by Sam Houston, on the day he crossed the Brazos, to the Coushatta Indians on the Trinity, where he spent several days trying to convince their chiefs to send 100 warriors to augment Houston's army. His efforts were unsuccessful; the Coushattas remained neutral. [145] Sheppard's son William operated a store and lived on two hundred acres of land in the John Corner League of the Lake Creek settlement which he purchased from William C. Clark in 1835. These two hundred acres of land would later be developed into the town of Montgomery. Although Sheppard and Groce had extensive business dealings, they did have a dispute over a $1,000 loan that prompted Shepperd to run a notice in the San Felipe newspaper warning the public against buying the note from Groce because he (Sheppard) had other claims against his cousin that offset the loan. [146]

The list of people connected to Bernardo goes on and on, prompting some to observe that anybody who was anybody in Texas knew the Groce's and had visited Bernardo.

Aiding the Texas Revolution

War clouds were sweeping over Texas in late 1835. After having driven the Mexican army from San Antonio and Goliad late that year, most Texans knew they had to remove themselves from the Mexican confederation, and fully expected a war to ensue. A group of delegates from every municipality met in San Felipe and elected Henry Smith as provisional governor. His first action was to ask for volunteers to organize an army for defense against the anticipated Mexican advance following their defeat on October 2 at Gonzales and later at San Antonio. Leonard Groce volunteered and received his commission as Colonel from Governor Smith during this period. Support for the Texians in the United States was widespread, including distant Groce relatives. The minutes of a meeting to support the Texains held in Macon, Georgia on November 9 - 12, 1835, reads as follows: "Lt. Hugh McLeoud, recently from the Military Academy at West Point, addressed the meeting in a spirit-stirring appeal, pledging himself to resign his commission, and embark as a volunteer, in the cause of liberty; that the struggle in Texas needed Soldiers, not resolutions; that we should tender from them [illegible] and our arms on the contested field; that these would best express our sympathies in their behalf". There is a list of the men that volunteered that day, offering Texas "all of the aid in our power, not forbidden by the laws and constitution of our own government, to save them from despotism. to correspond with the provisional government of Texas, to provide donations, to gather a list of persons willing to fight in Texas, and to solicit help elsewhere in Georgia. Among them were Wm. Ward [of Goliad fame] and Jared E. Groce, son of Shepperd Groce, brother of Jared II. [147]

Provisional Governor Henry Smith had a close personal relationship with Leonard Groce. In a letter from San Felipe to Groce dated January 18, 1836, Smith described his struggles involving public mudslinging with the governing council that had been appointed in November and was now trying to remove him from office. He mentioned the Texan's paltry defensive position at Bexar, and the recent arrival of troops at Goliad, expressing hope that Sam Houston would go there to take command. He also mentioned recent information that the Mexican army was advancing on Bexar and the residents were fleeing. Smith closes his letter with: "An unequivocal Declaration of Independence will save the country & that is all that can. You will certainly be alive to this, come down and see me, don't stay at home --- up with the Hypo. I am not thus troubled, and I know no reason why you should. If you had half of my troubles you might complain, so come down, and see me and hear what is going on. I can not write half - two hours with me would cure you - Please remember me to your brother and Ladies. It is late and I have much writing to do yet. Accept the good wishes of your Sincere friend. Henry Smith" [148]

Among the visitors to Bernardo in early 1836 was Pamelia Dickinson Mann, one of the more colorful and notorious characters of early Texas. Pamelia and her husband arrived in Texas in 1834 and settled originally at San Felipe; later she was an innkeeper at various locations in Texas, including a temporary inn at Washington during the constitutional Convention of 1836. Traveling from San Felipe to Washington, she stopped at Pleasant Hill and wrote a letter to Sam Houston dated February 2. [149] In this letter she referred to the Consultation of San Felipe held November 7, 1835, in which delegates voted to take up arms in defense of the Mexican Constitution of 1824. She was forwarding letters to Houston from provisional governor Henry Smith that the governor feared would be intercepted by his political rivals. She also sent fifty dollars to be used to buy corn from Jared Groce.

Pamelia Mann came back to Bernardo after leaving Washington; in mid-April her oxen were impressed at Bernardo to pull the Twin Sisters cannons eastward. One 1837 publication discrediting Houston's role in the revolution states that the General was resting with his head in Pamelia's lap in his training camp on the Brazos across from Bernardo in early April, 1836, when he received word of the massacre of Fannin's men. Startled, he jumped up, causing Mrs. Mann to state that she nearly stuck her comb in his head. When she later learned that Houston was not retreating to East Texas, she personally intervened as the army marched toward Harrisburg and successfully demanded that her animals be released. She was one of the first residents of Houston where she operated an inn named the Mansion House that including a tavern and brothel. Sam Houston apparently stayed at Mansion House when he was in Houston during the period that it was the capitol of Texas; they were obviously friends and perhaps lovers. Accused of several crimes ranging from larceny to assault to fornication between 1836 and 1840, she was awarded executive clemency by President Lamar. Sam Houston stood as best man in the 1838 wedding of her son Nimrod. Pamelia Mann died of yellow fever in 1840. [150]

George Campbell Childress and his uncle were elected in February, 1836, to represent Milam Municipality at the Convention of 1836. Childress called the convention to order and subsequently introduced a resolution authorizing a committee of five members to draft a declaration of independence. Upon adoption of the resolution, he was named chairman of the committee and is widely acknowledged as the primary author of the document, which he drafted in late February while staying at Jared Groce II's Retreat home.

A letter from James W. Robinson to Sam Houston is marked by him as "Recd. 2nd Feb. at Col. Groces. All upon the surface. H." This letter thus places Houston at Retreat on February 2. At that time both Jared II and Leonard were addressed by the title "Colonel".   Houston replied to Robinson's letter, and Robinson sent another to Houston on February 14 from San Felipe. [151] The Pamelia Mann letter to Houston dated February 3 from Pleasant Hill makes it clear that he was not at Bernardo on that date.   It was around this time that George Childress was writing the draft of the Texas Declaration of Independence at Retreat. Perhaps Houston made some suggestions to Childress as they stayed at Retreat in early February.

On the February 3 Houston arrived in Washington and was trying to sort through the debilitating infighting in the fledgling government between provisional governor Henry Smith and the General Council as to who was leading the newly-declared republic. Houston probably had seen Mann in the previous few days, somewhere between San Felipe and Washington, perhaps at Bernardo or Pleasant Hill. He left for east Texas from Washington on Feb. 5, where he negotiated a treaty with the Cherokees signed on February 23 and immediately departed for Washington, arriving on February 29. [152]

Several surviving records from this period place Jared III at home during March and April of 1836, directing activities around Bernardo and interacting with the Texian army. Leonard apparently prepared for war by taking his wife, their two young children, Mary Ann Groce and her daughter to Louisiana to stay with Courtney's mother. No record has been found mentioning Leonard at Bernardo during this period. An invoice from a mercantile shop in Alexandria indicates Leonard's presence there at some time in 1836. [153] The death of Frances Ann Groce in August, 1836 in Louisiana suggests that at least Mary Ann and perhaps Courtney stayed there for a several month visit with relatives before returning to Texas. Some of the Bernardo slaves were sent to Groce's Retreat under the care of overseer Gee to put them out of the path of the expected Mexican army advance. Jared II arrived at Bernardo from Retreat around mid-April.

Both the Mexican and Texian armies marched east along the Gonzales - San Felipe road in March and early April of 1836. By late March scores of Texans, mostly women and children, began appearing at the Brazos River crossings, ahead of the advancing Mexican army in what became known as the Runaway Scrape. Many crossed at Bernardo; the facilities there were soon filled with refugees. Wm. Fairfax Gray, who was in Washington for the declaration of independence activities, traveled to Jared Groce's Retreat after the convention ended. He wrote: "Groce's is prettily situated. Houses numerous, but small, and much crowded.". He related that the entire newly-elected cabinet including President Burnet and Vice President Zavalla were at Jared Groce's Retreat during March 19 - 21 as they traveled from Washington to Harrisburg. Gray also noted that Wm. B. Travis' slave Joe was present and was interrogated concerning his recollection of the fall of the Alamo. Gray wrote: "Some gents had expressed an unwillingness to remain at Groce's, because they thought it imposing on the hospitality of a gentleman too much. This delicacy was cured when, on starting, he presented each with a bill for $3 per day, man and horse. My bill was $8 from Friday night to Monday morning." [154]

Benjamin Franklin Bryant recruited a company of about 42 volunteers in the "Redlands" or the East Texas region around Nacogdoches and San Augustine. He lived 15 miles southeast of San Augustine near Milam and Hemphill. He was elected captain, and along with a smaller company under Captain William Kimbro, rode down the La Bahia road toward Washington. From the Trinity onward, they encountered hundreds of people fleeing east in the Runaway Scrape. One of Bryant's men, Hardy W.B. Price, wrote that the ferry at Washington was blockaded and a struggle ensued to see who should cross the river first. When the ferryboat was sunk in the struggle, Captain Bryant ordered his men to leave the crossing and continue down the east bank where they arrived at Bernardo late Monday evening, March 30. Price recalled that Jared Groce III refused to let Capt. Bryant and his company occupy his large white frame house at Pleasant Hill. Groce did offer Capt. Bryant use of the negro cabins which were accepted. The next morning Capt. Bryant called a council of his company and the term of enlistment was discussed. It was agreed that Capt. Bryant should cross the river and interview General Sam Houston who was encamped in the bottoms on the west side of the Brazos and offer their services for 30 days. Bryant felt that a general engagement with the Mexicans would happen within that time frame. They agreed to return home to tend to their farms if Houston did not accept the order. Houston accepted, and Bryant, Kimbro and their men crossed the river and joined his army on April 1, 1836. [155]

The main house at Bernardo at this time was occupied by relatives, which made it unavailable to the Texian soldiers. The negro quarters utilized by Bryan were most likely those at Bernardo, as the quarters at Pleasant Hill were believed to have been built later. After joining the army, Bryan and Kimbro were stationed on the east side of the river at Bernardo. Houston issued orders on April 3 commanding them to remain well organized, to make daily status reports, and to respect and protect Groce property. An extensive list of 22 specific orders from Houston to Bryant and Kimbro were issued on the same day. [156] Houston reorganized his army at Bernardo on April 13, placing Bryant and Kimbro's units under Col. Sidney Sherman. A list of Bryant and Kimbro's men at San Jacinto likely represent those who spent from March 30 to April 14 at Bernardo. [157]

Houston and his Texian army had departed San Felipe on March 28 after ordering all buildings burned so they could not be utilized by the enemy. The army crossed Mill Creek, camped for the night, and the next day made only a few miles progress due to the heavy rains and soggy ground. They apparently camped this night on the Coushatta Trace at Dry Creek about half way between the Cummings' mill and Piney Creek. On March 30 they arrived at the edge of the Brazos River bottoms on land near the modern community of Cochran owned by Julia Bracey, Jared Groce's niece. A detachment of soldiers kept most of the horses on adjacent land owned by Pamelia Foster, Jared Groce's sister-in-law. The Foster's at that time were living on their land acquired from Jared II a year earlier, where the pasturage was better than in the wooded river bottom where the army camped. The Bracey's had probably recently arrived but apparently had not yet established their ferry. On March 31 some 30 men under Lt. Nicholas Lynch were detailed to clear a road through to the river and to prepare camp near a lake for the army. Wm. Physic Zuber, one of the Texian soldiers bivouacked at Foster's, described his efforts in helping prepare the camp site. [158] He said they reached the lake in only four hours due to an abandoned narrow road (the Coushatta Trace) through the saplings. The camp site was cleared, and the army arrived that afternoon. Here they remained for two weeks, during which Houston provided some sorely-needed training for his army.

The accounts of several of the soldiers at the training camp near Bernardo leave a vivid impression of the challenges that Houston faced as he led an increasingly fractious army of free-spirited volunteers in a rain-drenched, nearly flooded camp. Dr. Labadie of Captain Logan's company wrote that the new camp was pitched "near a deep ravine, which had the appearance of having once been the bed of the river, and which miserable hole was our hiding-place for about two weeks." [159] According to George Hockley, the new permanent encampment was "in a secure and effective position with excellent water from a lake immediately ahead, and one of the most beautiful parts of the timber of the Brazos River which is ahead about ¾ of a mile off in the road leading to Col. Groce's ferry." [160]

Private George Erath described shortages of food and salt, with the men allotted only one ear of corn per day. He noted that many of the men were sick and under strict discipline by Houston, and spent much of the day standing on guard duty in knee-deep water.

Major James Perry described the camp as being on a small lake of stagnant water which was rapidly becoming polluted from animal and human waste that washed into it during the heavy rains. He noted that on April 9 there were some 300 sick men, about half of the total who had reported for duty. He indicated that most of the men were armed with rifles, that there were not more than 100 muskets and bayonets, and some of the men had no arms at all. Rising water threatened to flood their camp and forced them to swim from camp to the adjacent prairie. [161]

The training camp was on the south side of the oxbow lake, today known as Stone Lake. The campsite location has been known locally for years and was positively identified by the Houston Archaeological Society in 1989. A state historical marker has been erected at the site. Additional archaeological work at the training camp site was conducted in 2010 and is described in Book 3 - The Archaeology.

When he arrived at the Brazos, Houston found the steamboat *Yellow Stone* docked at Groce's Landing loading cotton. Thomas Mckinney had purchased the *Yellow Stone* in partnership with Samuel May Williams, and in December of 1835 had sent her up the Brazos to get cotton from the various plantations. The *Yellow Stone* had seen earlier service plying the waters of the Missouri from St. Louis to the Yellowstone River, suggesting the derivation of its name. Noted artists George Catlin and Karl Bodmer both used the Yellow Stone for transportation to the upper Missouri where they painted many scenes of Native Americans and their lifestyles. The following paintings probably accurately represent what this famous steamboat actually looked like.

at St. Louis, by George Catlin

aground on the Upper Missouri, April 19, 1833, by Karl Bodmar

arriving at Ft. Union in 1835, by Robert Back.

Houston had learned that the *Yellow Stone* was at Groce's when he was at San Felipe, and this, plus the access to large quantities of food at Bernardo, may have influenced his decision to move his army there for training instead of crossing the Brazos at San Felipe. He issued several orders from his training camp to assure that the boat would remain in place and subject to his orders. He promised Lewis Ferguson, engineer of the Yellow Stone, one league of his personal land for his services. Houston specifically indicated that both Ferguson and captain John Ross were not being forced to join the Texian army but would remain neutral United States citizens. On July 13, 1836, the Texian government paid McKinney and Williams $4,900 for the detention and services of the *Yellow Stone*. [162]

Among the refugees at Bernardo during this period were Mrs. Wm. Wharton, her son John and her foster daughter Annie Wharton Cleveland, Mrs. Pamela Waller Foster, and her aged husband James and their daughter Evantha. They were at first urged by Jared Groce III to flee to Louisiana to join the other family members, but after the arrival of Jared Groce II they stayed, caring for the sick Texian soldiers and making large bags for use in filling with sand and stacked as a breast works in the event they were attacked by the Mexican army. At this time William Wharton, Stephen Austin and Branch T. Archer were in the United States on an official mission soliciting aid for the fledging Republic of Texas. Jared Groce II arrived from Retreat in early April. He insisted he be brought to Bernardo when he learned that Houston's army was camped nearby, but was so weakened by the buggy trip down from Retreat that he spent the whole time in bed.

The Twin Sisters, two six-pounder cannons, arrived at Bernardo on April 11. Gifts to Texas from the city of Cincinnati, they had been shipped by water destined for delivery to Houston's army. Due to bad weather and road conditions, after arriving at the mouth of the Brazos at Velasco they were sent by schooner to Harrisburg and entrusted to a Captain Smith who left on April 9, hauling the cannons to Bernardo with a team of oxen. Upon their delivery to Bernardo, Sam Houston immediately formed a thirty-man artillery corps to service the guns, the only artillery with the Texas army at that time, and placed this unit under the command of Lt. Col. James Clinton Neill. [163]

Texian Secretary of War Thomas Rusk arrived on April 4, having been dispatched by President Burnet to urge Houston to engage the Mexican army. Rusk and Houston were friends, and Rusk's appearance bolstered the morale of both Houston and his soldiers. Rusk wrote to Burnet on April 6 that he had been in Houston's camp three days, and that the army was in fine spirits, ready and anxious to meet the enemy. [164]

A battle flag used in an early Texian defeat in the Battle of Tampico on November 15, 1835 was briefly displayed at the training camp by Charles Hawkins, a naval officer of the United States and Mexico. Hawkins participated in the disastrous battle at Tampico, where he acquired the flag. Returning to San Antonio, he joined the army after the surrender of the Mexicans under Cos. [165]

During the time Houston's army camped near Bernardo (March 31 to April 14), Jared Groce III furnished them with large quantities of food and supplies, including a thousand of bushels of corn, cattle, hogs and ground meal. The attached invoice for $2,272.25 was presented by Leonard and Jared Groce III for the supplies they furnished to the Texian army. [166]

Republic of Texas Dr. to
  Messrs. L. W. & J. E. Groce

1000 bushels Corn @ $1.50 ♂ bush.		$1500.—
171 lbs Bacon @ 25 ¢ lb		42.75
18 Beeves @ 16.— ♂ beef		288.—
25 bushels Meal @ 1.50 ♂ bush		37.50
2 hogs weigh 450 @ 5 ¢ lb		22.50
6 beeves (3 yrs) @ 15.— ♂ beef		90.—
2 pair double trees @ 2.50 ♂ pair		5.—
2 do Stretchers @ 3.— ♂ do		6.—
8 Sets gear (complete) @ 6.— ♂ gear		48.—
7 Single trees @ 1.50 ♂ tree		10.50
8 Hauck Collars & 4 Tapwings		5.—
2 Pair Breechings for wagon		8.—
1 beef		15.—
4 bushels Meal @ 1.50 ♂ bush.		6.—
Cash advanced to Gov. Smith		100.—
do San Felipe Comittee		51.23
& paid Pr. Grimes (feeding troops)		4.75
Supplies (as ♂ a/c certified by D Pitman Lt. Z. M. Gen)		30.—
1 Bushel Corn (Capt C L Ripley Wheelock)		2.—
		$ 2272.25

Personally appeared before me A. Brigham Auditor, J. E. Groce, on behalf of Messrs. L. W. & J. E. Groce, and says on oath that the annexed documents and above account are just, true and original, and that the claimants are not indebted to the Government.

J. E. Groce also acknowledges to have received a draft on the Treasurer, favor of Messrs. L. W. & J. E. Groce for two thousand two hundred seventy two Dollars, twenty five cents in full for the accompanying documents—
Columbia 14th day of December 1836

Sworn to and signed
before A. Brigham Auditor

Jas. E. Groce
for L. W. & J. E. Groce

Groce family lore indicates that the lead on the plantation in water pipes and clock weights was used by the soldiers to mold bullets. A separate account of this activity is given by a family member describing the early Austin County settler John Atkinson's retreat during the Runaway Scrape. Upon receiving the news that their friend Wm. B.Travis had been slain at Goliad and that Santa Anna was approaching with an army, Mrs. Anderson loaded what she could of her possessions on an ox-drawn sled, buried the rest and headed east. Her husband was with Houston's army. At Groce's she obtained a cart to replace the sled. To avoid overloading the cart she left a large box containing the pendulum ball and weights of a clock. When she later returned, she found that the box had been opened and the lead had been molded into bullets by the Texian soldiers. [167]

Horses were also furnished by Groce. Captain J. P. Lynch gave a receipt dated April 17, 1836, indicating that he had received three horses valued at $120 from Jared III, each branded with the letter "G". They were used to assist the sick soldiers who remained at Donoho's when Houston departed for San Jacinto. Payment of $168.75 for the horses and other supplies provided by Groce was submitted by the Republic of Texas was approved by Comptroller Francis Lubbock on August 3rd. [168]

A hospital was established at Bernardo during this time to care for the many ill soldiers suffering from measles and from diarrhea caused by drinking polluted water. The army "Hospital", a wagon with medical supplies, had been kept at Bernardo since Houston arrived at the Brazos, under the charge of Dr. James Phelps. Physician N.D. Labadie, with Houston across the river, visited the hospital on April 10. He heard that two cannons were soon to arrive, and saw them standing in the yard of the main house on a repeat visit two days later. Labadie described several women in the house making flannel bags to be filled with sand and used in defense. Ladies of the household also assisted in nursing the ill Texian soldiers. Phelps also noted a warm reception by Jared Groce II, whom he had met crossing Groce's ferry in 1831. Phelps had a difficult time obtaining food and other supplies including "wine, brandy and whiskey" for his patients, and sent a letter to Sec. Rusk dated April 2 stating his problems and asking for help. Houston organized a Medical Staff for his army during this period and appointed Dr. Alexander Ewing as Surgeon General.

When the Texian soldiers in their training camp west of the Brazos learned that Santa Anna was at San Felipe, they immediately urged Houston to go to battle. Although opposed to this idea, he was finally forced to agree by threat of desertion, and a plan was laid in which the infantry would board the *Yellow Stone* and be transported downriver to offload at the mouth of Mill Creek. There they would be met by the cavalry and the entire army would march the remaining four miles to engage the Mexican Army at San Felipe. Only the news that the Mexican army had moved downriver to Fort Bend aborted this plan and kept the signature battle for Texas independence from occurring at San Felipe instead of San Jacinto. [169]

The Texian army began crossing on the impressed *Yellow Stone* at 10 a.m. on April 12. By noon the next day most of the army had crossed. They camped the nights of April 12 and 13 at Bernardo a few hundred yards east of the main house and departed the next morning for Donoho's and ultimately San Jacinto. [170]

Noted Texas artist E.M. Schiwetz drew the following illustration depicting the Texian army crossing the Brazos on Yellow Stone: [171]

James F. Perry and his family were in the Runaway Scrape. Perry wrote to his brother-in-law Stephen Austin from the west side of Lynch's Ferry on April 8 that he and hundreds of others were fleeing east to the Sabine River. He noted that Houston was at Groce's with 2,000 men - a significant over-estimate. He said his wife Emily (Stephen's sister) and children were nearby and he intended to send them to Galveston and then by sea to New Orleans, but the vessels at that port were already overcrowded and he might have to take them with him by land. He had brought his slaves this far, and was undecided as to leaving them there or taking them further east. Perry stopped briefly at Bernardo on his return home. In a letter from Groce's Landing dated April 28 he described the battle, that Houston had been wounded, and that a unit of the Mexian army was still active. He expressed his sentiments succinctly: "I hope they catch Santa Ana alive and hang him high for what he done at the Alamo and others. Maybe now at least we can have peace in this land." [172]

An invoice from James Wells to Jared and Leonard Groce written in Houston on February 24th, 1838, reads as follows: "Gentlemen - Please pay Louis Knipp Twenty Two dollars for my bringing yours Nigroes (sic) in from Victory [Victoria] in July, 1836 by order of T.J. Rusk." Rusk was Secretary of War at San Jacinto, but shortly thereafter was appointed Commander-in-Chief of the Texian army following Sam Houston's removal to treat his injuries suffered in the battle. Rusk followed the Mexican troops westward as they retired from Texas to be certain of their retreat beyond the Rio Grande. He stopped in Victoria, where he held some 2,500 troops as his scouts tracked the movement of the Mexican army. Both Wells and Knipp were in Houston's army and at Bernardo before San Jacinto. A receipt written on March 15, 1836 at Bernardo certifies that Lewis Knipp provided one large paint horse valued at $1,000 to the Republic of Texas. Another document signed by Thomas Rusk on October 2nd at Dimmit's Point certifies that James Wells joined the army on March 13th and "having faithfully discharged his duty to the present date is honorably discharged from the service." [173]

Rusk likely impressed several of Groce's slaves to assist him in the campaign, then had one of his men (Wells) return them in July. This practice was specifically condoned for officers above the rank of lieutenant. The invoice from Wells was dated several months after he delivered the slaves, unusual in that it was not presented upon delivery. No note on the invoice indicates it was paid - a common addition to other invoices presented to and paid by Leonard Groce. Perhaps Groce felt nothing was due Wells as he was an enlisted man carrying out an order from his superior officer at that time. The slaves probably joined Rusk at Bernardo in mid-April, and would have been at or near the battle at San Jacinto. When Rusk arrived in Victoria he went on to Goliad and discovered the remains of Fannin's men where they were left - partially burned - by the Mexican army. He then conducted a military ceremony and reburied the remains. One can only wonder if the Groce slaves were not engaged in digging the grave for the reburial.

Although they had contributed significant financial resources to aid the revolutionary effort, neither Leonard nor Jared III actually saw military action. Both "joined" the Texian army after independence was won by hiring a third party to serve in their stead, a common practice for wealthy men at that time. Leonard Groce "entered service" in the Texian army on June 4, 1836, in the form of a substitute named W.W. Davis who served until September 4, 1836 in Captain James Chesshire's Jasper Volunteers. Leonard received 320 acres of land for Davis's having "served faithfully and honorably". Jared E. Groce III also received 320 acres of land, by virtue of John Dorsey, his substitute, having served faithfully and honorably for the term of three months from May 23 to August 23, 1836. [174]

Leonard Gross testified in 1871 that R.R. Peebles was in the Texas army and fought at San Jacinto: [175]

The State of Texas
County of Austin

Before me the undersigned Authority personally came and appeared L.W. Groce who on Oath deposes and says that he has lived in the State of Texas Forty nine years, and has been intimately acquainted with Dr. R.R. Peebles between Thirty and Forty years has often heard him speak of being in the Texas Army of 1836. Was or belonged to a Company at the battle of San Jacinto. has often heard others speak of him as being in the Army. So that he feels very certain in saying that he believes Dr. R.R. Peebles was a soldier in the war of 1836. and as such did his duty faithfully.

L.W. Groce

Sworn to and Subscribed before me this 30th day of January A.D. 1871

W S Wright
Notary Public

Family Feud Over Estate Distribution

After the death of Jared Groce III in 1839, Leonard Groce completed the probate process of Jared's estate and became guardian of his brother's children while providing financial and other support for Jared's widow. A large number of documents related to the probate and later challenges to it were filed with the Austin County probate judge, and remain today in the files of the Austin County Clerk.

On April 4, John Sharp, husband of Mary Ann Groce's sister and a lawyer in Brazoria, filed a copy of Jared III's will that he testified was "signed, sealed and witnessed in my presence and that Jared Groce did at that time acknowledge and declare to me that the same was his last will and testament." It was dated October 9, 1838. The will contained the following provisions:

1. gave $1,000 to his sister-in-law Courtney Ann Groce,
2. gave to his sisters-in-law Sarah Jane Sharp and Mackall Calvit, sisters of his wife, $500 each.
3. "in consideration of the love and affection which I entertain for my wife Mary Ann Groce, as well as from a great desire to see her comfortably provided for in this life, and placed beyond the wants of this world, and in further consideration of her renouncing the benefits of the community of accord and gains subsisting between us and renouncing all right, title, claim or interest which she may have either in law or otherwise to Estate of my children in case of their decease I give and bequeath to her the sum of $8,000 either to be paid in money or property at her option … and in further proof of my love and affection and for the consideration for the above named, I give and bequeath to my said wife the sum of $400 as an annuity to be paid at the end of each year and the annuity is to continue until the death of my wife or until she contracts another marriage, in either event it then ceases and finally for the considerations above explained I renounce in favor of my wife all that property which she brought into the marriage contract."
4. to his children Jared E. IV and Barbara Mackall Groce "all the remainder of my property both real, personal and mixed" upon their reaching age 21. If they die before age 21, the property is left equally between JEG's brother Leonard Groce and sister Sarah Ann Wharton.
5. He appointed Leonard and F.I. Calvit (Mary Ann's uncle) to be Executors of his estate. If they cannot act in this regard he appointed Wm. H. and John A. Wharton as Executors.

6. He appointed Leonard Groce as Guardian of his children, specifying that they be raised as good and moral children, and receive an education including the instruction of French and Spanish,

7. He specified that the partnership between he and his brother should continue until his son reaches age 21.

8. That his Executors and the Guardian of his children shall have the power to sell any property in his estate as it might benefit his children, except one league of good land which is to be reserved for each child,

9. That Mary Ann, whether at home or with her relatives, be given the services of such servants as necessary for attending to her household affairs, cooking, etc. and that they shall obey her as mistress of the place as in my own lifetime and this shall not be out of her annuities nor shall she without her own affirmation purchase anything for the interest of the plantation or house but that necessities for the plantation and house shall be bought for her in similar quantities and qualities as in my lifetime and paid out of the proceeds of the estate. She shall have a good carriage and horses and servants to attend she and my children whenever she desires of traveling.

10. And it is my wish that she shall reside at home most of the time so that she may attend to the interests of my children.

Jared signed this will, as did eight witnesses including Edwin Waller.

Mosley Baker, a captain in Houston's revolutionary army and also his biggest detractor, provided a receipt dated March 2, 1844 to Leonard for $500 in payment for "professional services for cases instituted by him in the District Court of Brazoria County, Austin and others for himself and as executor of the estate of Jared E. Groce, Jr. deceased." On May 14, 1844, Leonard paid $240 "as a balance of the principle of two legacies of five hundred dollars each bequeathed by said J.E. Groce to Sarah Jane Sharp and B.M. Calvit". The two women mentioned here were Mary Ann's Calvit sisters and had been left $500 each in Jared's will.

The probate records clearly indicate that Leonard was very diligent in carrying out all of the provisions of Jared's will. However, Mary Ann Peebles apparently decided that she was entitled not only to the property specified her in her deceased husband's will, but also half of his remaining estate, despite the fact that Jared's will specifically left this solely to his two children. Her new husband had not yet amassed the fortune that he would in later years, and perhaps she soon tired of living on a smaller budget after Leonard stopped support payments from the estate after her marriage. At any rate, on February 5, 1846, she and her husband Richard Peebles filed a lawsuit against Leonard and her uncle Frederick J. Calvit, the two executors of Jared's will. The petition was directed to Austin County Probate Judge Edwin Waller, a Groce relative and close family friend. The petition stated that Mary Ann had rights to the estate beyond what was spelled out in the will by virtue of her marriage to Jared. She claimed a share of the community property, despite the revocation of community rights clause in Jared's will. The Peebles challenged Leonard's earlier administration of the estate, saying that "no legal probate of any adequate testament" took place. They also challenged the validity of Jared's will and accused Calvit of collusion with Leonard regarding the earlier testimony. They asked the judge to cite Leonard and Calvit to appear in court and produce Jared's original will. Judge Waller issued the summons as requested.

Leonard responded on February 10, asking Waller to dismiss the lawsuit and to order the Peebles to be banned from bringing these accusations against him. He stated that between the time of Jared's death and the date of Peebles marriage he, as Executor, paid Mary Ann $724.35 and $500 plus the $4,000 on June 5, 1843 and another $2,000 on January 1, 1844, and that during this time Mary Ann was allowed the "enjoyment of the premises of Pleasant Hill". Leonard reminded the court that he was granted Letters Testamentary and Guardianship of Jared's children in 1839, and stated that by these actions he had fully paid to Mary Ann all that she was due from Jared's will and thus there was no basis for the recent lawsuit claiming that Mary Ann was owed more from the estate. In March the court sent a list of questions to ask Sarah Ann Wharton concerning her knowledge of Leonard's actions toward Mary Ann relative to the administration of Jared's estate. Other interrogatories were sent to Abner Lipscomb of Washington County, who had acted as Leonard's lawyer in the original probate. The Peebles' attorney at this time was David Portis, a lawyer and state senator from Austin County who had married Rebecca Cummings, the fiance of William Barrett Travis prior to his demise at the Alamo.

Sarah Ann Wharton's answer to these questions indicated that relationships between Mary Ann and the Groce's began to sour not long after her marriage to Peebles, and apparently over money: "Mr. Peebles requested me to assist her in separating her account from her children - which she had kept. I did so, during this conversation the impression clearly left on my mind was - that she had been receiving the annuity left her by the will of her former husband … from … the Executor Leonard Groce in monies and such articles as she needed & by the payments of debts which she contracted. … I was on intimate and cordial terms with (her) until some months after her second marriage. … When she was a widow she spent a portion of her time at home and a portion in Brazoria County with her relatives - so I do not know that she particularly sought or avoided society." The specified payment of the annual $400 annuity was of particular interest in these interrogations.

In May Judge Waller ruled that the original probate of Jared's will was not valid. Leonard appealed this ruling to the District Court in Galveston. On July 15, 1848 the Galveston court reversed the decision of the lower court, validating Leonard's original probate of Jared's will, but the key issue of more money for Mary Ann went in her favor. She was awarded community interest in Jared's estate as well as the legacy specified by the will. The probate records do not indicate the particular legal precedent leading to this decision. All records indicate that Leonard had very carefully abided by all the provisions of his brother's will. He certainly provided all the cash, goods and services she wanted, certainly more than $400 per year's worth, and probably assumed this was in accordance with the annual annuity requirement. Failure to provide a specific annual payment of $400 apparently provided a technicality by which Jared's estate could be challenged. In hindsight, the Peebles challenge could have been avoided had Leonard simply given Mary Ann $400 per year and let her manage her personal purchases herself instead of allowing her to charge goods at mercantile stores which he paid for from Jared's estate.

After the Galveston court ruling Leonard began taking action to liquidate his brother's estate and acquiesce to the court's orders. In April of 1849 he gave notice of his intent to sell a number of properties in Jared's estate at public auction. A month later he filed a document with the court in which he provided a list of debts and expenses of the estate totaling $3,500, indicating that he had paid most of this with his own money and not from the estate. He asked the court's permission to sell some of the unimproved lands in the estate to reimburse himself for these expenses. By June he had requested and been released of his duties as executor of Jared's will and as guardian of his children. Peebles was then appointed guardian. Also in June Leonard listed with the court all of the land that he and his deceased bother had owned at the time of Jared's death, and asked for a partition between himself and Jared's estate. [176]

Commissioners appointed by the court prepared the partition by dividing each of the tracts into two parcels of equal value. The parcels were then divided into two lots of equal value and by random choice Leonard was granted one lot and the other went to Jared's estate. Each received ten parcels with a combined value of $41,888. On January 8, 1850, Peebles acknowledged receipt of $84.55 from Leonard as his final duty as administrator of the estate. He also received title to all the living slaves that were named in the inventory of the estate as well as their increase since that time, and to all of the estate property - personal, real and mixed, as delineated in the estate inventory. An inventory of these slaves is given in Appendix IV.

Later in 1849 the legal activity regarding Jared's estate continued within the Peebles family. Title to one of the properties in the estate, the Hall league, had been held up in litigation between Leonard and Wm. L. Austin. At Peebles' request, the court issued an order forcing Leonard to work with him to reach an agreement on the title dispute. This agreement was finally completed on July 28, 1850. Three commissioners then partitioned the lands jointly held by the brothers between Leonard and Jared's estate. Pleasant Hill and a reduced Bernardo had previously been divided between the two brothers and were not included in this partition. The 2,000 acres in the original Bernardo Two League tract that were below Pond Creek and jointly owned by the brothers was divided into two lots of 900 and 1100 acres, as shown on a survey sketch of the division:

Having finally completed this painful chapter in his life, Leonard penned a lengthy letter to Jared's children Jared IV and Barbara, in which he described to them how he had managed their interests after their father's death. He told of the partnership he and their father had with Thomas McKinney managing their father's property until Jared III married in 1833. He then described how he had continued to run the plantations "in their interest" as executor as he had promised his brother before he died. Leonard stated his desire that Jared IV and Barbara "should have all the property your father intended you to have". He said that Dr. Peebles was staying with him at Bernardo, where he met and married their mother Mary Ann. He wrote of the court battle which the Peebles eventually won. During this process Leonard stated that "I consequently closed up and gave up the Estate - Dr. Peebles applied and was appointed your Guardian - your mother then brought suit against you - in the probate court - and claimed a large portion of that property - willed to you by your father. You had no one to represent you - or to see to your interests, and the old English - ignorant Probate judge granted all that was asked." Leonard went on to say that he and Peebles had "buried the tomahawk" and agreed to continuing friendship.

The fight over the estate continued however, now evolving into a struggle over whether all of it would pass to Jared IV and Barbara when they reached age 21, or if Mary Ann was to receive half in her own name. Mary Ann sued her children to obtain half for herself. Her husband Richard refused to join her in this suit, probably because he was the children's guardian at the time of the lawsuit and thus had a conflict of interest. At issue was the legality of a married woman to sue on her own behalf instead of in her husband's name. Leonard successfully petitioned the court to have Peebles removed from guardianship and appoint an *ad litum* guardian. Z. Hunt was appointed to serve in this capacity and on May 6 Hunt and Leonard's lawyers petitioned the court to disallow her lawsuit against her children. Their petition claimed that Mary Ann was not entitled to community rights nor the dower because she had not pursued it. When she accepted the legacy left her by the will she waived her dower.

The court ruled in favor of Mary Ann, saying that "she is permitted to sue in law in her own name, to file this petition and to prosecute her own suit." After this decision Peebles was reinstated as guardian of the children. A May 30 court summary of the case stated that the Peebles "learned that the right to claim the legacy under the will or dower in lieu thereof as well as any community interest that might exist in the matter of the succession of Jared Groce, Jr. - and it appearing to the court that the said Mary Ann declining to take anything under the said will, but elects to claim and now claiming her dower in the separate estate real and personal of Jared Groce .." The document goes on to describe how Mary Ann was entitled to her share of the community property, including a list by names of slaves, cash money and lands individually listed. It further spells out division of all the property among Mary Ann and her two children Jared IV and Barbara.

Legal definition of marriage rights were in limbo during the early days of the Republic of Texas. Spanish (and Mexican) law recognized the concept of community property, which gave title to half of the assets accumulated during a marriage to each spouse. Another form of marriage rights called dower was commonly practiced under English law, and by many American states at this time. Dower (or morning gift) is defined as a provision accorded by law to a wife for her support in the event that she should become a widow and survive her husband. Typical dower law called for a widow to be allowed access to one-third of her deceased husband's assets to provide support for the remainder of her life. Texas in 1836 had a background of community property, but also had many new residents who came from the dower-based America. Confusion reigned on this issue during the first few years of the Republic. The Texas Congress passed an act on January 26, 1839, which attempted to end the confusion by adopting the English dower rights concept into law and discarding the concept of community property. The act proved very unpopular among the public, and less than a year later, in 1840, Congress repealed the Dower Law act and replaced it with the older Spanish custom of community property. As a result, the law in Texas provided for a widow's ability to claim one-half of the community property of her former marriage, <u>unless she agreed to a different arrangement</u>. The case put forward by Leonard Groce was that Mary Ann had lost her ability to claim community assets when she voluntarily accepted the legacy left her by her husband's will, in lieu of community property rights. Mary Ann successfully proved that she, under existing law, was entitled to her share of the community property, and that she had never been paid the specific $400 annuity described in the will, despite all the cash and personal purchases she received from Leonard from the estate during her three years as a widow. This technicality ultimately allowed her to claim half of the estate.

Court appointed commissioners met at Pleasant Hill on June 17, 1850, to partition the estate again, this time between Mary Ann and her two Groce children. All the land was evaluated and divided into two parts. Mary Ann was awarded Pleasant Hill and four other tracts of land, a total of 13,139 acres worth $33,002. The children were awarded seven tracts including 900 acres of Bernardo for a total of 14,323 acres worth $28,855.

The commissioners then split the tracts above destined for Jared IV and Barbara Groce into two equal parts for distribution to each child at their maturity. Following this they divided the forty community-owned slaves into two twenty-person "moeities" by name, age and value, selecting by random lot which moiety went to Mary Ann and which one went to the children, and further dividing the 20 assigned to Barbara and Jared between the two of them. These forty slaves were all under age 16 with one exception, representing the slave children born after Jared III married in 1833 and thus community property. The commissioners then identified by name, age and value the forty-two slaves owned by Jared III as his separate property. All except two were over age 16. These were divided into two groups of twenty-one individuals each. From one of these groups fourteen individuals valued in total at $8,501 were selected by name and assigned to Mary Ann. Details of this redistribution of slave ownership are shown in Appendix IV.

The commissioners identified $4,298 in cash or other property of which they assigned half to Mary Ann and the other half spilt equally between the two children. They also identified $18,655.33 due the estate from R.R. Peebles, arising from his rent of the plantation and hire of the negroes from the initial contract with LWG dating from December 31, 1842. This amount of "payable" indebtedness was was assigned 1/2 to Mary Ann and 1/4 each to Jared IV and Barbara. This act finally completed the lengthy family dispute over the estate of Jared Groce III.

Leonard and family moved from Bernardo to Pleasant Hill in 1853, ostensibly because they needed a larger house for their ten children. Another reason may have been the fact that they no longer owned the land under the Bernardo main house. It had been transferred to Mary Ann Peebles in 1850.

Children of Privilege

Richard Peebles, in his role as guardian of Jared and Mary Ann's two children, was required to make periodic reports to the court regarding his administration of their inheritance from their father. Many documents regarding these activities from 1850 to 1859 are in the Austin County probate court records. Providing a proper education for the children was among the duties of a guardian, and the records filed by Peebles in this regard provide a fascinating insight into the lives of wealthy plantation owners of the time. The first such report was made in July of 1850 and included expenses totaling $293 for two teachers at Pleasant Hill, $350 for a new piano from New York, music lessons for Barbara and $200 for clothing to equip Jared to attend a private school in Kentucky. A few months later Peebles reported that he had found it "utterly impossible" to provide educational opportunities for the two Groce children at home, and had recently sent Jared, then aged 14, to "a celebrated school in a beautiful portion of the state of Kentucky" and that Barbara, age 12 or 13, "is still at home enjoying such privileges of instruction as I can obtain for her from time to time but in a couple of months plan to send her to a Female Seminary of good report in Tennessee." Peebles asked the court for an allowance of $350 per annum for each child to support this schooling, room and board. Both children were apparently sent off to private schools in late 1851. A receipt from the Columbia (Tennessee) Female Institute dated October 17, 1851 states that Peebles paid $150 in advance tuition and expenses for Barbara's enrollment, indicating that he accompanied her to her new school. An invoice covering expenses for Barbara from February - April, 1852 included $273 for tuition, board, several pieces of sheet music and other musical supplies. She took guitar, piano, singing, drawing and French, and bought $52.42 worth of clothes. Peebles reported that because of discord between the rector and trustees, the Columbia school dissolved in April and Barbara had returned to Pleasant Hill "until another suitable school in Texas or one of the older states can be found".

Jared apparently did not fare well at his first private school. On June 15, 1852 he left the school with the concurrence of the school administrators and Peebles, arriving back at Pleasant Hill in early July. Peebles had arranged for a Capt. Bratlinger to go to Kentucky and Tennessee and escort the two children home for summer vacation. A July 6 invoice for $45.39 from Galveston paid by Bratlinger for Barbara buying several items of ladies clothing and Jared buying one pair of shoes called "lad's brogans", 1 dozen socks and 1 man's hat at J. Hackleford & Co. In August Peebles reported that from what he had seen of Jared's character and accomplishments he felt it would not be advantageous to immediately send him back. He was to remain at home while Peebles sought another educational opportunity for him "known to be better adapted to his immediate educational needs". The search must have been prompt because in September Jared was enrolled at Western Military Academy in Georgetown, Kentucky. An invoice from the school treasurer for expenses between September, 1852 and June, 1853, included several cash draws, tuition, dancing lessons, drawing lessons and materials, books, clothing and a trunk, and for broken glass - 2 window panes, 1 cup & saucer and 1 bowl.

Shortly after Jared returned to school Peebles escorted Barbara back to continue her studies at Columbia. A detailed report described in detail the $788 spent on this trip, which began with shopping in Galveston for clothes and supplies for the children, then taking a boat to New Orleans, up the Mississippi to Memphis on a steamboat, transferring to a stage to Columbia where he left Barbara, then proceeding by stage to Nashville and Georgetown where he visited Jared. After his visit Peebles returned to Louisville, then took two boats to get to New Orleans, another to get to Galveston, and then paid $2.50 steamboat fare to Houston and $5 for stage fare home, arriving in early December.

Peebles routinely asked the court's approval for more expenditures from the estate for education, children's support, reimbursement for his time and expenditures, and more money for Mary Ann. As an example of the support expenses, J.H. Edington Co. presented an invoice covering $27.30 in purchases made by Jared between January and May, 1853, for clothing, shoes, hats, boots, a tie, a knife and 4 boxes of sardines; and another in March, 1854 totaling $36 for a black coat, buck gauntlets and a pair of brogans purchased in Columbia at Nash

Baytin and Co. In another report, Peebles said he found a $2,063 error in the accounting of how much Mary Ann Peebles should have received from the estate, and asks that he be allowed to sell some of the children's portion of the estate to provide this money for Mary Ann. His request was approved. Between August, 1852 and April, 1854 Peebles listed $2,026 in expenses on behalf of the children, including schooling for Jared at Washington, $75 at White Sulfur Springs, $250 for a saddle horse for Barbara and $400 to a Miss Wilson for teaching Barbara.

The children did receive good medical attention. Their stepfather was a physician. The following invoice from dentist E. Edmundson for work done on Jared in January, 1854 is an interesting printed invoice of the work both offered and performed, complete with a price list for all services offered.

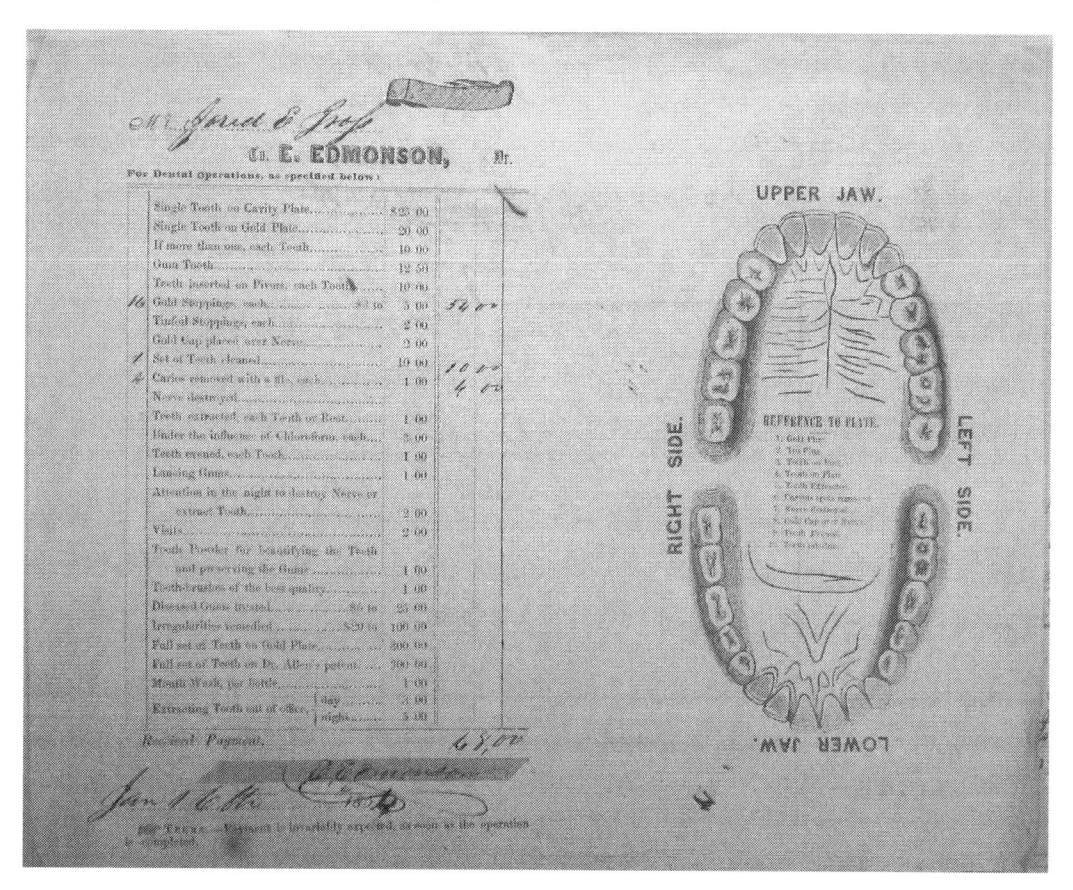

In March of 1854 Peebles reported to Judge Waller on the financial affairs he had conducted as guardian of the two Groce children. He stated that since the expiration of the Pleasant Hill lease contract with Leonard on December 31, 1852,

"I have since had the services of the working portion of said negroes without any understanding from the court relative to the disposition, maintenance and hire thereof; But I would now greatly prefer, if your honor please to make some definite and proper arrangements respecting to the employment and wages of he effective ones, and the support and care of all the others, such and one as would be clearly acceptable, and mutually beneficial, to all the parties of interest." Peebles also asked that the annual allowance for maintenance of his wards, set by the court in 1851 at $900 per year, be substantially augmented, "especially during the coming year as we expect to travel extensively with them over different portions of the United States, and would wish them duly prepared to derive all the natural pleasures and advantages of observation and instruction that this trip may afford." In July, 1858 the court allowed Peebles $1,154 for expenses of the children on "their travel to the North". Presumably the other Peebles children also accompanied their parents, but not at the estate's expense.

Barbara was being schooled at home in July of 1857. Peebles paid $50 for tuition to Elinar Wright and $83.35 to A. Fose for musical instruction.

Jared reached the age of 21 in May of 1858 and promptly began legal actions to receive his share of his inheritance from his father. He told the court that debts of this estate had been fully paid and the estate had been divided between Mary Ann Peebles, Barbara and himself, EXCEPT an interest in a league of land granted to John W. Hall on the east bank of the Brazos River in Brazoria County and an interest jointly owned by the estate and Leonard of 800 acres in Brazoria County granted to Wm. Harris and known as the Bolivar league that was and is still in litigation. He listed the lands set aside for himself and Barbara, as detailed in the June, 1850 court term. He also listed the negroes set aside to himself and Barbara from the JEG III estate partition, and provides a list of these 44 slaves by name and age (included in Appendix IV).

In July Peebles wrote to the Austin County court pointing out that he lost the use of the Groce negroes upon the expiration of the Lease Contract in 1852 and that, despite asking the court in March of 1854 for help with maintenance of the negroes, the court had declined to so order, and that he had to pay for their maintenance himself, and intends to charge the estate for these expenses before the soon-anticipated settlement with the Groce children. He stated that he has educated the children "as benefits their condition in life … without consuming a single dollar of their estate proper." He says that all of their property "that came into his hands is still in his possession, to be returned to them very shortly, of treble value, partly from the natural course of things and partly, I think, to my own efforts and contributions to that end." He mentioned that Jared had recently come of age and had asked the court for his share of the estate, and that Barbara would do similarly in about a year. The court promptly responded by appointing commissioners to effect the property division and to report back by August. The commissioners included Jared F. Groce, Leonard's son and Jared IV's cousin.

The commissioners met at Pleasant Hill on August 28, 1858 and completed their task, sending a letter and an inventory of the estate to the court on that same date. They considered the size, shape and boundaries of the various tracts of land and decided that it would be more advantageous to distribute whole tracts rather than divide each in two. With the agreement of the Groce children and Peebles, they divided the lands into four lots of approximate equal value, and by random drawing assigned two lots to each child. Jared E. Groce IV was assigned Lot 1 valued at $29,805 being 900 acres at the lower end of the original Bernardo grant (later sold to Wm. Wharton Groce for Bonny Nook) and two parcels in the Irons league totaling 4,428 acres. A sketch of this land indicates that at this time Jared F. Groce (son of Leonard) already owned the 1,100 acres of the original Bernardo grant immediately above the 900 acres distributed herein. Jared IV also was assigned Lot 4 valued at $18,016 consisting of 2,252 acres, being all of the W.C. White grant in Austin County excepting 400 acres previously given to Julia Bracey and 400 acres sold to C. Railey. Barbara was assigned Lot 2 valued at $26,585 consisting of 2,214 acres in the Thos. Stevens league, and Lot 3 valued at $17,712 consisting of 2,214 acres in the W.W. Sheppard league in Fayette County. The commissioners listed the slaves by name, age and value in two lots of 22 each of identical $11,675 value.

Barbara Groce married Philip Clarke on March 3, 1859, and by this act she became legally "of age" and no longer under the guardianship of her stepfarther. In May Peebles presented his final accounting as Guardian of the Groce children to the Austin County court. He credited their account with $20,025 "for the hire of their negroes" for six years at $3,337.50 per year. He then charged the children's estate with $1,000 per year each for six years for "personal and all other expenses" plus $5,025 as the value of Mary Ann's Dower Right released to them, ending with a total of $3,000 due from him to Barbara and Jared, of which he paid $1,500 to Jared on October 16, 1858 and $1,500 to Barbara on February 25, 1859. He asked the court for release from guardianship. Also included in this report is a worksheet detailing each of the slaves, showing their occupations and assigning each a value based on their contribution. This was used to arrive at the annual rent shown above. Healthy working men were valued at $100 - 150 per year, with the higher values assigned to more diligent or skilled workers. Women were valued at about half that of men. Children and old adults no longer able to perform hard work were not valued and termed "expense".

In his final report to the court on October 25, 1859, Peebles attached documents showing the detailed distribution of Jared IV's and Barbara's inheritance, completing his duties as Guardian, and asked to be officially relieved of this duty. His final act was to request the court to examine all of his efforts and to order some compensation from the estate to him for these efforts. The twenty-year wrangling over who got how much of Jared III's estate was finally over.

Among the 750+ pages of probate court documents related to the prolonged estate settlement were several that provided a detailed listing of the slaves at Bernardo initially and Pleasant Hill later. Names, ages and family relationships were often included. A nearly thirty-year record of these slaves is thus available, providing a rare look into family relationships among slaves during this period. Most African Americans today have little chance of learning any specifics about their lineage before the end of the Civil War. Census records of 1850 and 1860 list slaves by age and gender but do not provide names nor family relationships. Descendants of these individuals who spent their lives operating the Bernardo and Pleasant Hill plantations may actually be able to trace their forefathers back to at least 1831, and in some cases to arrival in the United States from Africa in 1818. Appendix IV is a summary of the eight slave inventories from 1831 to 1859, showing the evolution of the family units during that time. The records indicate that there was very little buying and selling of slaves at Bernardo and Pleasant Hill before the Civil War. The growth in numbers came largely from new children born to parents who were already on the plantation. Divisions did occur over time; first to Sarah Ann Groce Wharton, and then to Jared IV's wife and children. Family units were generally maintained during these divisions.

Descendants of Bernardo Residents

Most of the extended Groce family and their former slaves remained close to the plantation they had shared for a half-century. The Peebles family continued to live at Pleasant Hill, while Leonard Groce lived at Liendo. Many of the African Americans who had worked on the plantation before the war continued to do so after, sharecopping on Groce and Pebbles lands and working as hired household helpers for the white families. As their children and grandchildren came of age, most of the Groce descendants migrated away from the area while the black descendants tended to remain in Waller County.

Tracing the Groce family through two generations after the Civil War is relatively easy. The family genealogy provided by Sarah Berlet is nearly complete through the 1930's. The names of the children of Leonard and Jared Groce III are known, and their whereabouts can be determined from census and other records. All of the children of Leonard and Jared Groce III lived in Austin (today's Waller) County in 1870. The 1870 census indicates that Leonard was living at Liendo with three sons, Marcus, Charles and Ellison, and his daughter Martha McKay. His son Jared F. was living nearby with wife Asenath and children Abner, Courtney, Margaret and George Fulton (aka. Jared Jr.). William Wharton Groce was living nearby at Bonny Nook with his wife Kate and three children, Frances, Courtney and Leila. Leonard Jr. was a physician living in Hempstead as a single man. Mary Henrietta and her husband Wm. Bennett had five children - Fulton, Wm. Jr., Leonard Groce, Arthur and Wade.

Richard and Mary Ann Peebles were recorded in the 1870 census at Pleasant Hill. With them resided Mary Ann's son Jared Groce IV and his sister Barbara with her husband Philip Clarke and their three children Mary Ann, Jared and Philip. Next door lived their housekeeper Luanna Childs, one of their former slaves, and her two young mulatto children, Bertie and May. The father of Luanna's children was Jared Groce IV. [177]

Tracing the descendants of the African Americans who had lived as slaves at Bernardo and Pleasant Hill is more difficult. Before emancipation, slaves were almost never mentioned as having last names. Census slave schedules listed bondsmen by gender and age only. Inventories in deed and probate records provide a little more detail, usually giving first name, age and sometimes descriptions of family units. The first records of African Americans in which their full names - first and last - are given are the Texas Voter's Registration List of 1867 and the U.S. Census of 1870. The ages and birthplaces of an individual often do not agree in the subsequent censuses. Enumerators were careless, names were recorded as phonetic renditions, and the illiterate former slaves were unable to check the record for accuracy. In many cases the individuals did not accurately know their age, or where they or their parents were born. All of these factors introduce uncertainty in tracing family genealogy of African Americans.

A census search for descendants of Bernardo and Pleasant Hill slaves using the first names and family units as given in the 1831 - 1859 slave inventories has been successful in connecting many of these people to their enumeration in the 1870 census. The data used in this evaluation are not precise and so the conclusions are not necessarily 100% accurate. Nonetheless, the existence of the slave inventories which provide family relationships allows a reasonable projection of the genealogy of the black descendants of Bernardo. Several instances in the 1870 census show two or more families with the same last name living as neighbors and have first names and ages which match siblings in the older inventories. A reasonable assumption is that these people are siblings in 1870, and the same as those given in the inventories. In other cases elderly individuals with first names and ages matching the inventory data are living with an adult child in 1870 whose first name and age match children of the elder in the inventories. As an example in 1870, Thamer Lilley, age 87, was living with her daughter Charlotte Livingston and next to her son Hampton Lilley. All three as well as Charltte's husband Pickins Livingston (deceased by 1880) show in the inventories with matching first names, ages and family relationships. Thamer came to Texas with Groce in 1822 and probably arrived from Africa in 1818.

Selection of a last name was one of the important decisions made by the newly-freed African Americans in 1865. Some adopted the name of their recent owner if they respected that individual; Robin and Ben were young male slaves at Pleasant Hill and took the name Peebles after emancipation. Some wanted no part of their former owner and adopted the names of famous people such as Jefferson and Washington. Some took the name of the place they lived, as in the Bellville family of neighboring Austin County. Many of the families associated with Bernardo apparently carried an unrecorded but recognized by them last name which originated before they came to Texas. The surnames Livingston, Lilley, Coleman, Colllins, Boyd, Childs and Spriggs were adopted by children of Bernardo slaves listed in 1831 who had moved to Texas with Jared Groce in 1822. The fact that they did not take the name Groce, and all or most in a family took the same last name, suggests a heritage which they understood and perpetrated. Slaveholding families with surnames Livingston, Collins, Childs and Boyd lived in Edgefield County, South Carolina, in 1820. Jared Groce lived near this area, had relatives and bought slaves in this county. Perhaps he also acquired slaves from these Edgefield County families, and they remembered the name of the person who owned the plantation on which they were born, thus explaining the surname origins of the Bernardo residents. Lilley family lore among current descendants suggests their last name was chosen by patriarch Abraham Lilley because he had "always wanted to be a lilly of the field."

At least four families who lived around Bernardo consisted of white men from the plantations or their sons, and black women who were former slaves. The first such relationship began when Philip Cuny moved to Texas in 1840, founding

Sunny Side Plantation just south of Bernardo. Philip was a cousin of Courtney Groce; both came from prominent families in Rapides Parish, Louisiana. Leonard Groce helped Cuny get his start in Texas by cosigning a note in which Cuney borrowed $10,000 to buy the first portion of Sunny Side. During a period in which he had three successive white wives, Philip and his household servant Adeline Stuart had eight children in Texas, one of whom, Norris Wright Cuney, became the most prominent African American in nineteenth century Texas. Among Cuny's slaves brought with him from Louisiana were Abram and Kitty. Abram was born on the Rapides Parish plantation of Ettiene Malafret Layssard, and took this last name after the Civil War. Their daughter Amy Lasarde began a relationship around 1872 with James B. Gee, son of Bernardo overseer Alfred Gee, that lasted for about 13 years and produced seven children including daughters Addie and Eva Gee. They lived near Sunny Side Plantation in the Pine Grove community. From around 1890 to 1914, Addie and Eva Gee lived with George Fulton and Abner Jackson Groce, sons of Jared Fulton Groce and grandchildren of Leonard and Courtney. Several children were born to each of these two families. Addie Gee was living in Waller County in 1900 with her brother Curtis Lee Gee and two sons by George Groce. Living next to her was Abner J. Groce, a single white man who lived with Eva Gee and their three children. Nearby at a convict camp whose inmates were used for farm labor on adjacent lands was George Groce, a single white man who boarded at the prison camp and worked as a guard over the convicts. George and Addie had several children between 1900 and 1910.

Eva Gee died about 1913. George Groce died in 1914, leaving his 96 acre farm on which he and Addie lived to their children. Abner Groce also died in 1914, leaving his 56 acre farm to his children. [178] Addie and her family continued to live in Waller County in the rural community near the old Bernardo plantation until she died in 1959. Addie was apparently a highly respected member of the community; a road close to the Bernardo plantation is named after her. Addie and her children are listed in the censuses of 1910, 1920 and 1930 with the last name Gee. In their later years, all of Addie's children went by the last name of their father, Groce.

Oral interviews in 1959 with descendants of the slaves at Bernardo indicated that some eventually settled in the Sunny Side community south of Bernardo on the former Cuny plantation of that name. [179] However, several oral interviews by Debra Sloan in 2011 revealed that a large number of former slaves at Bernardo and Pleasant Hill also lived in the rural community of Lewisville near Hempstead. [180]

Sarah Groce Berlet described a conversation with a former Bernardo slave at a dinner with a group of her friends: "Several years ago, the writer spoke of the old log house at Bernardo plantation, to Wharton Collins, an aged negro, and a one-time slave of Leonard Groce. He leaned toward her and whispered, 'it was a log house, Miss, but it didn't look like one, so you don't have to tell it.' The poor old man was trying to uphold the dignity of the family before her lady friends who were in the party." Wharton Collins was born about 1860. He married Frances Spriggs, daughter of George Spriggs, also a Bernardo slave. Frank Edd White in his Master's Thesis on Waller County history included an image (opposite) of "Wharton Collins, former slave of Leonard Groce". Abigale Holbrook mentions a September 23, 1935 interview with Mr. and Mrs. Wharton Collins as providing source material for her article about life on plantations in Texas. [181]

The following photo of former Bernardo slaves is from a magazine for cotton farmers, "ACCO Press", June 1936 edition. The article told of the Centennial celebration of the founding of the Republic of Texas at Hempstead on May 15, 1936. The caption reads: "Two interested spectators at the celebration are shown at left. They are original Groce slaves. The one on the right is 105 years old - was four years old when the battle of San Jacinto was fought." What fascinating stories these women could have told!

The first official record in which the emancipated former slaves were recorded with last names was the 1867 Texas Voter's List. [182] A transcription of this list for Austin County contains 136 pages of names of individuals. [183] The following excerpts from this list indicate black individuals who were likely residents of or closely associated with Bernardo and Pleasant Hill Plantations. The apparent boundary between Hempstead and Pine Grove Precincts in 1867 was Pond (Clear) Creek. In 1869 the Precincts changed - Waller's Store precinct appears in what was formerly called Pine Grove. This apparently includes modern Sunnyside.

#	Name	Precinct	born	TX	Years in county	Bernardo connection
242	Wesley Childs	Buckhorn	TX	24	24	son of Winston and Kizzy
1011	Jefferson Childs	Hempstead	TX	29	29	son of Winston and Kizzy
1013	Alexander Spriggs	"	TX	42	42	son of Jim (1831 inventory)
1019	Spencer Lasade	"	TX	24	24	son, Abram/Kitty,SunnySide
1034	Daniel Livingston	"	TX	24	24	son of Spencer and Maria
1044	Spencer Livingston	"	TX	24	24	son of Spencer and Maria
1057	Washington Collins	"	AL	49	48	son of Daniel and Delphy
1052	Winston Childs	Pine Grove	SC	44	39	Kizzy's husband.
1064	Hampton Lilly	Hempstead	SC	46	46	son of Jack and Thamer
1067	Pickins Livingston*	"	SC	46	46	son of Fielding and Sally
1077	Edom Livingston	"	TX	25	25	son of Pickins and Charlotte
1078	Eli Spriggs	"	TX	23	23	son of Jim
1079	Sampson Sherrill	"	GA	5	2	hsbd. of Charlotte Livingston
1108	George Spriggs	"	TX	30	30	son of Jim (1831 inventory)
1124	Spencer Livingston	"	TN	47	47	husband of Maria
1144	Robin Peebles	Forkston	AL	23	23	son of Lame Jake and Eliza ?
1150	Abraham Lilly	Hempstead	SC	46	46	husband of Harriet in 1831 ?
1176	Moses Boyd	"	GA	46	46	son of Peter and Suckey
1184	Robert Boyd	"	AL	46	46	son of Peter and Suckey
1199	Samuel Pease	"	TX	25	25	traded from Gov.Elisha Pease
1201	Leven Childs	"	TX	38	38	son of Winston and Kizzy
1249	Charles Coleman	"	TX	36	36	son of Elbert & Fanny
1252	Emanual Coleman	"	TX	37	37	son of Elbert & Fanny
1274	Albert Coleman	"	TX	31	31	son of Elbert & Fannny
1436	Abraham Lasade	Pine Grove	LA	26	26	husband of Kitty, Sunny Side
2002	Samuel Lilly	"	TX	27	27	son of Abram and Matilda
2100	Washington Collins	"	AL	48	48	second entry, this in 1869
2202	Colbert Coleman	"	TX	26	26	son of Abram and Harriet ?
2235	Nero Boyd	"	TX	21	21	unknow, prob. connection.
2236	Armstead Coleman	"	TX	24	24	Olmstead, son,Elbert &Fanny
2336	Phelon Collins	"	TX	21	21	Fielding, son, Fielding /Sally
2411	Allen Groce	Waller's Store	TX	27	27	"Budge", son, Chunky Issac
2419	Nelson Livingston	Waller's Store	TX	46	46	son of Mira

* Pickins later was listed as Peter Livingston, beginning with the 1870 census.

The U.S. Census of 1870 was the first to include the former slaves enumerated with their full names, ages and family units. A supplement to the main census, titled Schedule 3, Production of Agriculture, Austin County, Texas, Beat 2 (Hempstead) contained listings of several individuals formerly enslaved at Bernardo and Pleasant Hill, indicating the number of acres they farmed and the crops and animals raised.

Agent, Owner or Manager	Improved Acres	Horses	Mules	Milk Cows	Oxen	Other Cattle	Swine	Bushels Corn
Washington Collins	22	1		2			5	30
Felon (Fielding) Collins	18	2					2	
Robert Coleman	15	1						30
Emanual Coleman	15	1					1	40
Justin Boyd	20							75
AbrahamLilley	15	1					1	100
Moses Boyd	30	1			2		12	100
Jacob Boyd	25							50
Nero Boyd	20	1	1				3	50
Stephen Livingston	30				2		7	50
Bohe (Bowie) Lilley	20	1	2				9	55
Sampson Sherry (ill)	40	1					13	200
Sutton Israel	40	4					12	200
Peter Livingston	40	2	1				10	100
Edom Livingston	20	2					6	80
Boyd Jackson	20	2					5	80
Hampton Lilley	30	1					11	200
Eli Spriggs	25	2					6	110
Sam Coleman	20	1					6	110
Spencer Livingston	20	1					1	
Alick Spriggs	20	1					7	110
Martha Spriggs	20							80
George Spriggs	20	2					6	110
Samuel Lilley	20	1			8		20	100

Book Three: The Archaeology

Site Identification and Preliminary Fieldwork

Glimpses of Bernardo have gradually been reemerging in recent years, with scope and pace rapidly expanding since 2009. Relic collectors using metal detectors uncovered artifacts in the 1970's. Unfortunately, these uncontrolled and unrecorded activities have resulted in total loss of the information that these artifacts could have lent to understanding the history of the plantation. More recently beginning around 2007 avid Texas historian Glenn Collins, with the permission of the landowner Greg Brown, collected a number of artifacts and preserved these in displays for public viewing as opportunities to do so were presented. Collins' finds include a wide array of artifacts including iron cotton weeding hoe heads, many examples of hardware used for horses and wagons, Civil War relics such as uniform buttons and gun parts, Spanish and U.S. coins dated 1784, 1841 and 1847, brass lamp parts, candlestick holders, bells, finger rings, shoe accessories and buckles, and many lead bullets ranging from round musket and rifle balls from the 1820's to Minie' balls of the Civil War era. Pieces of broken ceramics found by Collins and others have been identified as having been made from the 1820s through the Civil War.

A brass button with a seal of the state of Virginia determined to date to the early 1800s is an especially interesting find. This artifact was found near the Bernardo house complex, and may have been brought to Texas by Jared Groce II from his ancestral Virginia home.

Texas Militia and Confederate Infantry buttons attest to visitors during the Civil War period.

And a heel plate from the boot of a proud Texan must have made quite a distinctive track! Could this have been lost by Leonard Groce, or his brother Jared? Or by Sam Houston or any of several other icons of early Texas who visited Bernardo?

Gophers conveniently brought buried pieces of broken ceramic vessels to the surface; examples are among the artifacts collected by Collins.

Glenn Collins' efforts to conserve and preserve the artifacts he found have added significantly to the story of Bernardo, and represent the beginning of archaeological work at the plantation. Many of these artifacts were placed on display at the Sam Houston Memorial Museum in Huntsville in 2011.

Creation of the Bernardo Archaeology Project

Organized archaeological activities began at the site in early 2009, led by two avocational archaeologists and Texas history buffs, myself (Jim Woodrick) and Gregg Dimmick, author of "Sea of Mud", the definitive story of the retreat of the Mexican army after the battle of San Jacinto. I had written about the Bernardo plantation in my book about the history of Austin County, and had been trying to locate the current owner of the land to request a visit to see if any remains of the famous plantation were still present. Driving together near the plantation site on a trip to scout another, unrelated historical site, I mentioned to Dimmick that I was interested in visiting the Bernardo site. Subsequently, a remarkable set of circumstances fell into place that led to the launching of a major archaeological project and ultimately to this book.

Gregg had been invited in March of 2009 to provide an interview for a documentary of his "Sea of Mud" work with Houston television station KTBU Channel 55 for their series called "Postcards From Texas". After the interview Gregg learned that station CEO Greg Brown owned a ranch in Waller County that encompassed the former Bernardo plantation. Dimmick met Brown at that time, described my interest in the plantation and asked if we could come for a visit. Brown agreed, and on April 25 the two of us were warmly received at Brown's Mossy Oaks ranch and given a tour of the property. A hour of surface scouting and probes with a metal detector around the purported site of the main house produced ceramic potsherds and metal artifacts believed to date from the Civil War period and before. The site was relatively undisturbed, and we immediately knew that Bernardo was an archaeological treasure that warranted proper recording and evaluation; with Greg Brown's full support we began to involve others in the archaeological community.

Dimmick organized a tour on July 14 in which about 50 interested individuals attended. Jim Bruseth, Archaeology Division Director at the Texas Historical Commission (THC), was on this tour and immediately offered THC's assistance in getting the project started. The sites were recorded with the state by Woodrick as 41 WL 28 (Bernardo) and 41 WL 29 (Pleasant Hill). A volunteer work party met at the site in early August to establish survey markers for future grids to be used to precisely record the locations of artifacts as to be uncovered. The week of August 17 was spent by THC staff and volunteers in performing ground penetrating radar and magnetometer surveys to identify underground features for future detailed excavations. This image shows these two scientific devices in use in the vicinity of the main house.

Project leadership was transferred to professional archaeologists Carol McDavid and Robert Marcom of Community Archaeology Research Institute, Inc. of Houston. Marcom became the Principal Investigator. Funds were sought and obtained to begin the Initial excavations in late 2009 and early 2010. These focused on the site of the main house at Bernardo as determined by THC remote sensing work. Features identified by the THC remote sensing work in the following composite image proved to be buried brick foundations of the main house and brick and sandstone fireplace foundations. Remarkably, the house dimensions as discovered in the excavations matched exactly those given in the sketches of Sara Berlet from the 1930s. [184]

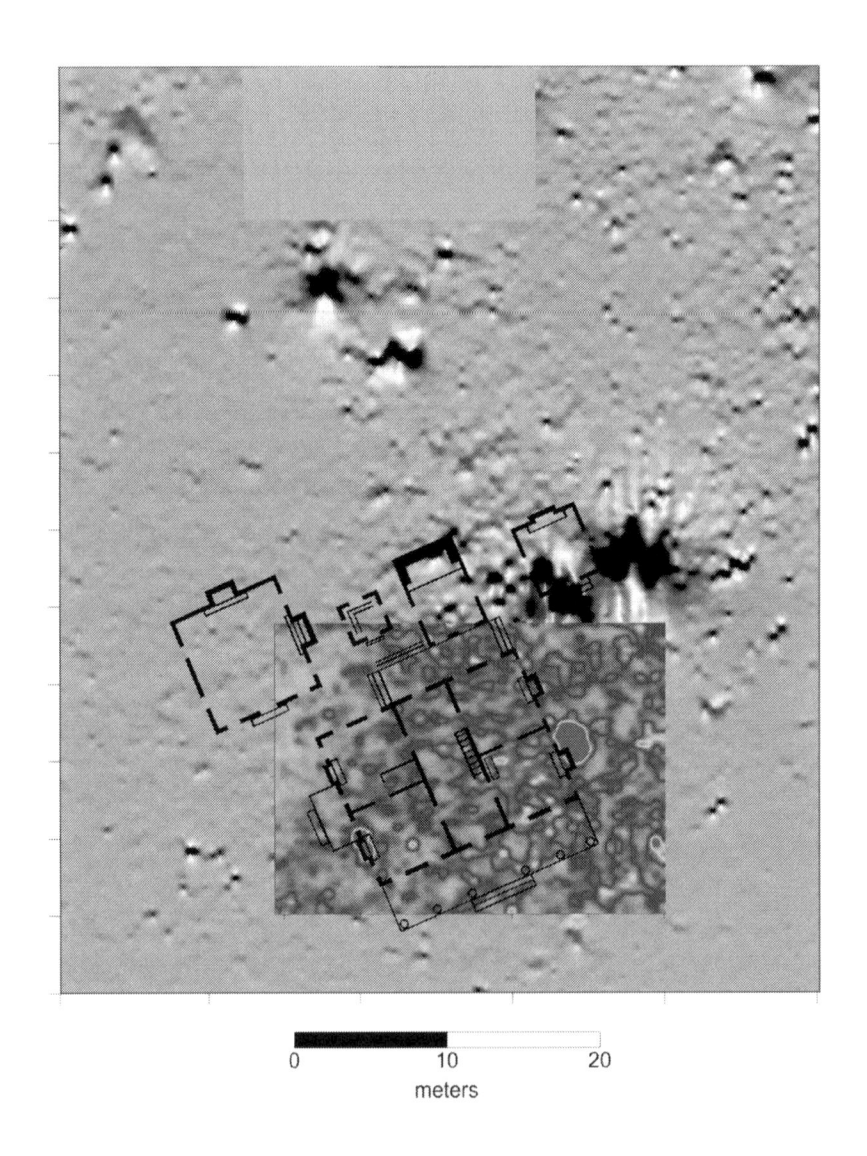

The Bernardo Plantation Archaeology Project (http://wiki.bernardoplantation.org) began in 2009 as a result of this work, with Dimmick, Brown and myself as Founders. I became the Project Historian and for most of 2009 and 2010 compiled archival information on the plantation and those who lived there, and transformed this information into this book. Several newspaper and magazine articles between July, 2009 and March, 2010, covered the archaeological work underway at that time.[185] THC publications also covered the archaeological activities in 2010.[186]

Excavations and Findings

An analysis of the artifacts found during the early excavations revealed that the nails in the original western portion of the house with sandstone chimney foundations were of a type used in the 1820's. However, nails found in the eastern half of the house with brick chimney foundations were made only after 1833, suggesting a major addition to the house was made during that period.[187] None of the hundreds of pages of archival information on Bernardo had mentioned a major renovation to the main house. Armed with the archaeological information that different nails were employed in constructing the house, a box containing the Groce papers in the Briscoe Center for American History was reexamined, and in it was found one of the several sketches of the floor plan of the main house that contained a unique penciled addition saying that "additions and improvements were added in 1838 …". The historians had finally found proof of what the archaeologists already knew from the story of the nails![188]

The following photos of excavations conducted in December, 2009 show the original 1822 sandstone chimney foundations as well as the carefully laid brick chimney foundations added in 1838. The same fireplace pattern was present at Pleasant Hill; the first phase in 1833 contained two sandstone fireplaces and the early-1840's expansion added two brick fireplaces. Bricks had been manufactured at Bernardo since its early years; their use in fireplace construction apparently began in 1838.

Dozens of volunteers participated in the excavations, directed by professional and avocational archaeologists. Several descendants of the Groce family visited and participated; this photo shows Max Petty excavating the fireplace foundation in the room of his great-great-great-great grandmother Courtney Groce.

In this photo Principal Investigator Robert Marcom poses with the family of Elaine Cobb, a great-great-great-great granddaughter of Jared Groce. With Elaine

164

are her son and three grandchildren. From let to right are William Bennett Siler, Doris "Elaine" Bennett Cobb, Robert, Nathan Porter Cobb, Christopher Tyler Cobb and Evan Lawrence Cobb.

A total of 7,192 artifacts were found and catalogued during the 2009 and spring, 2010 field work overseen by THC. Broken window glass, square nails and brick fragments were the most prevalent finds. Other finds included items from firearms, clothing, and household items, and many pieces of broken ceramics dated to the occupation period. Later excavations by CARI in 2010 and in spring, 2011 produced thousands of additional artifacts, including a sample shown in the following two photographs.

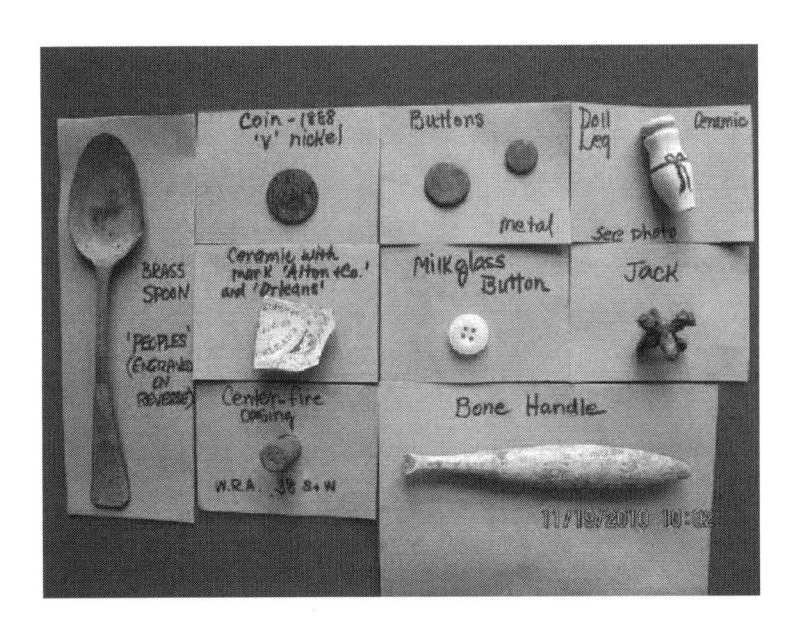

During this time, metal detecting surveys were performed in the large field west of the main house were successful in locating the stables and the wash room. Many used cotton hoe heads were found in these areas, as well as several flat or "sad" irons used in the laundry. One of the slave cabins located about 150 yards behind the main house was also located, with an intact occupation zone. The location of the main house and slave quarters at Pleasant Hill was identified in late 2011. Future excavations will be directed at these features.

The site of Sam Houston's April, 1836 Texian army camp across the Brazos from Bernardo was surveyed by THC and several visits made with metal detectors to locate and record artifacts. The site had been extensively surface collected in the early - mid 1900's by a local collector, and was recorded and tested by the Houston Archaeological Society in 1989. A large collection of artifacts from this training camp are currently in the possession of the landowner and the grandson of an early relic hunter. They consist primarily of lead rifle and pistol balls dropped by Texian soldiers, along with a few buttons and belt buckles. Some of these artifacts are exhibited in the Austin County Jail Museum in Bellville. A complete account of all of the archaeological activities at this site was published in 2011. [189]

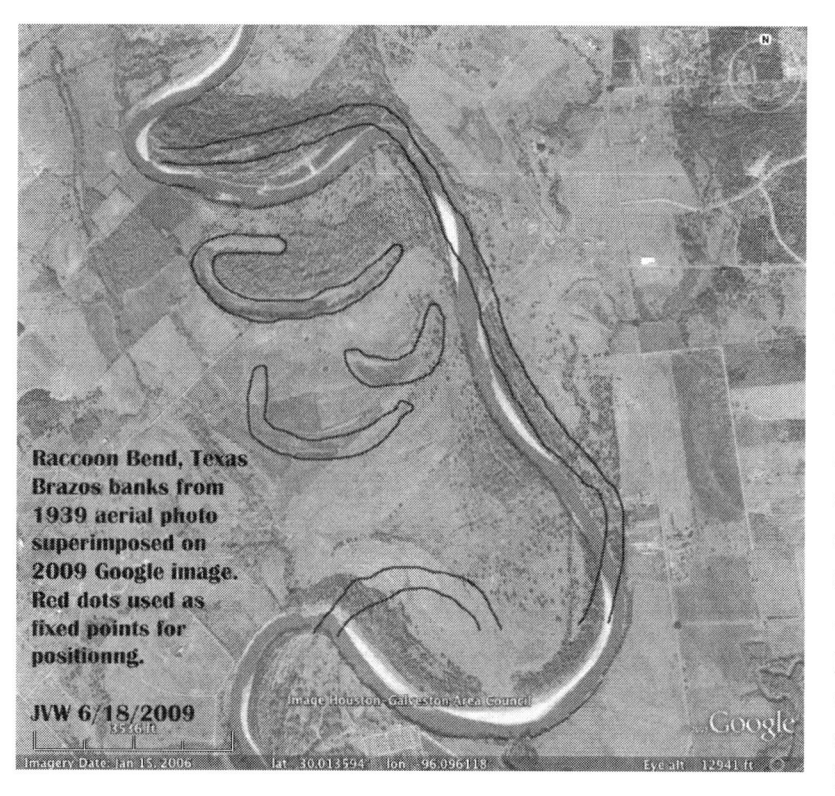

The Brazos River has changed its course over the years through the natural processes of floods and erosion. Determination of the extent of these river changes is important when seeking archaeological information near the waterway. An accurate picture of the changes in the main channel of the Brazos during the past seventy years is shown in the attached image. A 1939 aerial photograph was superimposed on a modern image and adjusted to match selected known reference points in both photographs. An outline of the 1939 river channel was then drawn on the modern image. Additional undefined river migration must have occurred between the time the first settlers arrived in 1822 to 1939; the direction and extent is estimated to have been approximately that of the last 70 years. It appears, based on measurements since 1939 and estimates before this date, that most of the land near the river in the early 1800's is intact, in some cases no longer on the river bank as it has retreated over the years.

The following image projects the Bernardo area with key features indicated. Some of these features are known and some are as surmised from the historical record but generally not yet supported by definitive archaeological evidence.

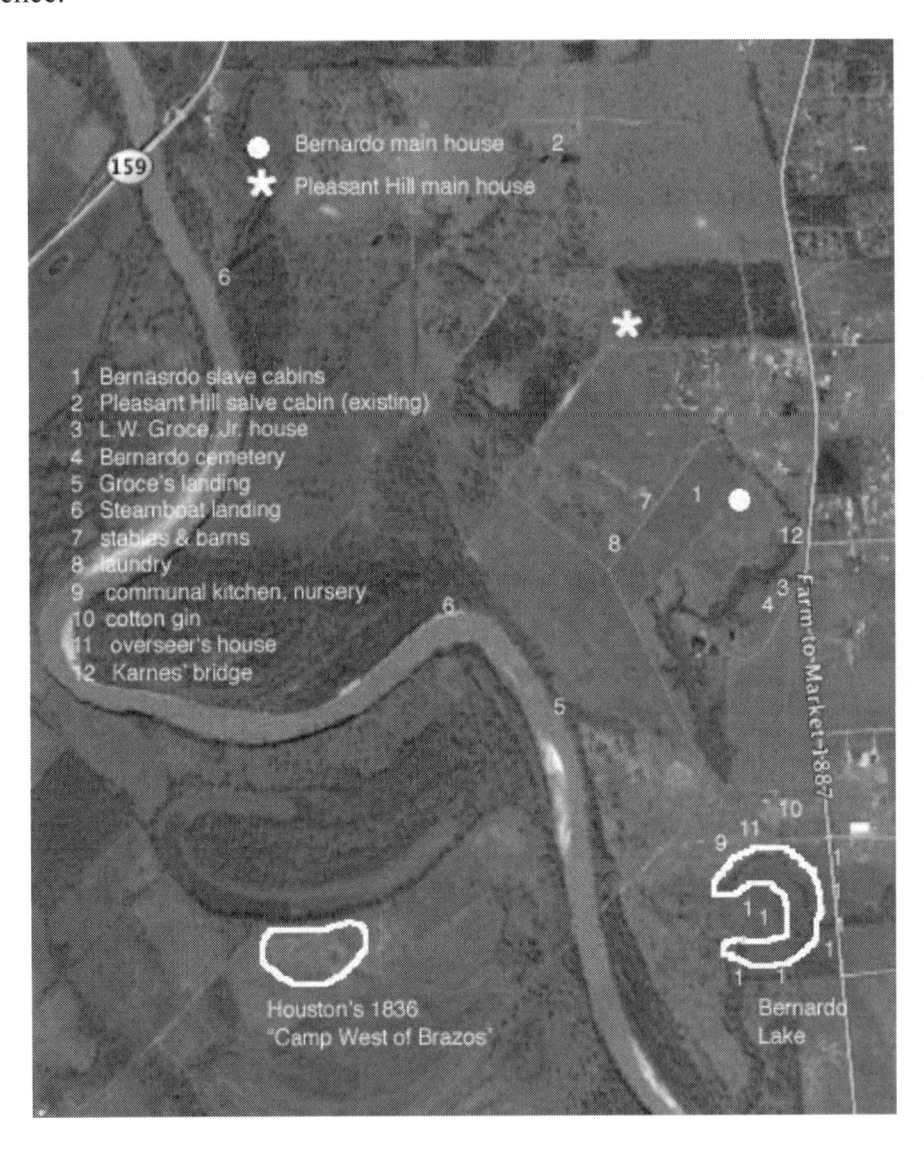

Appendix I: Public Business Disputes

Jared Groce II had at least two extended, publicized business disputes. The first of these began when he lived in Georgia and was in partnership with Andrew Erwin and his son James in a company known as A. Erwin, Groce & Co. A lengthy letter from James Erwin to Stephen F. Austin (Austin Papers, #1213, 9/30/1825) describes Groce in very derogatory terms and accuses him of failure to make a $10,000 payment on debts incurred from his failed partnership with the Erwins. According to Erwin, Groce did "runaway" or "fly his country" to avoid payment. A Mexican traveler who visited Bernardo in 1828, Jose Maria Sanchez y Tapia, also stated that Groce had fled the United States to avoid creditors and with stolen slaves.

A letter from Andrew Erwin from Georgia dated April 6, 1833 states that Jared III had visited him and had paid $6,086 cash and that this payment allowed them to finally close the affairs of A. Erwin, Groce and Co. So it appears that Groce finally acknowledged at least a portion of his debt to Erwin and paid him in full in 1833. [Ref: Box 240 - "Groce Family Correspondence", Woodson Research Center, Fondren Library at Rice University, Houston].

Andrew Erwin was an innkeeper and merchant at Wilkesboro, North Carolina, a member of that state's House of Commons from Wilkes County (1800 - 1801), and Ahseville's first postmaster, and in 1814 moved to Augusta, Georgia, where he established a mercantile business with connections in Savannah, Charleston, Nashville, and New Orleans. He was also engaged in developing extensive land holdings in Tennessee and Alabama. By 1819 he suffered severe financial reverses and at this time had shifted his residence to Bedford County, Tennessee. Erwin was also a rival to the Austin's for the Mexican grant to be the first *empresario* in Texas. On March 2, 1822, seventy citizens of Tennessee and Kentucky met in Nashville where they adopted a memorial addressed to the Mexican government asking permission to establish a colony in Texas. They called themselves the "Texas Association". Among the group were Andrew Erwin, Samuel Wharton, Sam Houston, Ira Ingram, and John P. Erwin. This group chose Andrew Erwin and Robert Leftwich to take the memorial to Mexico. On March 22, 1822, they arrived in New Orleans. Erwin called on Joseph Hawkins who had already loaned money to Stephen Austin for his Texas colonization project. Hawkins made a small investment in the Tennessee Association project, covering his bets to be a major participant with whomever won out in Mexico to become the primary purveyor of new lands in Texas.

Erwin departed for Mexico in April, arriving before the 26th. Austin arrived on April 29th. Both were then engaged in asking the Mexican Congress for colonization rights in Texas. Erwin also had extensive interests and involvement in Mexico, where he was an associate of Augustin de Inturbide, leader of the Mexican revolution against Spain and Emperor of Mexico in 1822 and 1823.

A horse race scheduled in Nashville in 1806 between two prize horses owned by Andrew Jackson and Andrew Erwin resulted in these two prominent individuals becoming lifelong enemies. Erwin pulled his horse out of the race just before it was scheduled to occur, evoking a previously agreed-upon penalty. Erwin initially refused to pay the forfeit fee, creating a public dispute between himself and Jackson. Charles Dickinson, a local attorney and son-in-law of Erwin, apparently made a derogatory remark about Jackson's wife Rachel in a local tavern. This led to more public name-calling, and ultimately to a challenge by Jackson to a duel to settle the matter. In the duel, Dickinson shot first and hit Jackson in the chest with a non-lethal wound. Jackson then took careful aim, fired and killed Dickinson.

In 1808 Jackson and Erwin sparred over ownership of a large parcel of land in Tennessee - Jackson won the deed dispute. [Ref; Robert Vincent Remini, "The Life of Andrew Jackson"]. In 1828 Andrew Erwin published several articles in newspapers accusing Jackson of slave trading, timed to harm Jackson's chances of reelection to the presidency. [Ref: Robert H. Gudmestad, "A Troublesome Commerce: the Transformation of the Interstate Slave Trade" p. 148]. In a direct appeal to President Monroe designed to thwart Erwin's later political ambitions, Jackson accused Erwin of slave trading.

Andrew Erwin's son was married to Henry Clay's daughter. Jackson's friend John Eaton fought a duel with Andrew Erwin during the Jackson / Erwin litigation over the Tennessee land.

Groce's second public dispute began on a positive note as he attempted to hire Imla Keep of Rapides Parish, Louisiana, as an overseer/ doctor for one of his plantations. Keep came to Bernardo in company with Leonard Groce as the latter returned to Texas after completing school in 1824. Keep soon returned to Louisiana, where he was to attend to some personal matters, buy a list of supplies for Groce in New Orleans for which Groce had given him $3,000 in cash, and promptly return to Bernardo to begin his employment with Groce. Keep was delayed in Louisiana, caught up in a personal bankruptcy. He kept the cash that Groce had advanced, engaged in a duplicity involving Leonard Groce who was in Louisiana at that time on his mission to obtain a cotton gin for Bernardo, and bought the supplies on faked Groce credit. To make matters even worse, some of the goods were damaged from water that leaked into the sailboat that transported them to Velasco. Groce sued Keep and lost, being ordered to pay court costs and other damages. He appealed the verdict; the ultimate outcome is unknown. Keep left Texas around 1826.

Keep was born in Groton, Middlesex County, Massachusetts on July 31, 1785. In Townsend, Massachusetts he studied medicine and had a good practice. He married in Townsend in 1807, and soon decided to move south seeking more opportunity. His wife would not leave, so they separated. Keep went to South America for a while, where he was a surgeon in the army of revolutionist leader Simon Bolivar. Returning to the United States he settled in Lincoln County, Georgia, where he married a second time in 1810. This wife was killed in a carriage accident. Keep then married a third time in 1817 in Mississippi, where he stayed for a while before moving to Louisiana. His third wife died in Alexandria before he went to Texas. When he returned to Louisiana he married a fourth woman in New Orleans in 1828; they promptly moved to Vicksburg, Mississippi where Keep remained for the rest of his life. He was listed as a physician there in the 1850 census. His presence in Lincoln County, Georgia in 1810 overlaps the period that Jared II lived there, making it possible that Groce knew Keep from that period. Imla Keep died in Vicksburg on June 13, 1855. [Ref: www.rootsweb.ancestry.com/~msissaq2/keep.html and "John Keep of Longmeadow, Massachusetts, 1676 - 1680, and his descendants"]

James Erwin also alleged that Keep was a long-time associate of Samuel May Wiliams, and that both Keep and Williams had fled to Texas to avoid murder charges. Williams did enter Texas in 1823 under a pseudonym before reverting to his real name.

According to historian Gregg Cantrell ("Stephen F. Austin - Empresario of Texas", p. 179): "Austin had to ignore whatever misdeeds Groce might have committed in the United States and any small transgressions in Texas. For all his shortcomings, Groce was an asset to the colony, and as usual that was all that mattered to Austin.".

All of the following accounts are taken from the Austin Papers headed by their page number in Volume 2 of that collection. The original documents in this collection are housed at Center for American History in Austin, Texas. They were published in three volumes by Eugene C. Barker, Washington: USGPO, 1924-1928.

933 JARED E. GROCE TO AUSTIN 11/6/1824
"November 6th, 1824
"Dear Sir,
"I promised to Select a Track of Land for Doct. Keep and one of Thomas Purvis and Capt. Brown and for the Ranols. But in consequence of my Bad health and other Misfortunes I shall not be able to attend to it and must request you to make the selections for them. as to my Own business I Leave it to yourself and J.P. Coles to decide on it as you may Think proper which will be satisfactory to me I have Expalind my self to Coles - whom will Explain to you. I am in Bad helth But something on the mend
"J E Groce"

1148   Deposition   7/18/1825 -   apparently taken at Velasco on the brig "Texas".
"Mr. Jared E. Groce, having called on me to state what passed between him and Doctor Imla Keep at the time the Goods were landed which were brought on from Orleans by said Keep I have to State that a difficulty arose between Keep and the owner of the vessel in which they were brought as to the freight, and Groce repeatedly stated that he had plac'd Money in Keep's hands to purchase sundry articles for him in New Orleans, and that he should hold Keep responsible for the manner in which that money was expended - that he had nothing to do with the Goods until he rec'd them of Keep and would credit him for this amount on the Sums due by Keep to Groce, on account of Monies placed in Keep's hands. *Texas* July 18, 1825 (signed) S.F. Austin"

1150 Judicial Procedure: Maritime Insurance
"It appearing by the protest of the Master and Mate of the Schooner Lady of the Lake of and from New Orleans and other evidence herewith presented, that a part of the   merchandise shipped on board of said Schooner were damaged by sea water that leaked into her, and the said goods have been insured by the Louisiana Company and there being no port warden or other Officers here specially appointed to attend to such matters   -   Therefore the Undersigned Consignees and Owners of said Goods petition that appraisers be appointed to examine said Goods and asses the damage under oath and should the damage amount to more than 5 per Cent on said Goods your petitioners pray that the goods so damaged may be sold at public sale under the direction of said Appraisers for the benefit of the Underwriters.
"Keep and Groce"

"To the Honbl. Stephen F. Austin   Judge of the Brazos, Colorado and San Jacinto

"United Mexican States   Department of Texas

"Jurisdiction of the Brazos, Colorado and San Jacinto

"I   Stephen F. Austin   Principal Judge of the Jurisdiction aforesaid having seen the above petition of Keep and Groce have thought proper to appoint and by these presents do appoint Samuel Sextant, Samuel M Williams and Elias R Wightman inspectors or appraisers to examine and estimate the damage done to the Goods referred to in the said petition and should the damage on any of the articles amount to five per cent that they assess the proportion of said damages and sell the articles so damaged at public sale, after giving 10 days public notice for a/c of the Concerned and that the said Appraisers furnish the parties with a Certificate specifying the proportion of damage said goods may have sustained. Given under my hand this [19th ?] day of July 1825   In the District of San Felipe de Austin.

"Stephen F. Austin [rubric]"

1151   Jared Groce to Hyde and Merit in New Orleans   7/19/1825

"Brassos *Texas* July 19th 1825   Messrs. Hyde and Merit.   Doctor Imla Keep has just arrived from New Orleans with some goods - and let me have the greater part of them for which I paid him - by crediting him for money that I placed in his hands to purchase some Articles for me.   I likewise gave him Authority to receive from me a considerable amount of money   -   which he received, and made use of and has not returned me one cent.   after buying the goods of the Doctor and paying for them as above stated I found out that he had not paid money for the goods - but got them on a credit, and made use of my *name* in getting them   he was not authorized to do so - and he is a man that never will have it in his power to use my name in any way - And I was much surprised to see you allow him the liberty of acting so with you - for he had not my name on paper - except he wrote it or got some one to do it.   neither was he authorized either verbally or in any other manner whatever to use my name. -- it is true, about twelve months since I promised to give him a birth as an overseer on one of my plantations, on conditions - he would perform certain acts and come out last winter - but he has disappointed me in every case, and not come until now, and now, without my money.   If he had complied I would have employed him, for he says he is anxious to make money to pay you and myself.

"I have a right to find fault of all the confidence, I placed in him, but was more displeased when I found out he was tampering with my name, than anything else. I have given him no employment as yet, and am so much displeased - I do not know wither I will or not, the doctor appears to be very *desirous* to get in some business, - to make money to pay you and myself; it is a duty I owe my feelings to notify you of this immediately - I have no credit in Orleans, for I sent my son there to purchase a few articles - he got a letter from Mr. James Brown of Alexandria, and had the goods charged to him - and I have to pay Brown; Why did I do this? Because Keep - as I heard, had made way with my money - and could not get the articles I wrote for but in Orleans he informed my son that he could not get such and such articles - And then applied to my son, to go get his security - and he could get what he pleased it made my son very angry for if I wanted a credit I did not want any assistance with his credit   for the last time I saw Keep, until now, he affirmed if I would send in my son - he would raise my money at Alexandria - and go in company with my son to New Orleans, and purchase the articles I wanted, and then he, Keep, would come round by water with them, and my son by land - and bring my money, that is, the overplus - that Keep had after buying the goods,   he advanced my son ten dollars out of the thousands that I had placed in his hands - and said that was half what he had.
Jared E. Groce"

1185   ANDREW ERWIN TO AUSTIN
"Nashville August 29, 1825
"Dear Sir
"Strange as it may appear it is true that I have never until two days ago seen your lengthy epistle to me on various subjects of 18th February last. this is owing I presume to my absence from this State in Georgia and South Carolina from November until April last and my attention to my election for congress from that time until the 5th inst. in which I was again 2nd on the list having 3 others to console with me in disappointment since when I visited this place for the first time since November last and here find your letter previous to seeing of which however I have seen our old fellow suffer Genl. Leftwich and his grant and several meetings of the Texas association. They had some difficulty in arranging matters with the Genl. about his compensation expenses etc. etc. which now however appears settled by allowing him his expenses and about $200 pr. month for services and the stock is selling at about 100 pr. cent advance   It is now believed that Doctr. Robinson one of our most worthy citizens will go out as agent and take with him a large connexion and many respectable friends you will find

hum a great acquisition to the settlement of your new Country, he possesses sterling integrity good sound sense mildness of manners and conduct and firmness suitable to the undertaking and with all a good stock of practical experiences in the ups and downs of life. - I was a stockholder but poverty prevents my holding on to it - The old business of A. Erwin Groce & Co. and Erwin & Co. of which you have heard so much and so varies from the true state of the case keeps me in poverty and at present on the limits prescribed for unfortunate debtors from which I shall be released in about twenty days as I have twice within the last 7 years given up my last knife and fork to creditors. I did expect to have escaped this ordeal but so it is owing to party feelings growing partly out of my defending myself and neighbors against Genl. Jackson & Co. with eventual success excites feelings of hostility from that quarter and the circumstance of Mr. Groce leaving the country with property causes some to suppose I had knowledge of it which he knows is not the fact and the circumstances of my living on a good tract of land and having the use of 14 negroes which are mortgaged to the government for three times what they would sell for furnishes a pretext for some illdisposed persons to say that I hold property and withhold it from creditors. Even your neighbor Mr. Groce who knows these facts as well as I do sometimes I am told indulges himself in saying we are all rich and owe him and refuse to settle with him etc. etc. In your letter you ask how this matter is above you have the answer all of which I could prove by Mr. Groce himself in a court of the United States by Record Testimony in the city of Agusta were he here - no man wishes Mr. Groce to prosper more than I do It is true he joined me in a mercantile business in which business I had been prosperous for more than 20 years - Both our objects were to make money in which I lost upwards of $100,000 of my own capital and Mr. Groce near $50,000 leaving us jointly bound for large sums which both he and myself exerted ourselves to settle and at our last meeting in Augusta James Erwin Mr. Groce and myself each executed our notes to Col. McKinne for about ten thousand dollars which each were to pay and was to exonerate Mr. Groce from all other liabilities in Georgia and he exonerated us from him for all claims by him on either of us. Mr. Groce left the country without paying his note. it was paid by us and I presume the claim about which James Erwin has been writing Judge Thomas to which you allude in your letter in this latter part, however, I may be mistaken as I seldom see James Erwin and when I do we speak and feel somewhat different about Mr. Groce. I make more allowances for his misfortunes and his disposition to turn molehills into mountains than he does I have no knowledge of any other unsettled business between him and us which would require references as to what was said in Mr. Groce's letter to which you allude and which I have answered which answer Mr. Groce has not shown you - I viewed it all as intended for your eye and others and his own gratification whilst talking about it. as to either myself or family having anything to fear from any thing Mr.. Groce could publish either in this country or that it is all a mistake - we have no fears of the kind As to your expressions of personal regard I assure you it is reciprocal - I view you as instrumental in doing much good for yourself and friends and wish you long life and continuing prosperity.

" Yours very respectfully,

"Andrew Erwin

"P.S as I write a bad hand and dislike Copying I send you the above written by my son George Washington Erwin, from a Copy written by myself Since writing the above Doctor Felix Robertson has been appointed sole agent for the Texas association and will depart thence in October or November next.

"P.S. In addition to all I have said I wish to be remembered affectionately to Mr. Groce and all his Children that are with him, my regard for all of them as old acquaintances is undiminished and had Mr. Groce been as cautious in speaking of my means and Intentions to relieve him as was his duty and his Interest I do believe I should have Effected that Desirable object long since, he has Injured me without Benefiting himself - I however am blessed with a family who view Enemies and Misfortunes as removable by time and proper Exertions where truth and Justice
is right in front as the poler star. this rule we adhere to and of Course fear nothing man can do or say - my best respects to Mr. Westall and family and all other acquaintances with you

"AE

[Addressed:]   Stephen F, Austin Esqr.   Care of Jacob Cable   Natchitoches Louisiana"

1213   J ERWIN TO AUSTIN   9/30/1825

"S.F. Austin, Eqr.   Shelbyville Sept. 30th 1825

"Sir, Altho I have not the pleasure of your personal acquaintance, I take the liberty of writing you, the object is more to reply to your letter of Feby 18th to my father, than to make any explanations of our former business with Mr. Groce for whom you express so lively an interest - how he has created that feeling I am unable to say. I am too conversant with your character, too well informed of your capacity and discrimination, for a moment to believe that you can be deceived in the man. Three days of acquaintance to a man of intelligence, will show, Groce to be a vain foolish Gasconading Bragadocia a man of considerable energy or rather industry, acute and subtle in small matters, ready to see and take advantage, ambitious, and vain, the latter two qualities so predominate as to expose him readily to an observer, he is entirely void of the high and honorable feelings of a gentleman, destitute of principles, and without the least pretensions to credit for veracity or integrity of character, all this can not have escaped your attention, and if so how can you give attention to Statements made by him affecting the character and standing of men of Reputation. Why hesitate about the opinions you seem at a loss to form about transactions between such men and a Renegade like Groce - What evidence have you to create a doubt - Whatever Groce may tell you to the contrary, I now can tell you I can substantiate by Groce's own hand writing that up to the last transaction of business that ever took place between us in any shape whatever, that there was no difficulty or complaint and that I have his rects in full up to the last transaction signed and sealed by him acknowledging that all was satisfactorily settled from the beginning of the world to that date, and it was then and on that very day - in order to bring the entire business of A. Erwin Groce and Co to a close we agreed to divide amongst us individually the remaining out debts which were all in the hands of Col. McKenni of Augusta Geo. and amounted to $30,000 - it was the earnest entreaty of Groce, himself - that McKenni divided this amount into three equal sums say $10,000 -   and took Groce's individual notes for $10,000, my note for $10,000 and my father's note for $10,000 - I refused to give my note at first until Groce begged me to do so, urged the object of a final settlement - his rect in full - and finally agreed to assist <u>me</u> who was then void of means to pay my note, he gave his note payt at such time as would allow two crops of cotton to intervene and promised McKenni on his Honor that his note would be punctually paid - what was the result, my father paid his note, I paid mine, and Groce <u>runaway</u> - and left his endorser to pay that note has fallen in my hands - the individual note of J E Groce - 2 notes of $5,000 each which I did not expect to have collected thro your assistance as I learned you intend to pursue a course of policy, not calculated to encourage flying renegade debtors who contract debts in this country and fly to your colony - I had hear that you sent my claim to Maj. Thomas for that purpose   - If it is contrary to your regulations of course I have no course of complaint - If its only justice and truth you wish to arrive at I have ample Means - to establish all I wish by testimony that would outweigh the verbal statements of Groce -   The fact is Groce and myself quarreled But not about our business -   at our last meeting to his face I gave him the same character, I now give you of him, which he patiently heard. If I had injured him then why not assert his wrongs he had acted ungentlemanly and I told him so - he felt it - he left this part of the country and the next news I hear he had <u>runaway</u>   I remained firm at my post - I have settled up the old business of A E G & Co - Groce complains of suits - I have been sued too But I have successfully defended those suits   - and so might Groce have done. But he chose to fly his country as the safest and most glorious mode of settling matters - he pretends to you and to the world that he and I had an agency in having him sued he knew better, and now knows better, I have tendered my assistance in defending   - How could I suffer him made liable without becoming so - you say My Brotherinlaw was selected as the channel - that is also false - Mr. Crawford the partner of my Brotherinlaw Brot the suits, he was selected by the other parties because he is the most eminent Lawyer in that State, and better able to conduct a Base cause - If Groce had remained at his post he could have easily defeated as I have done the claim - "

"But there is one claim he can not defeat that is his individual notes given to McKenni - now in the hands of Thomas - those he must and shall pay - or remain exiled from his native Country he can not pretend to have any offsets against this claim. If my eye was upon him he could not have the assurance to deny this to you. I know he will tell Some other tale, he will say anything that best suits his purpose; and I have myself seen him voluntarily subscribe to an oath - which made me shudder - which I can any day produce - these things are only mentioned to give you more particular information of his character and standing while in the UStates - and altho you have a much better opportunity of observing his course in Texas - than me, I can not help remarking that even there he gives you some small cause at least to suspect if all I hear to be true, that he is not very particular in his conduct - or select in his associates and coadjuters -"

"The last remark Brings to my mind his Celebrated letter written to my father last year by the assistance of his friend and Secy Mr. Williams who acted also as a certificate man and certified that all Groce wrote was true, which he must have been well qualified to do - as it related to transactions with men, the fellow - had never seen - that who is Mr. Williams - a Renegade also - who fled to avoid capital punishment - his friend also and the inmate of his House from Missouri whose name I do not recollect - who fled for murder - Doct Keep - quite as well known   - these are his associates his men of business - what can you expect from such a man - and is the same Mr. Groce   - who is to be so powerful in a chancery suit - who is to publish a Book - and demolish by a stroke of a pen all the Erwins - Unfortunately for this Hero, who is mightiest when far off - the word Renegade, would present itself in large letters in every page and obliterate all he could say   - to which might be added some equally strong and true - I must now Sir - in justice to my own feelings apologize to you for the tenor of this letter, and all I can say, is that I feel I am writing to J E Groce, and not to S F Austin - and I also feel that I am replying to J E Groce and not S F Austin - because I have with much pleasure read other productions from you to my father and others and I know that this now in question is not your own legitimate offspring   Groce may Borrow what plumage he will, yet he will be Groce still - I know as well as if I had been at your elbow - when you wrote that letter, that you did so by the importunity of Groce and that you were reluctantly urged to convey ideas repugnant to your feelings - I write this with freedom and frankness not to offend you, But to let you know I understand the man, I know his object - he wants under pretense of settling old disputes to make friends - But he can not be depended on, and there is no use in receiving the acknowledgement of so low minded a fellow - I have only one word for him, that is I want the $10,000 and int. - that he owes me - and until that is paid he may exert all his cunning for I will reach him before I have done trying - thro some sources or another, and I should be much obliged by your reply at Orleans - saying whether a just claim can be made under your regulations, that is done to a Resident of the U States -

"If he will pay his claim I have the done with him, as to any suits vs. him now in Alabama it only requires attention to set the aside that are not against him as one of the firm of A E Groce [A. Erwin, Groce & Co.] and Co - I have already sent him word that if he wants to see me, I am always in the winter to be found in N. Orleans - where I am ready - to defend a suit in chancery - rendering him personal satisfaction or receive $10,000 due me, and settle matters and let him alone - either alternative is always before him -

"From the Friendly intercourse that took place and continues between you and my father, I had hoped soon to have had the pleasure of making your acquaintance with you beneficial in both, which I yet hope may not be prevented by so unworthy an object as Groce -

"J Erwin"

Jared finally paid his debt to Andrew Erwin. A letter from Erwin from Georgia dated April 6, 1833 states that Jared III had visited him and had paid $6,086 cash and that this payment allowed them to finally close the affairs of A. Erwin, Groce and Co. [190]

1293   DEPOSITIONS CONCERNING BANKRUPTCY OF IMLA KEEP 3/20/1826

" 1. Isaac Thomas

"United States of North America, and state of Louisiana parish of Rapide. This day appeared before me Gilbert Legrass a justice of the peace in and for said parish Isaac Thomas who being duly sworn ... did depose that he was acquainted with Doct. Imla Keep in the years 1822, 1823 and 1824. That he was his near neighbor and had as he believes a pretty general knowledge of his affairs. During those years he is on opinion, that Doct. Keeps practice as a physician could not have yielded him on a fair estimate more than five hundred dollars a year. he also states that the Docts. attention was principally confined to the cultivation of his farm. The said Thomas further states - That Doct. Keep purchased part of the Land that he once owned in this parish and which is now owned by the deponent of Col. Thomas Patterson - [continues describing how Keep assumed liability for a $4,200 mortgage on the land that he was unable to pay when it came due. Keep was given an extension of two years to pay and did pay a part of what he owed and closed the matter by surrendering the land.]

Then Thomas Hooper was deposed, stating that he knew Keep from 1819 - 1824, that he was his near neighbor and had a general knowledge of his affairs. [Note: Thomas Hooper was the step-father of Courtney Fulton Groce, wife of Leonard]. He said in 1819 or 1820 Keep had an extensive practice and was for a time a popular physician. Hooper engaged him as his family physician but Keep was very unsuccessful and became very unpopular in those families in which he practiced medicine - they considered him unsafe. Hooper forgave a $90 debt owed him by Keep, and hired another physician. Hooper stated that "during the latter part of the year 1824 deponent [Hooper] started from this Parish in company with Dr. Keep and Colonel Gross's family and that they arrived at Col. Gross's the residence in the Providence [sic] of Texas on the 24th or 25th of December ... and was present when Dr. Keep and Col. Gross attempted to make a settlement, that the deponent understood from the parties that Dr. Keep upon settlement fell in debt to Col. Gross to a very considerable amount and that Col. Gross gave a bill for goods which Dr. Keep was to fill in New Orleans for the amount of two or three thousand dollars the deponent does not remember which but believes the latter, which money the deponent understood was in the hands of Dr. Keep and belonging to Col. Gross.

"The deponent further understood from the parties that a partnership was to be entered into after Dr. Keeps return from New Orleans between Dr. Keep,

Col. Gross and Wm. White and that said White and Keep were to take possession of the lower plantation. [signed by Hooper March 20, 1826]"

Sheriff Narrish Wright of Rapides Parish gave testimony stating that Keep owed three mortgages totaling $8,810.50.

On March 7, 1825, Imla Keep appeared before Hon. William Murray Judge of the Sixth District Court, Parish of Rapides stating that he has had a series of misfortunes that rendered it absolutely impossible for him to pay his debts. He mentioned a very expensive lawsuit in Mississippi. He provided a list of 22 creditors to whom he owed a total of about $6,500. He listed his assets totaling $100. He requested the Court to declare him bankrupt so he could call in his creditors and give them his estate.

Notice was posted to his creditors on May 4, 1825. On May 9, 1825, Keep and his attorney Isaac Thomas came before the judge. The creditors failed to appear and there was no opposition made to the surrender of Keep's property.

1328   Sheriff's Sale   about May 8, 1826

"The Sheriff of said colony is hereby commanded to seize and expose to public sale so much of the property of J E G the defendant in the above case as may be sufficient to pay Eighty five dollars and Seventy cents to the Secretary S M Williams   167.50 to the Sheriff J.H. Polly and 175.30 to the Jurors being the amt. of costs due in said case and ordered to be paid by said defendant Groce by the Judgement of the Jurisdiction and Supreme court of this Jurisdiction dated 8th May of this year - and the said Sheriff will make return of this execution to my office within sixty days from this day as respects to the Jurors fees -

"Stephen F. Austin"

1329   "Department of Texas   Austins Colony   Imla Keep vs Jared E. Groce 5/10/1826

"The Sheriff of said colony is hereby commanded to seize and expose to public sale so much of the property of Jared E. Groce the Defendant in the above case as may be sufficient to pay the Sum of Two Hundred and fifty three dolls. twenty five cents the amount of costs due in said case to the Secretary S.M. Williams and Sheriff J.H. Polly.

"Stephen F. Austin"
"Court Costs
"Imla Keep vs Jared E. Groce
"Jared E Groce Jr.

[follows a list of 11 items totaling $50.75]
"Sn Felipe de Austin May 10th 1826"

1433 James E.B. Austin to Austin   8/22/1826
"San Antonio August 22, 1826
"Dear Brother ..... "I would rather that you and J.E.G[roce] - would come to some understanding differently from the one you are now on - as to Keep from what I have learned from when I left you - it is his intention to leave the country shortly ..."

1596 Jared E. Groce to Saucedo   1/29/1827
"The Chief of Department
Citizen Jared E. Groce an inhabitant of Austins Colony in this Department before you with all due respect and as maybe due in right represent(s) that in the month of May last year [he had] a law suit with a man of this colony named Imla Kemp and as from ... his belief thinks he has been injured by the Judgement [rendered by the] Judicial Tribune he being sentenced to pay a Considerable amount of money and also to deliver to said Keep three Negroes which the said Keep had delivered to your petitioner in Consideration of money which he owed your petitioner. Besides this your petitioner has a very important Witness who was then in the United States of the North and when I Could not procure in time for the said suit he is now in this Colony and I do not doubt but his evidence would decide the business in my favor. In consideration of what I have set forth and the injuries I have rec'd. I supplicate your Worship to be pleased to give the necessary instructions in order that I may be heard anew in Court, and give an order that said Keep shall deliver said Negroes with the understanding that I will give bond and security to conform with the resolution of the Judicial tribunal that has to take Cognisance of the Case, and I supplicate you to instruct the Judicial tribunal that has to decide this Case not to permit the affair to be discussed before them by any other persons than the parties interested, in order to prevent the matter to be confused and justice perverted by the Cunning of Foreign Lawyers who are not licensed legally by the Govt. to exercise those functions in this Country. Therefore your Worship will be pleased to do as I have petitioned in order that I may receive justice.
Bernardo Place January 29th 1827   (signed by) Jared E. Groce"

1597   4/17/1827

"Sn. Felipe de Austin 17th April 1827 This petition is passed to Citizen Stephen F. Austin in order that he may inform on its contents declaring whether the business of which it treats is legally terminated or not. (signed) Saucedo"

1597   4/18/1827

"To the Political Chief   In Consequence of the subject treated on in the foregoing representation belonging exclusively to the Judicial Authority this petition will be returned to the interested person in order that with it he may apply to the first meeting which will be held by the Alcaldes of this Colony where they can admit him to bring forward the new proof which he has to present in favor of his right, oblige the opposite party to secure the property in question, and not admit foreign Lawyers should either of the parties object.   Sn Felipe de Austin 18th April 1827 (signed by Stephen F. Austin)"

Appendix II: Illegal Slave Acquisition

Other business dealings between Jared Groce II, Andrew Erwin and others involves a murky story of illegal importation of slaves into the United States, apparently involving some of those who came with Groce to Texas in 1822. Beginning in 1808, the United States banned further imports of slaves. Any new slaves would have to be descended from those already in this country before 1808. Internal American slave trade and international slave trade was not banned - only new imports to the United States.

Andrew Erwin and his son James, business partners with Jared Groce II in Augusta, were accused of being involved in illegally purchasing a group of slaves allegedly landed in the winter of 1817 - 1818 at St. Mary's, Georgia. [191] This very convoluted story opens with a document written by US Attorney General William Wirt dated January 21, 1821, in which Wirt says: "I proceeded .. to take up the case of General David B. Mitchell, the agent of the United States for Indian Affairs, at the Creek agency, under a charge from Governor Clark of Georgia, that he was concerned in the importation of Africans, in breach of our laws, in the winter of 1817-18, and have now the honor of reporting to you … my opinion, both of the law and the facts of the case. … I am constrained to adopt the conclusion, (painful as it is) that General Mitchell is guilty of having prostituted his power … to the purpose of aiding and assisting in a conscious breach of our laws… in prohibition of the slave trade, and this from mercenary motives."

Colonel Gideon Morgan then wrote an affidavit in which he said: "Before the arrival of the second parcel of negroes at the agency, and about the 20th December, 1817, Col. Gideon Morgan [referring in the first person to himself by name], of the state of Tennessee, being on his return home from Georgia, called at the agency at the request of Andrew Erwin of Augusta, for the purpose of inquiring if there were any negroes there, in which Mr. Erwin was interested, [and if so to remove them] to a place of more safety, or making such other disposition of them as he [Erwin] thought most advantageous for the benefit of the purchasers." The purchasers were not identified. Morgan testified that he had a letter from Erwin, Groce and Associates giving him unlimited authority to act in their interests. Of course the letter did not mention purchasing illegally entered slaves, adding to the intrigue. The letter simply stated that "Should he [Morgan] have occasion for funds, or any other services in your power, you will confer a singular favor to me by rendering him any service in your power. We will accept his drafts, at any sight, for any sum he may think proper to draw on us for."

Morgan repeated a passage of a letter from General Mitchell to the Secretary of War dated February 3, 1818, as follows: " The truth however is that so far from those negroes having been brought here by speculators, they were claimed by gentlemen of respectability, some of whom came to me with letters of introduction from the General [Morgan] himself, couched in the strongest terms of friendship."   Mitchell admitted that he was willing to have the negroes delivered to Morgan, who verified this fact adding that he had no bond nor security to deliver them outside of the United States. Morgan apparently finally declined to have anything to do with the disposal of these negroes.

A letter by General Mitchell states that "A certain Capt. Bowen who had for some time been employed by Col. Hawkins in the Indian department, is now engaged with some mercantile houses in Augusta and Savannah, and as their agent had purchased somewhere on the St. Mary's a small parcel of African negroes, and during my absence carried them to the neighborhood of the agency on their way to the Alabama territory."

Morgan states that "forty-seven of the Africans, only were delivered to … Groce, leaving still at the agency the forty-two brought by Tobler. … and you have the interest of Erwin, Groce, & Co., fixed at one half the number taken away by Groce."

Morgan references another affidavit by Andrew Erwin that states that Groce also is innocent -- "not only innocent but it seems Mr. Erwin had some difficulty in appeasing the virtuous indignation of Mr. Groce, upon the discovery that his partners had been concerned in a breach of laws, and that Groce convinced him, I believe, of my innocence in any such trade."

The following letter indicates that the US agent who headed the port at Darien, Georgia confiscated the 47 slaves that Groce was transporting to his home in Alabama, removing them back to Darien where they were appropriated by the Georgia authorities and given back to Groce.

"LETTER FROM THE SECRETARY OF THE TREASURY, TRANSMITTING,
In obedience to a resolution of the House of Representatives, of the 31st ultimo,
INFORMATION IN RELATION TO THE ILLICIT INTRODUCTION OF SLAVES INTO THE UNITED STATES: WITH A STATEMENT OF THE MEASURES WHICH HAVE BEEN TAKEN TO PREVENT THE SAME
January 13, 1820. Read, and ordered to lie on the table.
WASHINGTON: PRINTED BY GALES & SEATON. 1820.
Collector's Office, Dis. of Brunswick, Geo. Port of Darien, March 14, 1818.

"Sir: I had the honor to address you per last mail, and to enclose you papers respecting 47 African negroes, taken, by the surveyor of Darien, from one Jared E. Groce, on their way to the Alabama territory, through the Indian nation, and 41 others at the Creek agency, from the negro houses of the agent for Indian affairs. It is a painful duty, sir, to express to you, that I am in possession of undoubted information, that African and West India negroes are almost daily illicitly introduced into Georgia, for sale or settlement, or passing through it to the territories of the United States for similar purposes; these facts are notorious; and it is not unusual to see such negroes in the streets of St. Mary's, and such too, recently captured by our vessels of war, and ordered to Savannah, were illegally bartered by hundreds in that city, for this bartering or bonding (as it is called, but in reality selling,) actually took place before any decision had passed by the court respecting them. I cannot but again express to you, sir, that these irregularities and mocking of the laws, by men who understand them, and who, it was presumed, would have respected them, are such, that it requires the immediate interposition of Congress to effect a suppression of this traffic; for, as things are, should a faithful officer of government apprehend such negroes, to avoid the penalties imposed by the laws, the proprietors disclaim them, and some agent of the executive demands a delivery of the same to him, who may employ them as be pleases, or effect a sale by way of a bond, for the restoration of the negroes when legally called on so to do; which bond, it is understood, is to be forfeited, as the amount of the bond is so much less than the value of the property. And again, sir, an officer disposed to perform his trust with fidelity, is placed at the mercy of the state; for, to carry the intention of the federal laws into execution, great expenses may be inclined, and for which, the state seems not to have made any provision; but has, by its own law of the last session of the legislature, invested the executive with the power of becoming a speculator on the exertions and integrity of such federal officers as feel the weight of their responsibility, and who are willing to perforin their duty. For instance, sir: after much fatigue, peril, and expense, 88 Africans are seized and brought by the surveyor to Darien; they are demanded immediately by the governor's agents, notwithstanding the knowledge which his excellency had, that these very Africans were for some weeks within 60 miles of his excellency's residence, (the seat of government,) there was no effort, no stir made by him, his agents, or subordinate state officers, to carry the laws into execution; but no sooner than it was understood that, a seizure had been effected by an officer of the United States, a demand is made for them; and it is not difficult to perceive, by a compliance, that the very aggressors may, by a forfeiture of the mock bond, be again placed in possession of the smuggled property, at but little additional expense to him, but at the entire ruin of the officers who had executed, with fidelity, the laws they felt bound to observe. There are many negroes, (independent of those mentioned, as having been bartered in Savannah, &c. before any decision had passed respecting them.) recently introduced into this state and the Alabama territory, and which can be apprehended. The undertaking would be great; but to be sensible that we shall possess your approbation, and that we are carrying the views and wishes of the government into execution, is all we wish, and it shall be done, independent of every personal consideration.

I have, &c.   [Signed] WM. I. McINTOSH, Collector" [192]

Andrew Erwin then sent his son James to Augusta to explain the business dealings with Groce, "whose moral delicacy the Messrs. Erwin manifested so much solicitude to soothe is the same Jared E. Groce …." Andrew Erwin swore that Jared E. Groce had no interest in the negro properties. He did have an interest in the Erwin partnership in Augusta but not in Savannah. Did Groce materially participate in the slave deal, or not? Did the Erwin's affix the name of their partnership Erwin, Groce and Co. to slave trade documents without Jared's knowledge? Answers to these specific questions are lacking, but it appears that Groce was not directly involved in the initial acquisition of the negroes but did purchase 47 slaves after they were acquired by Erwin.

These slaves arrived in "the St. Mary's" according to Col. Gideon Morgan. St. Mary's, Georgia, initially settled by Spain in the mid-1500s and located on the St. Mary's River which formed the border between Spanish Florida and American Georgia. At least four towns were created: St. Davids, St. Patrick, St. Marys, and St. Thomas. These documents suggest that at least some of the slaves that Jared Groce II brought to Texas in 1822 arrived first in America at the mouth of the St. Mary's River in Georgia in 1817. Here eighty-eight Africans were acquired by an agent of A. Erwin, Groce and Co. and transported to the Creek Indian agency in Georgia (near Roberta in Crawford County). After an unsuccessful attempt by another A. Erwin, Groce and Co. agent to secure the slaves, Jared Groce arrived at the agency in person and left with forty-seven individuals. On his trip to his plantation on the Mobile River in Alabama he was apprehended by a U.S. Customs agent who confiscated the slaves and, after also confiscating the others still at the agency, took them to the Customs House at the Port of Darien near Brunswick, Georgia. With help from the state Groce apparently reacquired the forty-seven slaves and took them to Alabama. Some probably came with him to Texas in 1822.

Appendix III: Transportation Links

When Austin's Old Three Hundred settlers arrived in this part of Texas there was already in existence a network of known roads used by travelers, including the Atascosito Road, Coushatta Trace, La Bahia Road, and probably other trails occasionally taken. Building roads to connect the new colonists and their settlements became a high priority for the fledgling government of Austin's colony. Near Bernardo, the Coushatta Trace and the Atascosito road were routinely used prior to 1821 and only timely maintenance and improvements allowing wagon passage were needed so long as the routes remained in use.

New roads were built either by entrepreneurial individuals or when the colonial government assigned landowners specific responsibilities for laying out new roads or improving existing ones. All such routes were subject to final approval by the government. This began in Austin's Colony with the creation of the *ayuntamiento de San Felipe*. The 1829 decree defining powers of the *ayuntamiento* specified "Relative to the roads and public bridges of the jurisdiction, specifying the manner of establishing and laying them off, opening and completing them, either by means of a tax in money, or by the personal labor of the inhabitants, divided in just and equitable proportions according to the circumstances."

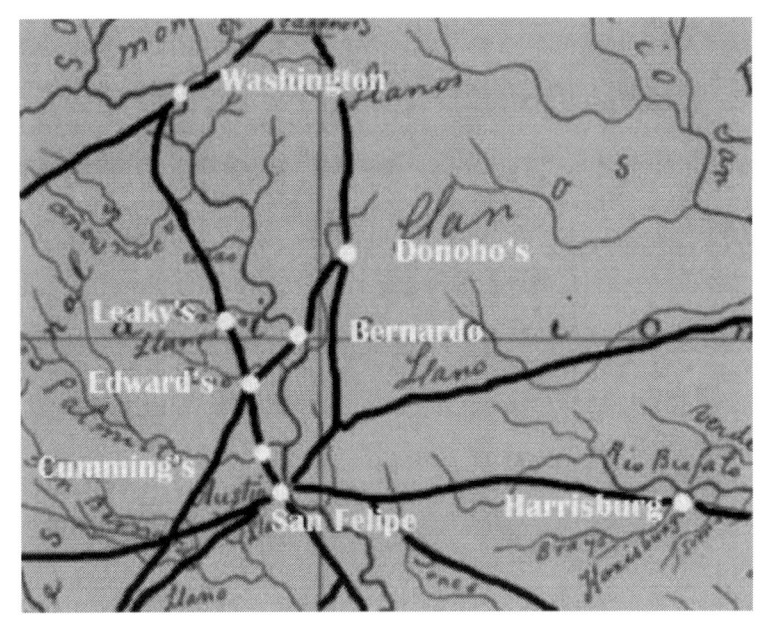

Stephen F. Austin's map of 1829 identified the main roads in use during the early yeas of his colony. A segment of this map has been retouched to emphasize roads and show towns and the homes of prominent settlers.[193]

The older La Bahia, Upper Coushatta Trace and Atascosito roads are shown, along with new roads created by the colonists since 1822 emanating from San Felipe to Holland's on the east side of the Brazos, to Gonzales, to Harrisburg, and to Oyster Creek and Brazoria. There was a secondary or "Lower" leg of the Coushatta Trace that was used occasionally during dry weather that also intersected at Donoho's but is not shown on the above map. The English Field Notes for the Donoho league made prior to April 12, 1831 indicate the points on the boundaries at which the "San Felipe to Holland", the "Groce to Holland" and the "Groce - Rankin" roads crossed. Francis Holland, his brother William and sister Mary Holland Peterson and their families were early settlers in Austin's colony who located on the Upper Coushatta Trace on modern Holland Creek near Anderson in Grimes County. The "Groce - Rankin" road at this time was an east - west corridor that began at Bernardo, went to Isaac Donoho's and from there followed the older Lower Coushatta Trace to Samuel McCarly's on the southern bank of Spring Creek and along this creek passing through Abraham Roberts' and back to join the Atascosito road at Burnett's, then east to cross the San Jacinto at Frederick Rankin's.

At McCarley's a road turned away from the east-west road that traveled the southern wooded margins of Spring Creek, crossed the creek and headed generally north. Survey notes of the McCarley league names this the Landrum - Grimes Road. A similar entry calls it the Landrum Road. The east-west road from Donoho's to Spring Creek is named the Grimes Road in these two surveys. Another road named Landrum is shown on a survey of the leagues around the Raleigh Rogers league in Montgomery County. This map shows the Landrum road passing through the Zachariah Landrum league and heading generally west to the John Landrum league. It also shows the Coushatta Trace (the "Lower") entering from the northeast and turning south at the "iron mound" shown on several extant maps. Zachariah Landrum was an early settler whose land grant was in Montgomery County some three miles southwest of the town of Montgomery. The Lower Coushata Trace crossed Spring Creek in the McCarley League. The extension of the Landrum Road mentioned in the McCarley survey apparently was the Lower Coushatta Trace to just before the Rogers "Iron Mound" league, where a fork turned west to pass by Z. Landrum and then J. Landrum on the way to Jesse Grimes. [194]

Recognition of the common use of the Coushatta Trace in the early years of Austin's Colony is evidenced by a land grant request by John H. Cummins. On February 3, 1830, Cummins petitioned for a grant to be located near the crossing of the Coushatta Trace over the Trinity River, identified as "six or seven leagues below the place known as the Falls [*el Salto*] on said river, which point is very suitable for a crossing on an outer road leading to Nacogdoches and the state of Louisiana, and considered more direct and less distance by 15 or more leagues from the town [San felipe de] Austin to said point of Nacogdoches..." He expressed his intent to establish a ferry crossing to assist travelers using the "soon to be opened road from Mr. Gros' [Bernardo] direct to Nacogdoches." [195]

The following entries from the minutes of the *ayuntamiento* of San Felipe de Austin cite the beginnings of the major new roads in Austin County:

February 10, 1829   "In view of the great necessity which exists that the road from this town to the mill on Palmitto [now Mill] Creek should be improved, in order that the resources of the first necessity, such as corn meal, may not fail the citizens, the president appoints two *regidores* and Ira Ingram a committee to carry into effect this important object".

The mill of the Cummings family on today's Mill Creek, established in 1822 and the first such in Texas, sawed logs in addition to grinding corn, providing lumber for buildings in San Felipe and beyond until its closure in 1836.

March 2, 1829   "The ayuntamiento passed to the consideration of the condition of the road from here through the woods on the other side of the river, and agreed that all the inhabitants of that side of the river within the following district shall work the said road and put it in condition for carts and wagons: This district is defined by a line which begins on the road, three leagues from the river, and follows the course of the river at a distance of three leagues to a little creek below the Hensleys; thence down this creek to the river; thence up the river to the upper corner of the labors north of the national road; thence following the upper line of said labors eastward to a point three leagues distant from the river; and thence southward, keeping the course of the river to the point of beginning. The *ayuntamiento* appointed Isaac Best to supervise the work of the inhabitants, under the instructions of the *ayuntamiento*. It was also agreed that the *Atravesia* road [Spanish for "crossing over"], known as the Madelana road [aka Coushatta Trace], which crosses the river at Jared E. Groce's house, shall be worked by the said Groce with his negroes, according to the instructions of the *ayuntamiento*, from his place to the intersection of the road that runs from here to Gustavus Edwards's."

The first road addressed was that very difficult stretch from San Felipe across the heavily timbered and swampy Brazos bottomlands to the prairie at Pine Grove near modern Pattison. Many early travelers mentioned the problems this passage presented. This road split after crossing Irons Creek and exiting the timbered river bottom to enter the prairie, with one branch running up the river initially following the older Atasosito road, then past Dononho's to a point opposite Washington. The other fork led to Harrisburg. The second road mentioned in this section was that portion of the Coushatta Trace (aka *Madalena* or *Atravesia* road) from Groce's crossing on the Brazos to Gustavus Edward's residence on Piney Creek at the crossing of the San Felipe to Lakey and Washington road. Gustavus Edwards was one of the Old Three Hundred settlers who operated Robinson's Ferry at Washington in 1825, He later moved to Austin County and lived on Piney Creek. He was postmaster at Piney in October, 1836. In 1837 he sold his Austin County land and moved to his headright league in Wharton County. His daughter Mary Jane married prominent San Felipe and later Washington County resident Robert McAlpin "Three Legged Willie" Williamson.

    December 31, 1830   "First that Citizens Horatio Chriesman, G. E. Edwards, James Lynch, Oliver Jones, and William Pettus be and are hereby appointed as Commissioners to lay out a road from the town of San Felipe de Austin to the present residence of Joel Lakey and report the same to this body as soon as possible. Second that Citizens John W. Hall, Amos Gates, James Bradbury, Gibson Kuykendall, and Joel Lakey be and are hereby appointed Commissioners to lay out a road from the present residence of Joel Lakey to the crossing of the Labahia road on the river Brazos. Third that Citizens Abner Lee, John P. Coles, Nestor Clay John Cole and George Erving be and are hereby appointed Commissioners to lay out a road from the present residence of Joel Laky to the garrison on the river Brazos."

    Joel Leakey (Lakey, Laky), one of Stephen F. Austin's Old Three Hundred colonists, was born around 1795. He married Nancy Calloway, with whom he had at least seven children. He came to Texas about 1826 from Louisiana. Four of his children came to Texas, and three remained in Louisiana. On May 28, 1827, he received title to a league of land on Caney Creek in an area that later became part of Washington and Austin counties. Between 1827 and 1832 he was awarded 2½ leagues in the same area. According to the census of 1826 he was a farmer and stock raiser, aged between forty and fifty, and had a wife, four daughters, and one servant. He died around 1840. The garrison mentioned here is the one established by the Mexican government in 1830 to Mexicanize Texas and to staunch the flow of Anglo immigration to Texas. It was located on the west bank of the Brazos River in northeastern Burleson County, north of the the Old San Antonio road and almost directly west of where the Robertson / Brazos County line meets the river. Called Fort Tenoxtitlan, the garrison was abandoned in 1832.

November 7, 1831 "A petition from the inhabitants of the precinct of Bastrop living up on the Colorado praying for a division of the precinct and for permission to open a road from the crossing of the San Antonio road to this town, the body decided that it was impracticable to accede to the prayer for a division of the precinct but granted the privilege of opening the road." This is the genesis of the road that would be blazed through the wilderness to connect Bastrop and San Felipe, known today as the Gotier Trace. It significantly shortened the previous route which passed through the settlements along the Colorado River. Friedrich Ernst arrived in 1831 with his family, marking the beginning of German immigration to Texas. Ernst settled on his league of land that straddled the Gotier trace; the location would later grow into an Austin County community named Industry. This road is shown on the Austin/Perry "Connected Map" of 1833 - 1838. Mexican General Gaona marched his troops down this road in 1836 after he departed from Bastrop and moved to join Santa Anna at San Felipe.

All of these roads with the exception of the original Gotier trace from Bastrop to San Felipe were already in existence before 1829 as evidenced by their presence on Austin's map of that year. Together they represent the main road network around Bernardo at the time of the Texian Revolution in 1836. At the Bernardo crossing from 1822 to 1836, travelers no doubt continued to use the sandstone - based ford of the Coushatta Trace when the river was low. At times of high water, travelers would either camp near the river bank and wait for the water to recede, or would be transported across the river by Groce slaves poling the flatboats they used to transport their cotton down river to market. The nearest public ferry during the colonial period was at San Felipe, having been established by John McFarland in 1822 before the town was sited, and operated by him and others after this time. Up river, Andrew Robinson established a ferry in 1822 at the La Bahia road crossing (later the town of Washington). This ferry remained in operation until the 1860's.

Two events in 1836 sparked significant changes in the travel network around Bernardo. First, the burning of San Felipe during the Revolution caused the center of government to be moved. The town never recovered, and ceased to be the draw for travelers that it had been prior to 1836. Travelers continued to use the roads around San Felipe, but only to pass through. Perhaps an even more important event in the evolution of roads during this period was the founding of the town of Houston, which rapidly grew and caused many existing main roads to be rerouted to connect with this new population and commercial center. Once a major crossroads location visited by many travelers, Bernardo gradually saw fewer and fewer travelers after 1836 as the road and travel networks migrated elsewhere.

Beginning in 1837, the newly created county of Austin, then including modern Waller County, assumed responsibility for roads within the county boundaries. The minutes of the Austin County Commissioner's Court located in the courthouse at Bellville provide the record of road development from 1837 onward. As settlers continued to flood into the area, many new roads were created.

The first of these that ultimately had an impact on travel through Bernardo was a new route to Washington on higher ground (hence better wet weather travel) than the existing Washington Road from San Felipe to Lakey's. On July 27, 1837, a road was ordered to be laid out from San Felipe to intersect the Washington Road at the Austin / Washington county line and to "cross Mill Creek at the most advantageous place on said creek that will not make the route too indirect." This was the beginning of modern Hwy. 36 between Sealy and Bellville. From Mill Creek the road continued to the later site of Bellville, then along Center Hill road to Buckhorn and Caney Creek. The first toll bridge in Texas was soon built, crossing Mill Creek: "Oct. 26, 1838 The petition of John F. Sapp was presented and heard .. building a toll bridge across the waters of Mill Creek at a place known and called Lawrence's Crossing on the road leading from this place to Washington County." This was the crossing used two years earlier by Sam Houston and his Texian army on March 29, 1836. Bridge tolls were set at $1 for each cart wagon and pleasure carriage, 50 cents for each one-horse cart or wagon, 6.25 cents per head cattle, and 12.5 cents per horse or mule.

This new road had already been renamed the Washington road by 1838; its extension from Mill Creek to the county line was authorized in 1839: "October 12, 1839 James Hall III, Nathaniel Reed, Benjamin Granville and ... were appointed to review, to lay out and to mark legibly a road from what is known as Sapp's Bridge across Mill Creek or Lawrence's Crossing in the nearest and best route to James Hall 3rd - from thence on the nearest and best route to this county line in the direction to Independence in Washington County." The original Washington Road that passed near Bernardo was still used by travelers after the new Washington road was established. The existence of a bridge over Mill Creek on the new road surely made it more appealing than the older road without a bridge, and the new one was more commonly utilized: "October 12, 1839. Whence on the notion of Ira Fisher it was ordered that the road leading from the town of San Felipe de Austin to Washington was taken under consideration and ordered that the road now in use commencing in the town of San Felipe from thence to Cummings mill on Mill Creek from thence to what is known as China Grove or Edward's old place on Piney Creek from thence to Ivy's old place on Spring (modern Ivys) Creek from thence to Lakey's old place on Caney Creek be called the old road and now used as such. And it is hereby declared a public highway and road."

Various historical records refer to either a "Groce's Landing" or a "Groce's Ferry" on the Brazos River at Bernardo. Jared Groce did have a "landing" or accessible location on the east bank of the river that he used to load his cotton onto flatboats for shipment downriver to Velasco, and later to receive steamboats such as the "Yellow Stone". He also provided a transportation service across the river for a fee, as several early travelers left accounts describing crossing the Brazos on "Groce's Ferry" for a fee. All commercial ferries were licensed and regulated by the local government, beginning with the *ayuntamiento de San Felipe* in 1829 through the Austin County Commissioner's Court into the late 1800's. The minutes of these proceedings include many references to ferries, roads and bridges, but not one entry mentions a ferry operated by Groce. He apparently never sought a license for a traditional public ferry, choosing to operate instead on his own terms using his flatboats poled by his slaves.

W.D.C.Hall was issued an invoice by Groce including "ferriage fees" in 1823. The diary of Mexican General Manuel de Mier y Teran mentions crossing the river at Bernardo in February, 1829 on a *chalán*, which was a type of flatboat that Groce used to transport cotton downriver. N.D. Labadie wrote that he had crossed on "Groce's Ferry" in 1831. Sam Houston's April 13, 1836 note written at Bernardo describes crossing his army over the Brazos using a steamboat and a yawl (presumably Groce's) and that there was no ferry-boat present. Shortly after the founding of Houston in 1836, Groce took his cotton to market there by ox-cart and reduced his use of the landing to load flatboats.

Groce's east bank landing location is approximately 300 yards downstream of the sandstone outcropping that provided the low water ford. A large gully, shown on Groce family sketches, enters the river at this point. The gully was utilized as a more gradual approach to the river than the nearby steep banks. Sketches by Sara Groce Berlet also show the ferry landing by the gully, between the Bernardo Main House and the slave quarters.

The first commercial public ferry at Bernardo was founded by McLin and Julia Bracey around 1836. The Bracey's originally settled in the northern part of modern Waller County at Beason's Creek; their league of land was granted on January 7, 1833. McLin operated a post office and a ferry at this location for a short period. In 1833 Jared Groce gave 400 acres of land across from Bernardo, in the northeast corner of the Wm. White grant, to his niece Julia Bracey. The Bracey's apparently moved to that location around 1836; they sold their original grant to James Bell on July 31, 1837. Joseph Kuykendall, in his account of the Texian army activities during the San Jacinto campaign, mentioned that the army arrived at the Brazos and camped "at Bracey's", indicating they were already here in April of 1836, although their ferry was apparently not yet established or had been moved as a protective measure in the Runaway Scrape. Despite the fact that Jared Groce was ordered on March 2, 1829 by the *ayuntamiento* of San Felipe to "work" the Coushatta Trace from his plantation to Gustavus Edwards on Piney Creek, the road was not significantly used in 1836. Wm. Physick Zuber described the road in March of that year as "an abandoned narrow road that lay through a continuous thicket of saplings". This suggests that the Bracey ferry may already have been established at its later location some two miles below Bernardo, resulting in abandonment of a short section of the Coushatta road west of the crossing.

An advertisement by Bracey in the August 28, 1839 issue of the "Telegraph and Texas Register" mentions this road:

> THE nearest Road and best Road to *Washington.*—From the city of Houston to Matthew Burnet's, 20 miles; from Burnet's to Bracey's Ferry on the Brazos, 20 miles; no streams or creeks on the way, and only two miles through the bottoms, two miles below Groce's Plantation. The Ferry is inferior to none in the country.   McLIN BRACEY

By this time Bracey's ferry was apparently located below Bernardo, just downstream of the mouth of Pond Creek, avoiding a crossing of that steep-banked Brazos tributary. The eastern bank of the river at Bracy's Ferry was part of the original Bernardo land grant and remained in Groce family ownership until after the Civil War. This ad confirms that a road ran from Bracey's ferry to Cypress Creek at the residence of Matthew Burnet. Here a fork went south to Houston and another east along the old Atascosito road to F. Rankin's home on the San Jacinto River. Minutes of the Austin County Commissioner's Court from 1837 to 1846 contain several listings of county roads in effect during this period. "Cross Road No. 4" led from Bracey's Ferry due east to the county line, and from the ferry west through Center Hill, Travis and to Industry." The eastern leg of this road was the one mentioned by Bracey in his 1839 advertisement.

The first mention of Bracey's ferry in the commissioner's court records orders a new road to be laid out from the ferry west to Industry: "October 12, 1839. The report of commissioners at last term of this court to review and lay out a road from Bracy's Ferry to Industry was read and approved. On motion of the President H.O. Campbell was appointed overseer of the hands liable to on road in Beat No. 2 and to work on the new road lately laid out leading from Bracey's Ferry to Center Hill to the east fork of Mill Creek in that Beat. McLin Bracey in Beat No. 5. Jno. P. Shelburn was appointed overseer of the hands liable to work on road in Beat No. 3 including all hands in the said Beat in the Forks of Mill Creek on the new road recently laid out & follow the newly laid out road to what is known and called Industry at the present place of residence of Friedrich Ernst."

Around 1840 the Austin County Commissioners ordered a new road to be laid out due east from Groce's to the Austin / Harris County line. This new road replaced the older Groce / Rankin road. Although no map is known to exist showing this road in then-Austin, later Waller County, its likely projection matches up exactly with a road shown on an 1841 Map of Spring Creek County. This county is one of the "ghost counties" of Texas, created by the legislature as a judicial district in 1841 from parts of Harris, Grimes and Montgomery counties. It was declared unconstitutional in 1842 by the Texas Supreme Court, and its lands reverted back to their original counties. A copy of this map was transmitted from Ann Wilson to the Texas General Land Office in January, 2002. Copies have been placed in the GLO Map Collection. Wilson indicated that Harris County surveyor Stinson was last known to have the original years ago. The original appears to have been lost.

A planned new road from Bracey's ferry southeast to Houston was first mentioned on January 1, 1844 "It was presented for commissioners to be appointed to lay out a road from Bracy's ferry to eastern boundary line of Austin County so as to intersect the road leading from San Felipe to Houston which was granted whereupon Edwin Waller, Josiah J. Lamothe, Charles Railey, Washington Floyd & McLin Bracy was appointed to lay out road aforesaid." It is not apparent that this road was ever built. The point of intersection with the San Felipe - Houston road was apparently at the county line at modern Katy. Another competing ferry established by Oliver Jones in 1840 at the modern Hwy. 529 bridge intercepted travelers away from Bracey, especially after Bellville was founded in 1848.

A road running east from Bernardo had existed in the 1820's. It was the older Orcoquisac road, used to connect Bernardo with the main road to San Felipe and the Atascosito road, the main thoroughfare to the east at that time. Small remnants of it still exist today, as evidenced by a short section named Groce Road adjoining Clear Creek on the eastern side at the Rocky Ford crossing of that creek.

On January 18, 1847, the commissioners ordered a new road from Bracey's ferry "over the best and most practicable route to Mrs. Foster's crossing over Caney Creek whence the Washington Road across same." This road went through modern Cochran to Caney Creek near Buckhorn.

The last mention of Bracey's Ferry in the Austin County Commissioner Court minutes was on February 2, 1858: "... it is ordered that the following .. be appointed a jury of review to lay out and mark off a road from Bellville to Julia Bracy's ferry." McLin Bracey had died on August 18, 1856.[196] The Bracey heirs sold their land in this location after the Civil War. The date that Bracey's ferry ceased operation has not been determined but it appears probable that this occurred around 1860. By this date other ferries located above Bernardo near the modern Hwy. 159 bridge, and downstream at the current FM 529 bridge were the primary crossing points for travelers between Bellville and Hempstead, and to Houston.

A map of the network of major roads around Bernardo ca. 1840 follows:

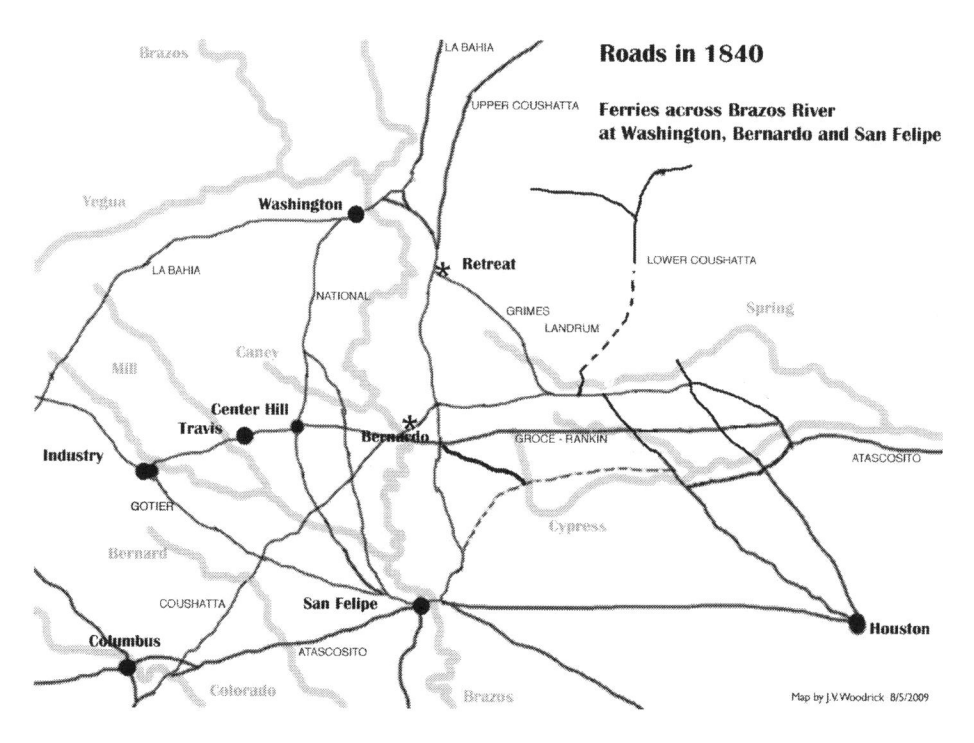

New ferries on the Brazos both up and down river were established in the 1840's, siphoning away some of the travel past Bernardo. On October 5, 1840, Oliver Jones was granted permission to establish a ferry. This site at the modern Hwy. 529 bridge was later known as Crump's ferry; it operated at this location into the 1930's. Roads on both sides of the river extending east and west were promptly established after Jones Ferry began operation, connecting it to existing roads, and directly to Houston. Up river, on September 13, 1844, Wm. B. Lipscomb was granted a petition to establish a ferry at his residence; also on the same date James Cochran, J.J. Davis, Wm. B. Lipscomb, JGW Mott & John McCloskey were appointed to lay out a public road "commencing at the residence of Chas. Donoho on the old Houston Road running west to said ferry and from thence westward to intersect the road leading from Jones Ferry to Caney Creek." David I. Hill was granted permission on November 21, 1848 to operate the ferry that had been Lipscomb's. Hill's ferry continued in operation until the completion of the first bridge over the Brazos in this vicinity (modern Hwy. 159) in 1873. At least one and perhaps two other ferries operated within a few miles upriver of Hill's. Thus, between the mid-1840's and 1860, three ferries operated on the Brazos in this region: Hill's, Bracey's, and Jones / Crump. Each of these three ferry locations was connected directly to Houston on the east, and to the main roads on the west side of the river.

When the new towns of Bellville (1848) and Hempstead (1858) were established, roads connecting these towns to the ferry crossings were promptly laid out by the Austin County commissioners. One of the commissioners entries dated July 5, 1858, indicates that Leonard Groce and other landowners in the area had not been able to agree on the route of the new road from Hill's ferry to Hempstead. The commissioners issued the following order: "report from review committee appointed Feb. 1,1857 to mark off road from Bellville to Hempstead by Hill's ferry. The action on the east portion of this road was postponed until those citizens interested in same should do something more definitive with regard to said road. Until further appearing, then the Report now made at this Term of the court is correct and in accordance with law. It is ordered that the same be received and adopted, and that said road shall be established as follows to wit: beginning at Hill's ferry and running with the Houston road about seventeen hundred *varas*, then in a northeasterly direction in nearly a straight line to the town of Hempstead...." The distinct straight portion of modern Hwy. 159 leading from the Brazos bridge into Hempstead is clearly the result of this order, and the 1,400 *vara* distance from this road to the ferry pinpoints the ferry location.

In the early 1900's the river changed course near Hempstead, cutting off and isolating Hill's and the nearby ferries from the new channel. The old river loop now cut off on which these ferries plied became Perry Lake, and the land between the new oxbow lake is now called Hinton Island.

An 1895 Austin County map shows the old Coushatta Trace and the first road from San Felipe to Washington, crossing Piney Creek in the Thomas Bell league. [197]

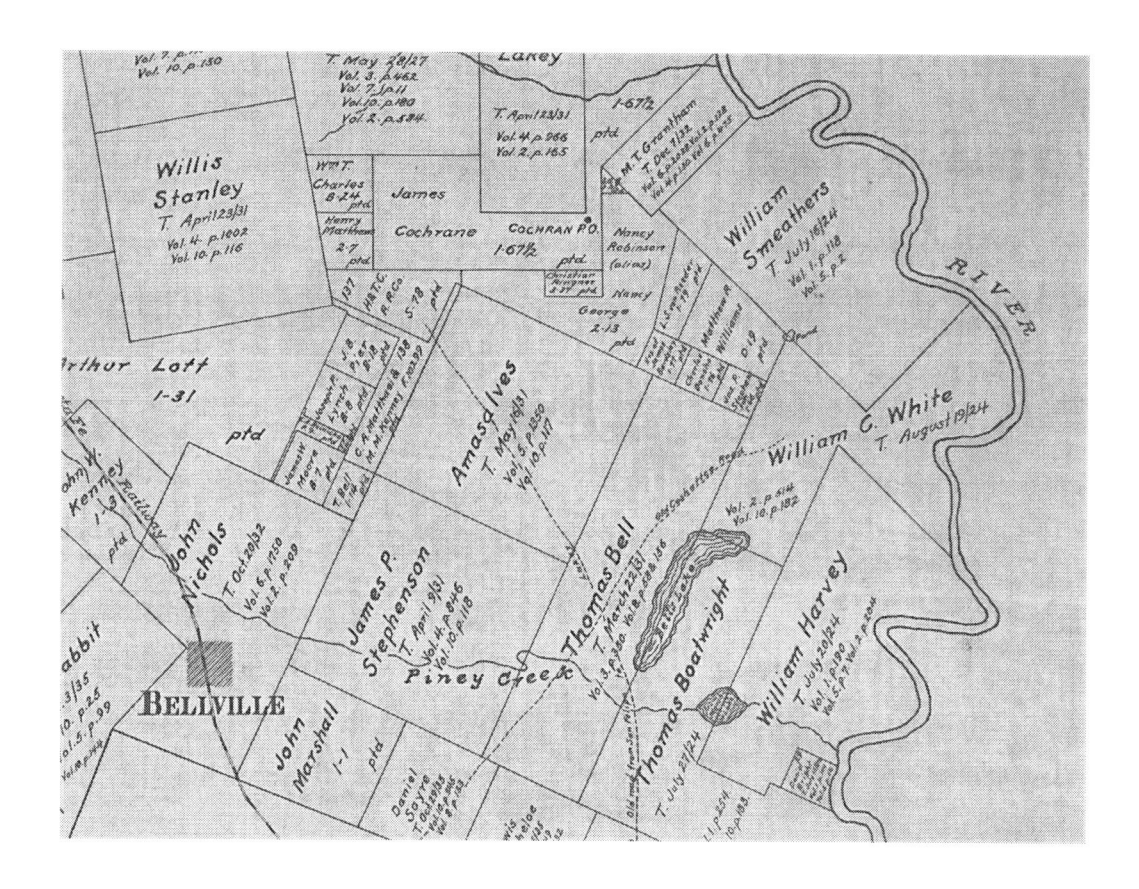

A map of the road network around 1865 shows that by this time public travel through Bernardo had essentially ceased:

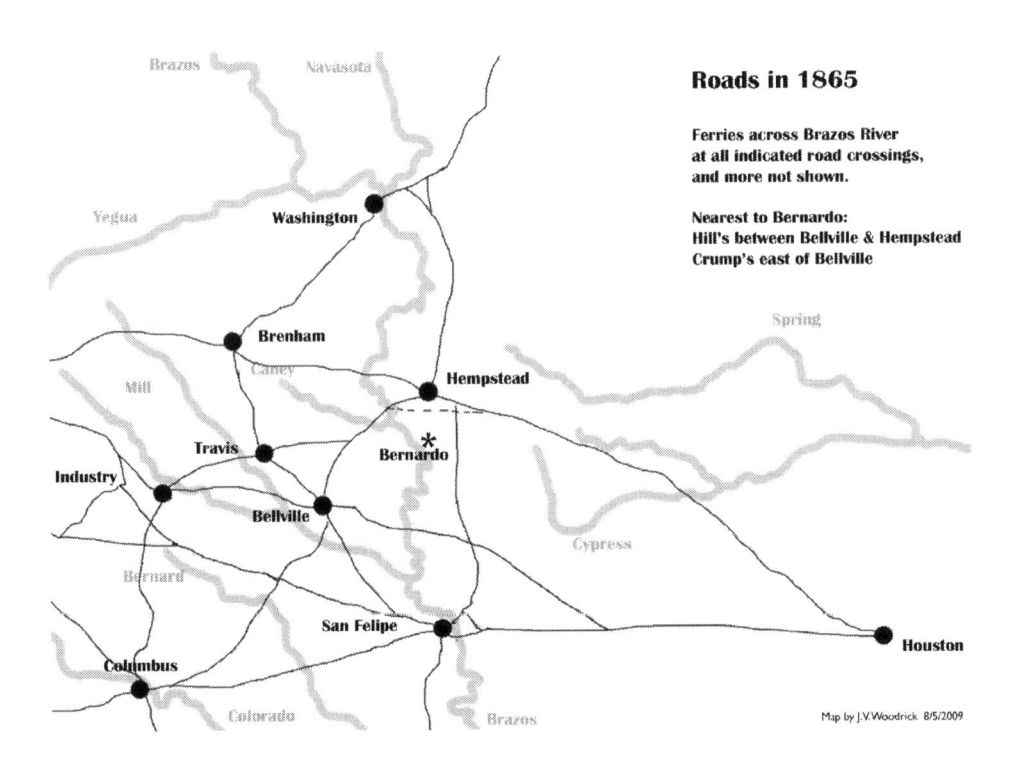

Roads in 1865

Ferries across Brazos River at all indicated road crossings, and more not shown.

Nearest to Bernardo:
Hill's between Bellville & Hempstead
Crump's east of Bellville

Map by J.V.Woodrick 8/5/2009

The first bridge over the river in this location (modern FM 159) was completed during or shortly after 1873, thus virtually eliminating a need for a ferry in this vicinity.

Steamboat traffic on the Brazos in the vicinity of Bernardo began perhaps as early as 1833 and lasted until the arrival of the railroad in 1858. A letter dated July 2, 1836 to Jared Groce II at Retreat from George Hockley and B.S. Lawrence says that they plan to ask Jared's sons Leonard and Jared III if they would sell them 50 - 100 acres on the river at Bernardo or Pleasant Hill in which to establish a steamboat landing. This plan never materialized. [198]

Steven F. Austin's nephew Guy Bryan, in an interview with the "Houston Post" in 1899 concerning Brazos River improvement, stated that about 50 years earlier he was a delegate from Brazoria County to a convention in Washington to take preliminary steps for the improvement of the Brazos River and to place steamboats thereon for the removal of crops. Dr. R.R. Peebles of Pleasant Hill was one of two leaders of this movement. Peebles' relatives in Ohio had steamboat interests on that river. "Through Dr. Peebles mainly arrangements were made to place two boats upon the Brazos". Named the 'Washington' and the 'Brazos', for several years they navigated that river parts of the year, taking off the crops. From the mouth of the Brazos the cotton was taken to Galveston. "… when Texas sold her New Mexican territory to the United States [in 1850], a portion of the money was appropriated by the Legislature to the improvement of the river."

In the *Austin Statesman* in 1899 Mr. Frank Brown of Austin wrote an article describing the history of Washington-on-the-Brazos. "Steamboats sometimes ascended the Brazos in the middle 30's. … The first steamer that I remember coming up to Washington was in 1842. It was a small stern wheeler called the 'Mustang'. Afterward, when a light rise was on, the boat went up to old Nashville. The 'Mustang' continued in trade a few years. In the early 40's another boat called 'Lady Byron' made frequent trips. … During the middle and late 40's and the 50's other boats continued to ascend the Brazos as high as Washington. They did not usually proceed higher because of the obstruction known as Hidalgo Falls, just above town. The village was considered to be the head of ordinary steam navigation. In the late 40's the people of Washington and vicinity, realizing that something should be done to build up the town, managed to purchase two small side-wheel steamers, named Brazos and Washington. These boats were placed in trade, and made regular trips for several years to Velasco and return. A boat usually left or arrived about once a week. Navigation was kept up most of the time each year. For a short time in the heat of summer trips were sometimes suspended because of low water. But it was generally the case that steam navigation was kept up for nine or ten months each year. … Completion of the [rail] roads to Brenham and Navasota completely ruined Washington. There was no more trade here. Produce thereafter was shipped by rail and merchandise came on the cars. Passenger travel was no longer in the old way. Steamboats quit running. Many houses were torn down and moved to Navasota. Most of the people went away." [199]

Bernardo and Pleasant Hill each had its own steamboat landing. Landings at "Groce's" and "Peeble's" are listed in an 1858 document as being one mile apart. There are two places above the rock crossing on the river which have old roads leading to them. Each approaches the river at the site of a gully which would have provided a naturally more gradual approach. The lower of these two sites is at the river termination of modern Joswiak Road. These two are almost exactly one mile apart and seem likely candidates for the two steamboat landings. At lower water levels steamboats may well have docked at the original location of Groce's Landing below the rock crossing. [200]

The following report to Jefferson Davis, Secretary of War, Washington, D.C. dated July 29, 1854, provides a good status of the obstacles to steamboat traffic on the Brazos and suggested improvements. [201]

"Indianola, April 1, 1854

"Sir: I have the honor to submit the following report of survey of Brazos River:

"The low water navigation of the Brazos river extends as far up the river as Washington, 400 miles, by water, from the mouth.

"Ninety miles below Washington [at Bernardo] is found one of the serious obstacles to low water navigation, viz.: Shoals of a species of soft transition sandstone. Cooper's shoal fifty-six miles below this, fifty-nine miles below this Randen's, and twenty-five miles below this one Thompson's shoal, all of the same character; ledges of soft rock crossing the river, and extended down its bed, requiring about two feet excavation through them to give depth sufficient for the low water boats.

"The snags to be removed as far down as Thompson's are trifling; not more than two month's work with the snag boat would be required. Below Thompson's there are two places requiring heavy snagging but for short distances only. Tide water extends sixty miles up the river, making the mouth more an arm of the sea than a river. For improvement of the bar at the mouth, I see no other way than adopted by the tow-boat association at the mouth of the Mississippi.

ESTIMATE OF IMPROVEMENT

Snag boat and apparatus,	$12,000
Six months' employment snagging, $1,500 per month	9,000
Making channel through first shoals [at Bernardo],	5,000
Making channel through Cooper's	4,000
Making channel through Randon's	6,000
Making channel through Thompson's,	3,000
Contingencies	5,000
	44,000

"Respectfully submitted,
        W.H. Stevens, L.U.S. Engineer's
Brig. Gen. Joseph G. Totten,
Chief Engineer, Washington City, D.C."

The "first shoals" ninety river miles below Washington stated as one of the most serious obstacles to navigation appears to be the sandstone crossing at Bernardo. The channelization project at this location was never completed; advent of the railroads only a few years later precluded any such river improvements.

Appendix IV: Slave Inventories

Summary of Slave Inventories at Bernardo and Pleasant Hill
Austin County Deed and Probate Records and U.S. Censuses

May 25, 1831 (Austin County Deed Records Book A/ 600 - 643) Jared E. Groce II liquidated all of his real and personal property to the highest bidder at public auction. The following is a list of all of the slaves sold in this auction.

----- Negroes ------

Lot #		$ value
1	Douglas, wife and 4 children to wit: Annis, Jane, Lynda & Lucinda	610
2	Jack, his wife and two children Mahala and Sally	1000
3	Ben, his wife and three children, Lavina, Phillip & Britton	810
4	Stephen and wife Harriet and 3 children, vis Martha, Lamar and Jim	650
5	and a boy 18 years of age named Abraham	960
6	Frank, wife and two children, vis. Sam and Jackson	610
7	Negro man called Quaker	405
8	Jack, wife and children, Louisa, Hampton, Charlotte and Edmund	820
9	Milly and three children, vis. Henderson, Margaret and Jared	900
10	Mira and son Nelson	855
11	Sally and three children, viz. Fielding, Pickins and Matt	965
12	Spencer, wife and infant and Luanna, age 14 years	1030
13	Molly & five children, viz. John, Caroine, Neva, Chloe & Willliam	1220
14	Abram, wife and two children, Emeline & Anna	1005
15	Rachal and three children, vis. Maris, Ephriam and Jackson	1115
16	Patty; Jacob, his wife and two children, Billy and Robin	600
17	Daniel, wife & two children, Cretia and Wash, & a boy Harry age 28	1775
18	Peter, wife and 6 children, Moses, Tom, Willis, Bob, Boyd & Peter	2000
19	Jack, wife and 7 children, William, Charles, Peggy, Katy, Charlotte, Franklin & Stepney	2505
20	Winston, wife and one child named Levin	1010
21	Elbert, wife and 2 children, Manual & Sumpter	1305
22	Jim, wife and 5 children, Alack, Agnes, Polly, George and Selah	2000
23	Hagar, and 3 children, Ely, Charles and Louise	1405
24	Isaac, wife and 3 children, Edward, Bernard and Edwards	1505
25	Kelly and wife	1205
26	Joe, wife and 3 children, Jasper, Sarah and Amy	2005

Of the above, 117 individuals, William H. Wharton is listed as having purchased lots 1-9, 13, 14, 18, 21 and Zeno Phillips Lots 10-12, 15-17, 19. 20, 22-26. Steven and Sally were likely among the slaves that Groce acquired in South Carolina in 1817.

On May 24, 1831 at Bernardo, Jared E. Groce for $13,295 "sold, conveyed and delivered unto to William H. Wharton of the Jurisdiction of Austin the following described negro servants and slaves, to wit - the Negro man Douglass, his wife and their four children Annie, Jane, Lynda and Lucinda; Jack, his wife and two children Mahala and Sally; Ben, his wife and their three children Lavina, Philip and Britton; Stephen his wife Harriet and three children Martha, Lamar and Jim; Abraham a boy aged 18 years; Frank, his wife and two children Sam and Jackson; Negro man called Quaker; Jacob his wife and four children Louisa, Hampton, Charlotte and Edmund; Milly and her three children Henderson, Margaret and Jared; Molly and her five children John, Caroline, Nerva, Chloe and William; Abraham his wife and two children Emeline and Anna; Peter his wife and six children Moses, Tom, Willis, Bob, Boyd and Peter; Elbert his wife and two children Manuel and Sumpter"

The final paragraph in this document reads "I hereby acknowledge that Leonard W. Groce and Jared E. Groce Junior are jointly and equally interested with myself in the within Negroes, they having executed their obligations for their proportionate parts of the purchase money. Signed and acknowledged by me in the presence of the subscribing witnesses this 24th day of May 1831. William H. Wharton" Witnessed by Walter C. White, Zeno Philips and one other unrecognizable signature. [Austin County Deed Records CA/2/635].

Also on May 24, 1831 at Bernardo, Jared E. Groce for $17,975 "sold, conveyed and delivered to to Zeno Phillips, a resident of the Jurisdiction of Austin, the following described negro servants and slaves - to wit, the woman Mira and her son Nelson; Sally and her three children Fielding, Pickins and Matt; Rachal and her three children, Maria, Ephrian and Jackson; Patty; Jacob his wife and two children Billy and Robbin; Daniel, his wife and their two children Cretia and Wash; Boy Harry about 28 years old, Jack, his wife and their seven children, William, Charles, Peggy, Katy, Charlotte, Franklin and Stepney; Winston, his wife and their child Levin; Jim, his wife and their five children Alack, Agnes, Polly, George and Selah; Hagar and her three children Ely, Charles and Louis; Isaac his wife and their three children Edward, Richmond and Edwards; Kelly and his wife,

Joe, his wife and their three children Jaspar, Sarah and Amy; Spencer, his wife and infant child; and Luanna aged 14 years."

The final paragraph in this document reads: "William H. Wharton, Leonard W. Groce, & Jared E. Groce, Jr., having assumed the payment for the negroes in the within mentioned bill of sale for that consideration I hereby assign and transfer to the said William, Leonard and Jared E. all my rights title and interest in and to all and every one of the negroes mentioned in the written bill of sale. Done at Bernardo on the Rio Brazos ." It is signed by Zeno Phillips with Walter C. White and Thomas F. McKinney as witnesses. [Austin County Deed Records CA/2/633].

February 29 and March 11, 1840 (Probate Book B p. 217, Probate File 20 (9) - Estate of Jared E. Groce [III]

This document is titled the Succession of Jared E. Groce III and provides an , Inventory including listing of slaves and personal property owned by the Jared's estate and lands jointly owned by he and Leonard. The 60 slaves are listed individually by name, gender, age, and value ($26,250 total).

"I, John H. Money, Judge of probate of Austin County proceeded to the last place of residence of Jared E. Groce, Jr. and made the following estimate inventory of the estate having appointed and administered the oath prescribed by law to James B. Miller ad McHenry Winborn appraisers, February 29, 1840.
Negroes:

1	Joe, a blacksmith	about 52 years old	$ 800
2	Jasper, a boy, Joe's son	16	600
3	Sarah, Joe's daughter	12	400
4	Amy, Joe's daughter	10	300
5	Philip, a boy, Joe's son	8	250
6	Charles, a boy, Joe's son	3	200
7	Elbert, a man	31	800
8	Fanny, his wife	28	600
9	Manual, their son	12	200
10	Charles, their son	8	250
11	Tilder, their daughter	6	200
12	Elbert, their son	4	200
13	Barbara, their daughter	2	150
14	Thamer, an old woman	58	300
15	Hampton, her son	28	800
16	Edmund, her son	18	800
17	Siscy, her granddaughter	6	200
18	Chunky Isaac, a man	45	800
19	Maria, his wife	32	600
20	Edwards, their son	14	500
21	Richmond, their son	12	400
22	Chickanaba, their son	10	350
23	Martin, their son	8	300
24	Sucky, their daughter	infant	100
25	Molly, a woman	about 45	400
26	John, her son	30	800

27	William, her son	10	300
28	Jack, her son	7	250
29	Mahala, her son (sic)	4	200
30	Winston, a man	32	800
31	Kissy, his wife	26	600
32	Levin, their son	10	300
33	Jefferson, their son	7	250
34	Wesley, their son	5	200
35	Horton, their son	3	150
36	Anthony	26	800
37	Caroline	25	600
38	Rhoda, child	3	150
39	Lame Jake	34	150
40	Elisa	30	600
41	Billy	12	400
42	Robin	10	300
43	Moses	8	300
44	Martha	6	250
45	Jane	4	200
46	James	2	150
47	Sarena	infant	100
48	Daniel	45	600
49	Delphy	40	500
50	Mat	22	800
51	Creesy	18	600
52	Patty	70	100
53	Pickins	27	800
54	Charlotte	18	600
55	Lavina	infant	100
56	Harry	38	400
57	Thom	27	800
58	Nelson	18	1000
59	Charley	21	800
60	Bob	22	800

October 27, 1841 (Deed Records Book B/274)

     Leonard conveys "all of that tract of land known as the Bernardo Tract, the same on which I now reside, …" and a group of 75 slaves (listed by first name of house heads plus number of children) in a Deed to Trust to Young Gaines Lipscomb. Leonard reiterates his marriage dower of $10k and the $5,500 given her by her guardian Thomas Hooper, stating that whenever Courtney asks for it, Lipscomb is obligated to sell all or as much of this property as needed to pay the $15,500 plus 10% interest from their marriage date and convey this amount to Courtney. Lipscomb is charged with holding anything left in from the Bernardo property in trust for the use and benefit of Leonard's children. Witnessed by Judge Edwin Waller and Wm. B. Lipscomb.

     "… the following described slaves, to wit, Dock and his wife Eliza & their eight children, Moses & his wife Louise and their two children, Rachel & her two children (Ephriam and Andrew), Spencer & his wife Maria & their four children, Cate and Letty his wife & their three children, Fielding & his wife Ann & their three children, Abram & his wife Harriet & their five children, Bill & his wife Cloe & one child, Jack and his three children, Peter & his wife Sucky & their three children, Lydia and her son William, Peggy & her two children, Caty and her two children Hagar & Lewis, Matt & Sally, Sucky the second and Moses the second, Moses the third, Titus, Willie, Charles & Fanny, Nell [no comma] Garrison, Lewis the second, Jerry, Minerva & James."

     In this latter list appears Lewis (the 2nd) and Fanny. These are the probable individuals who signed a contract to work for Leonard Groce for the year 1866. According to William Wharton Groce, Minerva was his nurse or nanny until age six, Jerry was their butler, Lydia oversaw operations at the dairy, Sally had been Jared II's nurse, Matt was the "cow hand", Fielding was Leonard's manservant and Moses was the hunter who provided deer and turkeys for the plantation.

January 8, 1850 (Estate of Jared E. Groce [III])

R.R. Peebles acknowledges receipt of and on behalf of his wife Mary Ann and as Guardian of the two children the sum of $84.55 from LWG in the final administration as Executor of the Estate. Also Peebles received all of the living slaves that were named in the inventory of the JEG III estate and their increase since that time, as well as all of the estate property - real, personal and mixed, as delineated in the Estate inventory. The slaves were not specifically named in this document.

April 3, 1850   (Probate Court File # 21(8) - Estate of Jared E and Barbara M Groce)

Report from appraisers J.E. Kirby, Wm. B. Whitfield and Chas. Donoho who were appointed to appraise the real and personal property, community or otherwise, of the estate of JEG III, based on information provided by R.R. Peebles. The inventory includes all of the slaves as of that date, showing the 40 who were present before the Peebles marriage in 1843 (valued in total at $25,825) and the 40 who were born or bought between 1843 and 1850 (valued in total at $14,050, less than the previous group because of their younger age). In the first group was listed Myrah (Jared II's housekeeper) valued at only $1 because "she is nominally free". She is listed as age 45, indicating a birth year around 1805. Of the 40 listed as coming after 1843, all were born into families already present on the plantation except one - Anthony, who was purchased in 1837. Also listed and appraised is all lands, debts, payables and other property for a grand total estate value of $89,078.

"Inventory of the Separate Property which Mr. Jared E. Groce Jr died possessed of on the 3rd day of Feby. A.D. 1839, and as received from Leonard W. Groce Esqr. Executor of his will & late guardian of his minor children, Jared E. Groce and Barbara M. Groce.

No.		Age	Value
1	Joe a negro man & head of a family	62	$ 200
2	Jasper his son	26	900
3	Sarah his daughter	22	700
4	Amy his daughter	20	700
5	Philip his son	17	675
6	Elbert a negro man & head of a family	40	700
7	Charles his son by Fanny who died Feby. 1843	20	850
8	Emanual his son by Fanny (afflicted with White Swelling)	18	700
9	Thamer an old woman and nurse in the Quarter	68	100
10	Hampton her son	38	500
11	Edward her son	28	900
12	Chunky Isaac head of a family	55	600
13	Mariah his wife	42	400
14	Edward their son	24	200
15	Richmond their son	22	750
16	Chick their son	20	750

No.	Name	Age	Value
17	Martin their son	18	750
18	Molly an old woman and head of a family	55	100
19	John her son	40	750
20	William her son	18	750
21	Winston head of a family	42	750
22	Levin his son by Kizzy who died in March 1848	20	750
23	Jefferson his son by Kizzy	17	750
24	Caroline wife of Anthony & daughter of Molly	35	500
25	Jake a lame man & head of a family	44	100
26	Eliza his wife	40	500
27	Billy their son	22	800
28	Robin their son	20	600
29	Moses their son	18	600
30	Daniel head of a family	55	200
31	Delphy his wife	50	200
32	Washington their son	32	900
33	Creesy their daughter	28	500
34	Patty an old woman	80	000
35	Pickins head of a family	37	800
36	Charlotte his wife	30	700
37	Goue (aka Willis) a man and son of Uncle Peter	37	800
38	Bob his brother and son of Uncle Peter	32	800
39	Charles son of Lydia at L.W. Groce's	31	700
40	Myrah, Harry's wife and nominally free	45	100
41	Harry a man about	48	600
42	Nelson a man about	28	1000

"*Negroes* born or bought after the marriage of the said Jared E. Groce Jr. on the 1st Oct. 1833 with Mary Ann Calvit now Mary Ann Peebles & which are deemed *community property.*"

No.	Name	Age	Value
1	Charles son of Joe	12	$ 600
2	Matilda daughter of Elbert and Fanny	15	600
3	Barbara or Fanny their daughter	12	500
4	Colbert their son	9	400

5	Omstead their son	7	300
6	Ailcy daughter of L.W. Groce's Louisa	15	600
7	Elbert son of Elbert and Fanny (Louie)	14	300
8	Budge or Allen son of Chunky Isaac	14	600
9	Ally daughter of Chunky Isaac	12	450
10	George son of Chunky Isaac	6	250
11	Ann daughter of Chunky Isaac	4	200
12	Lucinda daughter of Chunky Isaac	2	150
13	Suky daughter of Chunky Isaac	infant	100
14	Jack son of Molly	16	700
15	Mehala daughter of Molly	14	500
16	Wesley child of Winston and his wife Kizzy	15	700
17	Luana child of Winston and his wife Kizzy	8	300
18	Polly child of Winston and his wife Kizzy	6	250
19	Delia child of Winston and his wife Kizzy	4	200
20	Anthony Purchased in 1837	36	650
21	Rhoda child of Anthony and Caroline his wife	13	450
22	Anthony - Butten child of Anthony and Caroline	8	400
23	Carey child of Anthony and Caroline his wife	4	200
24	Martha child of Lame Jake and his wife Eliza	16	500
25	Jane child of Lame Jake and his wife Eliza	14	450
26	James child of Lame Jake and his wife Eliza	13	450
27	Syrena child of Lame Jake and his wife Eliza	12	400
28	Ambrose child of Lame Jake and his wife Eliza	10	400
29	Tom child of Lame Jake and his wife Eliza	7	300
30	Saveny child of Lame Jake and his wife Eliza	5	250
31	Sally child of Lame Jake and his wife Eliza	3	200
32	Jacob child of Lame Jake and his wife Eliza	2	150
33	Eliza child of Lame Jake and his wife Eliza	infant	100
34	Lavina or Pickaninny child of Pickins and Charlotte	11	450
35	Edom child of Pickins and Charlotte his wife	9	450
36	Harriet child of Pickins and Charlotte his wife	6	300
37	Seely child of Pickins and his Charlotte his wife	4	250
38	Charlotte child of Pickins and Charlotte his wife	infant	100
39	Amelia child of Sarah	3	200
40	Isaac child of Amy	2	200

May 30, 1850   (Probate Court File # 21(8) - Estate of Jared E and Barbara M Groce)

      District court record: "Jared Groce (III) at the time of his death left an instrument purporting to be his Last Will and Testament which was admitted irregularly by probate in the County of Austin" and that Mary Ann and new husband R.R. Peebles sued Leonard Groce to "set aside the irregular Probate, that said case was reached in favor of the petitioners" and that Groce appealed from the decision of the Austin county Court, and that the case was transferred by a change in venue to the District Court of Galveston County. At its spring term, 1848, the Galveston court overturned the decision of the Austin County court and declared that "the probate of Jared Groce III's will by Leonard Groce should remain established in all things the law permits, without prejudice to the Claim or Claims of the said Richard R. Peebes and Mary Ann his wife leaving them the right to claim the legacy under the will or dower in lieu thereof as well as any community interest that might exist is the matter of the succession of Jared Groce, Jr. - and it appearing to the court that the said Mary Ann declining to take anything under the said will, but elects to claim and now claiming her dower in the separate estate real and personal of Jared Groce .."   The document goes on to describe how Mary Ann was entitled to her share of the community property, including a list by names of slaves, cash money and lands individually listed. The document further spells out division of all the property among Mary Ann and her two children Jared and Barbara. Jared's will left both a dower and a legacy to Mary Ann - a $400 per annum dower and an $8,000 legacy.

      "It appears from the inventories, records and verbal testimonies that ... the following property Real and personal which is Community Property belonging to the Community and generating in the marriage of the said Jared E. Groce Jr. with the said Mary Ann. First. the following Negro slaves for life. Charles a boy, Matilda a girl, Barbara or Fanny a girl, Colbert a boy, Omsterad a boy, Ailey a girl, Elbert a boy, Budge or Allen a boy, Ally a girl, George a boy, Ann a girl, Sucundas a girl, Sukey a girl, Jack a boy, Makaly a girl, Wesley a boy, Luana a girl, Polly a girl, Delice a girl, Anthony a man, Rhoda a girl, Anthony Butten a boy, Cary a boy, Martha a girl, Jane a girl, James a boy, Syrena a girl, Ambrose a boy, Tom a boy, Saveny a girl, Sally a girl, Jacob a boy, Eliza a girl, Charlotte a girl, Amelia a girl, Isaac a boy."

"And it further appearing to the Court that the following negroes are the Separate Property of Jared E. Groce Jr. decd., to wit. Joe a negro man, Jasper a negro man, Sarah a negro woman, Amy a negro woman, Philip a negro man, Elbert a negro man, Charles a boy, Emanual a man, Thamer a woman, Hampton a man, Edmund a man, Chunky Isaac a man, Mariah his wife, Edward a man, Richmond a man, Chick a boy, Martin a boy, Molly a woman, John a man, William a boy, Winston a man, Levin a boy, Jefferson a boy, Caroline a woman, Jake a man, Elysa a woman, Billy a man, Robin a boy, Mose a boy, Mariah his wife, David a man, Delphy a woman, Washington a man, Creasy a woman, Patty a woman, Pickins a man, Charlotte a woman, Tom a man, Bob a man, Charles a man, Mira a woman, Harry a man, Nelson a man."

June 17, 1850 (#659 - 680) This is a 21 page report to the court from the commissioners charged with making the land partition. They met at Peasant Hill on June 14, 1850, in the presence of a Mr. Hunt, the then-current *ad litem* guardian of the children. The examined the "diverse and sundry" tracts of land comprising the community property of Mary Ann, Jared IV and Barbara. The commissioners listed and sketched each tract owned then split the tracts above destined for Jared IV and Babara Groce into two equal parts for distribution to each child at their maturity. Following this they divided the 40 community-owned slaves into two 20-person "moeities" by name, age and value, selecting by random lot which moiety went to Mary Ann and which one went to Jared IV / Barbara, and further dividing the 20 assigned to Barbara & Jared IV between the two of them. These 40 slaves were all under age 16 with one exception - Anthony Sr, age 36). The commissioners than identified by name, age and value the 42 slaves owned by Jared III as his separate property. All except two were over age 16. These were divided into two groups of 21 individuals each. From one of these groups 14 individuals valued in total at $8,501 were selected by name and assigned to Mary Ann.

The commissioners identified $4,298 in cash or other property of which they assigned half to Mary Ann and the other half spilt equally between Jared IV and Barbara. The also identified $18,655.33 due the estate from R.R. Peebles, arising from his rent of the plantation and hire of the negroes from the initial contract with Leonard dating from December 31, 1842. This amount of "payable" indebtedness was assigned 1/2 to Mary Ann ad 1/4 each to JEG IV and Barbara.

"We went on to arrange and divide [the slaves] into the two separate & equal lots or moieties ..

Negroes in Moiety No. 1

No.	Name	Age	Value
1	Jack	16	700
2	Pickaninny	11	450
3	James	12	450
4	Charles	12	600
5	Aily	15	600
6	Colbert	9	400
7	Tom (?)	7	300

Negroes in Moiety No. 2

No.	Name	Age	Value
1	Nelly	15	700
2	Fanny	12	500
3	Edom	9	450
4	Budge	14	600
5	Matilda	15	600
6	Ambrose	9	400
7	Ohmsted	7	300

8	Rhoda	13	450	8	Jane	14	450
9	Martha	16	500	9	Mihala	14	500
10	Syrena	12	400	10	Ally	12	450
11	Jacob	2	150	11	Isaac	2	200
12	Luana	8	300	12	Harriet	6	300
13	Delia	4	200	13	Ann	4	200
14	Suky	2	150	14	Polly	6	250
15	Lucinda	2	150	15	Amelia	3	200
16	Eliza	infant	100	16	Charlotte	infant	100
17	George	6	250	17	Anthony Butter	8	400
18	Saveny	5	250	18	Sooky	infant	100
19	Elbert	14	300	19	Anthony Sr.	36	650
20	Cary	4	200	20	Sally	3	200

Mary Ann Peebles drew and was awarded Moiety No. 1 and Jared and Barbara were awarded Moiety No. 2. The commissioners then "allotted, set aside and assigned the portion out of said Community negroes or personal Estate of the said Succession, to which the said Mary Ann Peebles ... is entitled under the provisions of said Dower Law - to wit 1/3 part thereof ..   accordingly we designate & set apart to the separate use & ownership of teh said Mary Ann, out of the said twenty negroes specified & assigned in Lot or Moiety No. Two, drawn as aforesaid, the following Seven negroes, to wit   Harriet, Charlotte, Edom, Anthony Butter, Anthony Sr., Fanny & Sookey to have & to hold in addition to those she drew [as] Moiety No. One .... and the balance of said 20 Community negroes in said Lot or Moiety No. Two drawn by said Jared & Barbara M. Groce To Wit   Wesley, Budge, Matilda, Ambrose, Omstead, Jane, Mehala, Ally, Isaac, Ann, Polly, Amelia, Sally - which 13 negroes we ... set apart to the separate use and ownership of the said Jared E. and Barbara M. Groce ..."

".. further specifying the following forty-two negroes as the Separate Property of the said Jared E. Groce To Wit: Joe a negro man, Jasper a negro man, Sarah a negro woman, Amy a negro woman, Philip a negro an, Elbert a negro man, Charles a boy, Emanual a man, Thamer a woman, Hampton a man, Edward a man, Chunky Isaac a man, Mariah his wife, Edward a man, Richmond a man, Chick a boy, Martin a boy, Molly a woman, Hohn a man, William a boy, Winston a man, Levin a boy, Jefferson a boy, Caroline a woman, Jake a man, Eliza a woman, Billy a man, Robin a boy, Mose a boy, Daniel a man, Delphy a woman, Washington a man, Emily a woman, Patty a woman, Pickins a man, Charlotte a woman, Tom a man, Bob a man, Charles a man, Myra a woman, Harry a man and Nelson a man." A list repeating these names and adding ages and values then follows:

No.	Name	Age	Value	No.	Name	Age	Value
1	Joe	62	200	22	Levin	20	750
2	Jasper	26	900	23	Jefferson	17	750
3	Sarah	22	700	24	Caroline	35	500
4	Amy	20	700	25	Jake	44	100
5	Philip	7	675	26	Eliza	40	500
6	Elbert	40	700	27	Billy	22	800
7	Charles	20	850	28	Robin	20	600
8	Emanual	18	700	29	Moses	18	600
9	Thamer	68	100	30	Daniel	55	200
10	Hampton	38	500	31	Delphy	55	200
11	Edward	28	900	32	Washington	32	900
12	Chunky Isaac	55	600	33	Creesy	28	500
13	Mariah	42	400	34	Patty	80	000
14	Edward	24	800	35	Pickins	37	800
15	Richmond	22	750	36	Charlotte	30	700
16	Chick	20	750	37	Tom	37	800
17	Martin	18	750	38	Bob	32	800
18	Molly	55	100	39	Charles	31	700
19	John	40	750	40	Myrah	45	1
20	William	18	750	41	Harry	48	600
21	Winston	42	755	42	Nelson	28	1000

" ... we proceeded to set apart to the said Mary Ann Peebles, her interest therein, which the said Dower law allows, & which the said Decree orders & requires us to assign her - To Wit the 2/3 portion of ... as follows - Daniel, Delphy, Wat, Creesy, Bob, Tom, John, William, Caroline, Pickins, Charlotte, Nelson, Harry, Myrah - which we value at Eight Thousand Five Hundred & One Dollars.

Recapitulation of the partition of properties:

to Mary Ann Peebles	to Jared E. and Barbara M. Groce
Lot No. 1 Community (20) negroes: Jack, Pickanniny, James, Charlie, Ailey Colbert, Tom, Rhoda, Martha, Syrena, Jacob, Luana, Delia, Suky, Lucinda, Eliza, George, Saveny, Elbert, Carey	Lot No. 2 Community (13) negroes: Wesley, Budge, Matilda, Ambrose, Omstead, Jane, Mehala, Ally, Isaac, Ann, Polly, Amelia, Sally
Seven negroes out of Community Lot: Harriet, Charlotte, Edom, Fanny, Anthony Sr., Anthony Butter, Sookey Jake,	28 Negroes Separate Property: Joe, Jasper, Philip, Edward, Amy, Elbert, Charles, Emanual, Eliza, Billy, Robin, Mose, Thamer, Chunky, Mariah, Rich, Chick, Jeff, Martin, Winston, Levin, Charles Hampton, Edmond, Sarah, Molly, Patty.
14 Negroes out of Separate Lot: Danl., Delphy, Nat (?), Creesy, Bob, Loue, John, William, Caroline, Pickens, Charlotte, Nelson, Harry, Myrah.	

~ July, 1858   (Probate Court File # 21(8) - Estate of Jared E and Barbara M Groce)

JEG IV petitions court, saying that he has lately turned 21, is one of the heirs of JEG III, that debts of this estate have been fully paid and the estate has been divided between Mary Ann Peebles, Barbara and himself, EXCEPT an interest in a league of land granted to John W. Hall on the east bank of the Brazos River in Brazoria County and an interest jointly owned by the estate and LWG of 800 acres in Brazoria County granted to Wm. Harris and known as the Bolivar league that was and is still in litigation. He then lists the lands set aside for himself and Barbara, as detailed in the June, 1850 court term. He also lists the negroes set aside to Himself and Barbara from the JEG III estate partition, and provides a list of these 44 slaves by name and age.

"For a more detailed description of all of said lands reference is made to the records of your Honorable Court June Term 1850. At the same time there was set apart to your petitioned [Jared IV] and his sister Barbara M. Groce as their portion of the negroes belonging to said estate [Jared III's] the following negroes to wit:

	Name	Age		Name	Age
1	Isaac	63	23	Jacob	52
2	Mariah his wife	50	24	Eliza	48
3	Chick	32	25	Rich	30
4	Martin	26	26	Jasper	34
5	Edward	32	27	Sarah	30
6	Amy his wife	28	28	Man [Emanual]	26
7	Isaac	10	29	Charles	24
8	Franky	2	30	Robin	30
9	Hampton	40	31	Levin	28
10	Philip	25	32	Mose	26
11	Jefferson	25	33	Budge	22
12	Billy	30	34	Winston	50
13	Lydia's Charles	39	35	Edmund	36
14	Wesley	23	36	Omstead	18
15	Elbert	48	37	Jane	22
16	Ambrose	15	38	Alley	20
17	Mahala	22	39	Ann	12
18	Matilda	23	40	Amelia	11

19	Polly	14	41	Rachel	3
20	Sally	11	42	Molly	5
21	Molly	65	43	Ransom	3
22	Patty	88	44	Thamer	75

August 28, 1858 (Probate Court File # 21(8) - Estate of Jared E and Barbara M Groce)

The commissioners appointed by the court on July 28, 1858 to partition the lands and negroes due JEG IV and Barbara Groce from their father's estate met at Pleasant Hill on August 28, 1858 and completed their task, sending a letter and an inventory of the estate to the court on that same date. The commissioners listed the slaves by name, age and value in two lots of 22 each of identical $11,675 value. Each child was assigned a lot by random choice.

"Being further Required and Commanded by said Petition Decree to value and divide certain negro slaves herein named, we next with the assistance and consent of all the parties at interest, made the following lists, No. 1 and No. 2, showing their names, ages, sex & relative value of same:

Lot No. 1	(To Jared)			Lot No. 2	(To Barbara)		
No.	Name	Age	Value	No.	Name	Age	Value
1	Chunky Isaac	68	600	1	Jacob	52	100
2	Mariah	50	400	2	Eliza	48	500
3	Edward	32	900	3	Hampton	40	500
4	Amy	28	750	4	Jasper	34	900
5	Richmond	30	750	5	Sarah	30	750
6	Philip	25	675	6	Chick	25	750
7	Jefferson	25	750	7	Emanuel	26	650
8	Billy	30	800	8	Charles	27	850
9	Wesley	23	700	9	Robin	28	800
10	Elbert	50	700	10	Levin	28	750
11	Charles(Lydia's)	37	700	11	Martin	26	750
12	Winston	50	750	12	Moses	26	750
13	Budge	22	750	13	Edmund	36	900
14	Ambrose	17	400	14	Olmstead	18	450
15	Mehala	20	500	15	Jane	22	450
16	Matilda	23	600	16	Ally	20	500
17	Polly	14	250	17	Ann	12	225
18	Sally	11	200	18	Amelia	11	200
19	Isaac	10	200	19	Rachel	3	200
20	Franky	5	200	20	Nelly	5	200
21	Molly	63	100	21	Randsome	3	200
22	Patty	70	000	22	Thamer	80	100
			$ 11,675				$ 11,675

May 23, 1859 (Probate Court File # 21(8) - Estate of Jared E and Barbara M Groce)

R.R. Peebles presents his final accounting as Guardian of the Groce children to the Austin County court - as of September 27, 1858. He credits their account with $20,025 "for the hire of their negroes) for six years at $3,337.50 per year. He then charges the children's estate with $1,000 per year each for six years for "personal and all other expenses" plus $5,025 as the value of Mary Ann's Dower Right released to them, ending with a total of $3,000 due from him to Barbara and Jared, of which he paid $1,500 to Jared on October 16, 1858 and $1,500 to Barbara on February 25, 1859. He again asks the court for release from guardianship. He included a worksheet detailing each of the slaves, showing their occupations and assigning each a "value" based on their contribution. This was used to arrive at the annual "rent" shown above.

Estimation Value per Annum of J.E. & B.M. Groce's negroes from 1st Jany. 1853 to 1st Jany. 1859

No.	Name	Age	Quality	$ Value
1x	Jasper	34	Field Hand	150.00
2*	Philip	25	Do.	137.50
3*	Edward	32	Do.	150.00
4x	Charles	24	Do.	125.00
5x	Man	26	Do.	137.50
6*	Rich	30	Do.	150.00
7x	Chick	28	Do.	137.50
8*	Jeff	25	Do.	125.00
9x	Martin	26	Do.	125.00
10*	Billy	30	Do.	125.00
11x	Rob	28	Do.	100.00
12x	Mose	26	Do.	100.00
13x	Levin	28	Do.	125.00
14*	Chs. Sr.	39	Do.	125.00
15x	Hampton	46	Do.	100.00
16*	Budge	22	Do.	125.00
17*	Natty ?	23	Do.	125.00
18x	Edward	36	Do.	100.00
19*	Elbert	50	Do.	100.00
20*	Chunky	68	Do.	100.00
21*	Winston	50	Do.	150.00
22*	Mariah	50	Woman Hand	50.00
23*	Amy&child	28	Woman Hand	75.00
24x	Eliza	48	Do.	50.00
25x	Sarah	30	Do.	75.00
26*	Matilda	23	Do.	75.00
27x	June ?	22	Do.	50.00

28x	Ally	20	Do.	75.00
29*	Mahalia	18	Do.	75.00
30x	Lame Jake	58	Stockhandler	50.00
31*	Ambrose	15	Good Boy	50.00
32x	Ohmstead	18	Do.	50.00
33x	Thamer	75	Nurses	
34*	Molly	63	Nurses	
35*	Patty	88		Expense
36	Joe	70 & ??? 58		Do.
37x	Ann	12		Do.
38*	Sally	11		Do.
39x	Amelia	7		Do.
40*	Yanky	5		Do.
41x	Nelly	5		Do.
42x	Rashel	3		Do.
43*	Gace ?	10		Do.
44x	Randon	3		Do.
45*	Polly	14		Do.

Those marked thus * to Jared E. Groce and thus marked thus x to Barbara M. Groce
(signed) R.R. Peebles

In A/C with Jared E. and Barbara M. Groce
1858 Sept. 29 to hire all of the above negroes as per List of estimated prices Stated,
for the period of six years from 1st Jany. 1853 to 1st Jany. 1859 @ $3337.50 per annum $20,025

By gross amount of expenses of every character incurred for x on account of the above
Hired negroes, and for those not hired but cared for and raised, also for taxes on their
[Jared and Barbara's] lands, and for their personal expense of every disposition during
said 6 years, assessed at $2,000 per annum- $12,000
Oct.   by value of M.A.P.'s established dower-right in each of the tracts of land,
Cancelled and Extinguished by the "Authentic Act" - $ 5,025
                                                                                          $ 17,025

Amount due to J.E. & B.M. Groce together - $3,000

1859 Feb 25th   B.M. Groce to R.R. Peebles

For his Note of Hand for his half of the above amount $1,500.00
    Recd. Pleasant Hill 25th Feb. 1859 of R.R. Peebles his due bill for $1,500 - The entire amount of my half interest in the above balance of $3000 due from Sd. Peebles to Sd. J.E. and B.M. Groce as established in the foregoing which I hereby acknowledge to be just, complete and wholly satisfactory and in full of my demand against him for and on acc. of his management and control of my portion of the Estate of my Father decd. lately rendered to me by Motion of the Order and Petition drawn by the Probate Court of Austin County at its August Term A.D. 1858.
                                            (signed) Barbara M. Groce

Appendix V: Clara Chappell Narrative

Texas Slave Narrative [202]
Clara Chappell

"I was born on de plantation of Colonel Grose, May 9, 1843. I remember much before de war, my father was Albert Williams, and he was a good slave 'cause my marster made him a nigger driver. Now den a driver is one who set de pace and all de rest must keep up. My mammy's name was Lizzie, she was cook for marster and missus. I had three brothers, William, Johnny and James, and I had four sisters, Betty, Frances, Cora and Lucy. We had a shack in de quarters. Marster had two quarters, one west and one south. I don't know how many slaves marster had but he had ten or twelve with large families. I had a easy time myself, 'cause I was maid to missus, I had to keep her dress and wait on her jes' like dey do now. Some of de niggers sho' did have to work 'cause marster's place was big. I don't know how many acres he had, but he had a league of land, 'course it wasn't all plowed but he didn't have enough niggers so some of 'em sho' did have to work. I may have earned lots of money, but I never did have any 'til after I's free. I had plenty to eat and plenty to wear but I sho' 'nough never had any money. Anyway, I didn't need any 'cause I never went to town nohow. We had plenty to eat 'cause marster had a whole field dat he planted taters and turnips and onions and corn and such, and we always had something good to eat. We had butter and 'lasses and bread and milk, too. We had 'possum and rabbit and fish, but I eat 'possum best. Oh man, I want to tell you dat nothin' can beat 'possum and sweet taters. De slaves had no garden of dere own, 'cause marster furnished us everything. We sho' had too much sometimes. We had de same dat marster had. We wore lowells in winter and striped cotton goods in summer and linen on Sunday. When we was big, marster furnished us shoes for winter and Sunday, but in summer we went barefoot. I was married after de war in a striped dress; I didn't have no weddin', jes' dress up and went to de judge and got hitched. Mr. J.M. Keys he done married me to my man at Hempstead, Texas.

"My marster was good to us, but de over-seer sho' 'nough was mean and some of marster's chilluns married to other folks and dey brought a change. We was woke up every morning before daylight, by a man dat de over-seer sent around over de quarters. He went from house to house and yelled, 'Roll out.' We worked in de fields from sun-up to sun-down. De slaves was not punished 'cept for dis'bedience. When a nigger didn't do what he was told, he was genteelly whipped with a whip. Dey was not chained 'cept when dey was expected to run away. 'Course dey had no jails on marster's place, 'cause marster was good and de niggers all loved him. Niggers den didn't care much what happened. I seen some sold for thirty and forty dollars a piece but dey don't care. Dey jes' stan' on de block and when de man say thirty dollars and dere marster say all right, den dey jes' step down off de block by de new marster. Dey was sold to neighbors and dey knowed dey could see dere folks, I'spect is de reason dey did not care. We could go some places if we would get a pass, but if we went without a pass the patarolas would get us and we would be whipped. The patarolas was policemen. We had no church of our own, but we went to church with missus. We never learned to read, so every Sunday morning missus would read the Bible to us an 'splain it. I 'member she told me I had a soul and de Bible was food for de soul. Den we would go to church. I 'member two songs, 'Amazin' Grace' and 'Soldier ob de Cross.' My mammy told me once dat if I was bad a ghost would sho' get me, and sho' 'nough one time I saw one. I know he was a ghost 'cause he come and went like de wind. I wasn't scared, but if he had ever spoke I would have keeled over. Some of dem, dey carried rabbits' feet for luck, but dey is no good 'less you is going to steal something, but if you is going to be a thief den you sho' better hunt you a rabbit foot and cat bone, 'cause if you have dem you sho' won't get cotched.

"We was sorry for marster and missus when we was freed, dey rang a big bell dat told all de niggers dey was wanted, and when we all got to marsters house he told us we was done free. Some niggers say, 'What do dat mean?' and marster say, 'If I slap you, you slap me. If you work for me, I have to pay you. If you eat here, you have to pay me. You can do what you please. You can go when you want to go and you don't have to ask anyone, you is your own. I hates to see you go, but I can't help it. I can use you all, and as many as want to stay can. As many as want to go can go.' Missus, she was cryin' and I didn' want to go, 'cause I loved her and I knows she loved us niggers, so I stayed a while. Den I marries in 'bout a year, in a striped dress, jes' dress up and go to de jedge and git hitched. Mr. Keys, he done marry me to my man at Hempstead, Texas. We had four chillun, all dead now, and I has six grandchillen. I come here to take care my gal [daughter] what was sick, and has stayed here. I has no place else to go, and I'll stay and meet de Lawd from here.. We have never had as good times as when we was with marster."

Clara Chappell was living in Grimes County in 1900; the U.S. Census lists her as a 40 year-old widowed head of household with three of her own children

(Joseph, age 9; Pearl, age 8; and Cora L., age 6) and two other children (James Stewart, age 9; and Willie C. Stewart, age 6). Her husband, unknown but presumably with the surname Chappell, must have died in in late 1899 or early 1900. She died in Brownwood on November 12, 1938, of "old age, natural causes". Clara's family does not appear on any of the several Bernardo and later Pleasant Hill inventories, suggesting they may have been purchased by Leonard Groce after the last Bernardo Inventory of 1841.

Research Sources

Information on the Groce family and their land holdings abound in the historical record. A very significant foundation is based on work done by Sarah Wharton Groce (Mrs. George) Berlet, daughter of William Wharton Groce, who was known by the nickname "Rosa". She began her historical research when, in 1915, she received a letter from E.W. Winkler, Associate Editor of the Southwestern Historical Quarterly, asking her to prepare a biographical sketch of her great-grandfather Jared E. Groce II. Before this time she had listened with interest to stories told by her father, making notes but nothing further. After receiving the letter from Dr. Winkler, she visited her father and recorded pages of oral interviews. Letters to family members in Georgia, Tennessee and Alabama added to the family history and lore, as did copies of related family papers and land records. She submitted her paper to Dr. Winkle, who published it as she had written it. She later found several errors in this initial work as she uncovered more information. By 1936 most of her research work was completed. The manuscripts she developed over two decades are found in several libraries in Texas. Some of these are about single individuals, and some are comprehensive, as "Groce and Kindred Families". Some of the original documents compiled by Sarah Groce Berlet are in the possession of her great-granddaughter Kate Patterson in 2011. These include two bound books titled "Groce Family 1936" and "Ancestral Records 1955".

Three articles and one book by Berlet and her father have been published:
1. Berleth (sic), Rosa [Sarah Ann] Groce, "Jared Ellison Groce", Southwestern Historical Quarterly, April 1917, 20: 358 - 368.
2. Groce, Captain William Wharton, "Major General John A. Wharton", Southwestern Historical Quarterly, January, 1916, 19: 271 - 278.
3. Mackey, Mrs. Mary Groce, "The Groce Family of Texas", Frontier Times periodical, October 1948, pp. 13 - 18
4. Berlet, Sarah Wharton Groce, "Autobiography of a Spoon, 1828 - 1856", (Houston, 1956) recounts the life of Sarah Ann Groce Wharton through the story of the Mexican silver dollars that were turned into silverware and silverplate.

Two Master's theses drew heavily on the work of Sarah Groce Berlet:
1. White, Frank Edd, "A History of the Territory that now Constitutes Waller County, Texas, From 1821 to 1884", MA Thesis, UT Austin, August 1936.
2. Hale, Laura, "The Groces and the Whartons in the Early History of Texas", MA thesis, UT Austin, August 1942.

Predating the Sarah Groce Berlet work is an article by Wm. Physick Zuber titled "Jared Erwin (sic) Groce - Biography and Life Work of a Prominent Immigrant of 1822" published in the Houston Chronicle in 1904. Zuber was a friend and neighbor of Jared Groce II at his Retreat home in Grimes County.

Collections of Berlet's work and other information on the Groce family and Bernardo are found in the following nine locations:

1. Center for American History at the University of Texas at Austin, named "Groce Family Papers" and contained in three archival boxes numbered 2D223, 2R6 and 2R301. Berlet's manuscript "Groce and Kindred Families", dateline Houston 1921, is in Box 2Q438.
2. The Texas State Library has a copy of Berlet's "Groce and Kindred Families" in Box 2-23/747.
3. Brazoria County Museum library in Brazoria, in a record titled "Austin Colony Old 300 Col. Jared Ellison Groce II Genealogical Report Forefathers & Descendants".
4. Fondren Library (Woodson Research Center) at Rice University. Box 240, "Groce Family Correspondence") has a number of original letters from and to Groce family members dating from 1824 to the 1850's, and the original typed manuscript by Sarah Ann Groce Berlet titled "Life of Jared Ellison Groce" is in Folder 159.
5. Hempstead Public Library
6. Corpus Christi Public Library
7. Clayton Library in Houston
8. Daughters of the Republic of Texas library at the Alamo complex in San Antonio.
9. Waller County Clerk's office in Hempstead. Deed and Probate Records.
10. Austin County Clerk's office, Bellville, Texas. Deed and Probate Records

    Courtney Groce estate probate: Succession Record Book R, pp. 40 - 47, 52 - 59, 109
    Jared E. Groce IV probate: Succession Record Book S, pp. 564 - 568.
    Jared E. Groce III Probate Records
        Book B, pp. 153 - 159; 215 - 220; 516 - 518.
        Book D, pp. 1 - 20; 292 - 296
        Book E, pp. 1-27
        probate minutes Book B pp. 81, 129 & 192
        "   "   Book C pp. 16, 17, 80 - 85.
    E. (IV) and B.M. Groce Probate records
        Book E, pp. 75 - 87; 231 - 256; 614
        Book H, pp. 288 - 293; 298 - 301
        Book K, pp. 120 - 125; 164 - 167

Other records of the Groce family and activities related to Bernardo are found in the Austin and Lamar Papers, in "Papers of the Texas Revolution" by John Jenkins and in the Bexar Archves.

Bibliography

Anonymous, "Houston Displayed, or, Who Won the Battle of San Jacinto:, by a Farmer in the Army [Algernon P. Thompson], printed in Velasco, 1837.

Austin, Stephen F., "Journal of Steven F. Austin on his First Trip to Texas, 1821", *Southwestern Historical Quarterly*: No. 7:305-307. This historical journal will be referred to hereinafter as SWHQ.

Barker, Eugene C. (editor), "The Austin Papers" (in 3 volumes) (Washington, USGPO, 1924 - 1928). Herein this collection will be referred to as Austin Papers.

Barker, Eugene C., "Recollections of the Campaign", Vol. 4 ,Issue 4, April 1901.

Barker, Eugene Campbell, "The Life of Stephen F. Austin, founder of Texas, 1793 - 1836" (Austin, University of Texas Press, 1969 - c1926)

Barr, Alwyn, "Black Texans: A History of African Americans in Texas, 1528–1995 (Norman, University of Oklahoma Press, 1996,2nd ed.)

Berlandier, Jean-Louis, "Journey to Mexico During the Years 1826 to 1834", Volume 2, (Austin, Texas State Historical Association, 1980).

Berlet, Sarah Wharton Groce, "Autobiography of a Spoon, 1828 - 1856", (Houston, Texas 1956

Berlet(h), Rosa [Sarah Ann] Groce, "Jared Ellison Groce", *Southwestern Historical Quarterly*, April 1917, No. 20

Bevill, James P., The Paper Republic (Houston, Bright Sky Press, 2009)

Brooks, J.W., "History of an Old Clock", the Bellville Times, March 8, 1910.

Bruseth, Jim, Tiffany Osburn, Bill Pierson, Pat Mercado-Allinger and Jef Durst, "2009 Archaeological Fieldwork at the Bernardo and Pleasant Hill Plantation Sites", published by Texas Historical Commission in September, 2009.

Campbell, Randolph B., "An Empire for Slavery: the particular institution in Texas, 1821 - 1865" (Baton Rouge, LSU Press,1989)

Cantrell, Gregg, "Stephen F. Austin - Empresario of Texas", (New Haven and London, Yale Univ. Press, 1999)

Carroll, John M., "Custer in Texas", (New York, Sol Lewis, 1975)

Cazorla, Luis, 1772 diary reproduced by Fray Jose Antonio Pichardo, "Pichardo's Treatise of the Limits of Louisiana and Texas - Part II", translated by Charles Wilson Hackett, (Austin: University of Texas Press, 1931)

Celiz, Fray Francisco, "Diary of the Alarcón Expedition into Texas, 1718 – 1719", translated by Fritz Leo Hoffmann

Chariton, Wallace O., "100 Days in Texas - The Alamo Letters", (Plano, Wardware Publishing, Inc., 1990)

Clarke, Mary Whatley, "Thomas J. Rusk",(Austin and New York, Jenkins, 1991)

Custer, Elizabeth Bacon. "Tenting on the Plains, or General Custer in Kansas and Texas" (Norman, University of Oklahoma Press, 1994 - c.1887)

Edward, David B., "History of Texas", (Cincinnati, J.A. James & Co. 1836)

"Muster Rolls of the Texas Revolution", by the Daughters of the Republic of Texas

Day, Donald and Harry H. Ullom, "The Autobiography of Sam Houston" (Norman, University of Oklahoma Press, 1954)

Day, James M., compiler, "The Texas Almanac 1857 - 1873 A Compendium of Texas History", (Waco, Texian Press, 1967): 648.

Dixon, Sam Houston, "The Heroes of San Jacinto", (Houston, The Anson Jones Press , 1932)

De Bow, James Dunwoodie Brownson, "De Bow's Review A Monthly Journal of Commerce, Agriculture, Manufactures, Internal lmprovement, Statistics, etc. etc. Vol. XIV No. 1, January, 1853

Folmer, Henri, "De Bellisle on the Texas Coast", *Southwestern Historical Quarterly*, October, 1940, No. 44

Gambrell, Herbert, "Anson Jones, The Last President of Texas", (Austin, UT Press, 1946).

Glasscock, Sally, "Dreams of an Empire - the Story of Stephen Fuller Austin ad his Colony in Texas", (San Antonio, Naylor, 1951)

Gray, Wm. Fairfax, "The Diary of William Fairfax Gray From Virginia to Texas, 1835-1837", Edited from the original manuscript, with an Introduction and notes, by Paul Lack . De Golyer Library & William P. Clements Center for Southwest Studies - Southern Methodist University, (Dallas, 1997) online at http://smu.edu/swcenter/FairfaxGray .

Greaser, Galen D., "Surveying in Mexican Texas", undated and unpublished manuscript . Greaser is with the Texas General Land Office and the leading expert on the Spanish archives at that agency.

Haley, James, "Sam Houston", (Norman, University of Oklahoma Press, 2002)

Hales, Douglas, "A Southern Family in White and Black - The Cuneys of Texas", (College Station, Texas A&M University Press, 2003).

Henson, Margaret Swett, "Samuel May Williams - Early Texas Entrepreneur", (College Station, TAMU Press, 1976)

Hogan, William Ransom, "Pamelia Mann: Texas Frontierswoman", Southwest Review, 20, July, 1931

Hollbrook, Abigale Curlee, "Glimpses of Life on Antebellum Slave Plantations in Texas", Southwestern Historical Quarterly Vol. 76, April 1973

Jackson, Jack "Almonte's Texas: Juan N. Almonte's 1834 inspecton, secret report & role in the 1836 campaign", (Austin, Texas State Historical Asociation, 2003)

Jackson, Jack and William C. Foster, "Imaginary Kingdom - Texas as Seen by the Rivera and Rubí Military Expeditions, 1727 and 1767", (Austin: Texas State Historical Association, 1995)

Jackson, Jack, "Los Mesteños - Spanish Ranching in Texas, 1721 - 1821", (College Station, Texas A&M University Press, 1986)

Jackson, Jack, "Texas by Teran"

Jenkins, John (compiler), "Papers of the Texas Revolution - 1835 - 1836" (Austin, Presidial Press, 1973)   Herein cited as "Jenkins Papers"

Krieger, Alex D., "We Came Naked and Barefoot - the Journey of Cabeza de Vaca Across North America", (Austin, University of Texas Press, 2000)

Kuykendall, J.H., "Reminiscences of Early Texans", SWHQ Vol. 7

Lafora, Nicholas de, "The Frontiers of New Spain - Nicholas DeLafora's Description 1766 - 1768 by Lawrence Kinnaird" (Berkeley:The Quivera Society, 1958)

Lutz, Eusibia, "Liendo - The Biography of a House", in "Southwestern Review", January, 1931

Miller, Clarence, "Forgotten Places of Waller County", (Waller County Historical Association, 2009)

Oglisby, Jackie Kindel, "How Cotton Came to Texas", *Farm and Ranch* magazine, Vol. 46, No. 44, October 29, 1927.

Sanchez y Tapia, Jose Maria, "A Trip to Texas in 1828", Southwestern Historical Quarterly XXIX (April 1926)

Schiwetz. E.M., "Texas Sketchbook - a collection of historical stories from the Humble Way", (Houston, Humble Oil and Refining Company, 1962)

Telegraph and Texas Register, March 17, 1836, Vol. I, No. 20, published at San Felipe de Austin by Joseph Baker & Bordens

Thrall, Homer S., "A Pictorial History of Texas" (Evansville, IN, Unigraphic, 1972):

White, Frank Edd, "A History of the Territory that now Constitutes Waller County", MA Thesis, University of Texas, 1936.

White, Gifford, "The 1840 Census of the Republic of Texas", (Austin, Pemberton Press, 1966)

Williams, Amelia W. and Eugene C. Barker, "The Writings of Sam Houston". 1813 - 1863", (Austin, University of Texas Press, 1938 - 1943)

Williams, Henry M., "Jared Ellison Groce in Texas From 1822 - 1836", thesis, August 1959, Texas Southern University.

Winkler, E.W., "Twin Sister Cannon 1836 - 1865", SWHQ, July, 1917, 21:63

Woodrick, James V., "Austin County - Colonial Capital of Texas", (Austin, 2007)

Woodrick, James V., "Archaeological Activities at the 1836 Texian Army Camp - 41 AU 82", a report submitted to the Texas Historical Commission - Archaeology Division dated May 24, 2010.

Woodrick, James V., "Elusive Dreams - Early Exploration and Colonization of the Upper Texas Coast", published for the Liberty County Historical Commission, (Houston, Kemp & Co., 2009)

Woodrick, James and Robert Marcom, "History and Archaeology Come Together at Bernardo", from Texas Archaeology, newsletter of the Texas Archaeological Society, Vol. 55, No. 1, Winter 2011.

Wooten, Dudley G., "A Comprehensive History of Texas", (Dallas, W.G. Scarff, 1898)

Wortham, Louis J., "A History of Texas", (Fort Worth, Wortham-Molyneaux Co. 1924)

Zuber, Wm. Physic, "Life of Jared Groce", Houston Chronicle, 1904.

Zuber, Wm. Physic, "My Eighty Years in Texas", (Austin, University of Texas Press, 1971)

Endnotes

[1] Geologist O.B Shelburn described the feature as: "The shallow water ford is formed by an outcrop of a resistant sandstone bed which strikes across the river. The sandstone is in the late Pliocene Willis formation and about 2 million years old. Its resistance is due to the small amount of carbonate cement binding the sand grains. Although the sandstone yields easily to a hammer it is strong enough to hold up a ridge up to 5 feet above low water level in the river. The sand grains are very poorly sorted, very fine to medium size, angular to round, about 95 % quartz with some pink feldspar, dark chert and rock fragments. The Willis here dips to the southeast, into the Gulf of Mexico at about 30 feet per mile (about ½ of 1 degree). Thus the outcrop strikes across the river NE-SW forming the sandstone ridges that support the ford. The span of the outcrop (1300 feet) plus the height of the exposure above water indicates this resistant bed is only about 15 to 20 feet thick. The sandstone at the ford is likely the hard sand reported at depths ranging from 20 to 90 feet about 2 miles south on the flanks of Raccoon Bend Oil Field; and the sandstone at 65 feet in a water well 2 miles SE on the Marshall ranch."

[2] Krieger, p. 187.

[3] Celiz (pp. 62 - 69). Another diary of this expedition by Fray Pedro Perez de Mezquia is in SWHQ Vol. 41 pp. 312 - 323.

[4] Folmer, pp. 210 - 222.

[5] Jackson and Foster, "Imaginary Kingdom", pp. 52 - 59.

[6] Barriero, Alvarez, *Plano, corographico è hidrographico.* Original in the British Museum; reproduced in Robert Weddle's "French Thorn", pp. 242 & 243.

[7] Although normally referred to in the Spanish archives as the Orcoquiza or Horcoquiza, the tribal name Akokisa was adopted by the Bureau of American Ethnology and is used herein to refer to this tribe. The Spanish word Orcoquisac is used herein to refer to the presidio and mission established on the lower Trinity in 1756, and to the road that connected this presidio with La Bahía and San Antonio.

[8] Woodrick, "Elusive Dreams", pp. 13 - 19.

[9] Woodrick, "Elusive Dreams", pp. 19 - 43.

[10] Jackson and Foster, "Imaginary Kingdom", pp. 135 - 138

[11] Lafora, pp. 174 - 176

[12] Woodrick, "Elusive Dreams", p. 36.

[13] Cazorla, pp. 392 - 397.

[14] Jackson, "Los Mesteños, pp. 173 - 221.

[15] Woodrick, "Elusive Dreams", p. 31.

[16] Austin, pp. 305-307.

[17] "Reminisces of Jesse Burnam", SWHQ Vol. 5 p. 14

[18] Clara Chappell's account is given in Appendix V.

[19] Sarah Berlet manuscripts of oral interviews with the father Wm. W. Groce.

[20] Woodrick and Marcom, "History and Archaeology Come Together at Bernard".

[21] The painting of the Bernardo main house is #1-76 in the Hunter Rose Collection at the Harry Ransom Humanities Center at the University of Texas in Austin. Mary Groce Mackey was the daughter of Robert Groce who married Willie Bethany. They had two children, Mary Bethany Groce (born ca 1925) and Florence Herndon Groce. The book "History of Grimes County" published in 1982 states on p. 84: "As Mary Groce Mackey, a Groce descendent said, "As long as the tradition of resourceful pioneers lives, the name of 'Groce's Retreat', where our most priceless document was drafted, will ever remain a part of the Texas pioneer story." The lineage of the artist is: Jared Groce II, Leonard Waller Groce, Leonard W Groce Jr., Robert Groce, Mary Groce Mackey. Mackey also wrote periodicals about her ancestors and Bernardo, including "Cotton Plantation - Texas First Cotton Crop Grew at Bernardo" in Texas Parade Magazine, and "The Groce Family of Texas", in Frontier Times, October, 1948, pp. 13 - 18.

[22] "Acco Press", a monthly magazine for the cotton farmer (Houston, June 1936) Vol XIV No. 6, p. 4.

[23] The letter is contained in the Bexar Archives at the Briscoe Center for American History at the University of Texas at Austin. It is in archival Box 2S145, indexed by the date July 12, 1822. Transcription and translation of this letter was made by Jorge Garcia-Herreros, Cultural Resources Director of the Gulf Coast Archaeology Group, LLP, in Houston, and edited by Jose Barragan, Spanish Archivist and Translator at the Texas General Land Office in Austin. The text of the letter follows:

"Mr. Governor, Political Chief [Gov. Antonio Martinez]

"I, Jared E. Groce, write this petition in my name and in the names of Ferman Pettus, Martin Varner, Walter Drane and Juan Crawford. All of us are of the American nationality and have established ourselves on the banks of the Brazos River. Now in this city, with my respect and profound wishes to Your Lordship, I affix my signature below.

"I have established my residence on the east bank of the Brazos River four leagues [10 miles] below the Navasota creek under a temporary license previously issued by you. This temporary license was to remain in effect until the sovereign congress gives its ultimate resolution relative to the immigration of foreigners to the domain of the Mexican Empire.

"I am widowed with four children and owner of ninety black slaves in which there are blacksmiths, carpenters, shoemakers, and tailors. I ask for a superior license [permanent permission] from Your Lordship to establish myself on the same side of the Brazos River, but below the Retreat location. I will draw the boundary lines in accordance with all of the resolutions of the sovereign congress regarding colonization in this province.

"Fermam Pettus is married with two children and nine slaves. Martin Varner is married with one child. Walter Drane has three slaves. They and Juan Crawford have all established themselves on the western side of the Brazos River but now ask you for a license to locate on the east side of the Brazos below my location.

"We obligate ourselves and our property to maintain the Political Constitution of this Empire, to defend the treaties against the barbarian Indians or any other enemy that would try to invade the domain or frontiers, and to abide by the religious, criminal, and civil laws that exist now in this Empire.

"Gladly I await your notarized justification.
San Fernando de Bexar July 12, 1822.
Jared E. Groce"

[24] Greaser, Gaylen D., Texas General Land Office report, "Surveying in Mexican Texas".

[25] Texas General Land Office, Waller County, Abstract 30, File Number SC 000002-49, Patent No. 258 and English translation #1679.

[26] TGLO book F/N, Book 5, p. 111

[27] TGLO book F/N Book 2, p. 71

[28] Barker, Eugene C., "The Influence of Slavery in the Colonization of Texas", Southwestern Historical Quarterly, Vol. 48, p. 32.

[29] Minutes of the *Ayumtamiento* of San Felipe, March 2, 1829. The minutes can be found in a series of twelve chapters in four volumes of Southwestern Historical Quarterly from Volume 21, No 3, January 1918 through Volume 24, No. 2, October 1920.

[30] Texas Sate Library (TSL) map # 409C.

[31] Austin Papers, Vol. I, p. 1204

[32] Austin County Deed Records Colonial Archives, Volume 2 Page 641 [CA/2/641]

Item	Purchasers name	
10 horses & mules - 1st choice	Zeno Phillips	$105
10 do. do. - 2nd do.	Ditto	$100
10 do. do. - 3rd do.	Zeno Phillips	$ 63
14 do. do.	William H. Wharton	$ 60
30 do. do.	Ditto	$135
20 beeves -1st choice	Isaac Donohoe	$250
20 do. -2nd do.	William H. Wharton	$190
20 do. -3rd do.	Ditto	$130
10 do. -4th do.	Ditto	$ 50
16 cows and calves & 60 head of young cattle	Zeno Phillips	$330
2 large steers and one yoke of steers at Brown & Millers	William H. Wharton	$ 52
135 head of cattle at Brown and Millers	Isaac Donohoe	$742.50
a note for 5 cows and calves on George Roberts	Zeno Phillips	$45
(125 ?) head of cattle at Wiliam Wharton's	William Wharton	$340
(?) do. do. at Bernardo	Zeno Phillips	$645
550 head of hogs at Bernardo	Ditto	$505
50 head of hogs at Retreat	Ditto	$41
Household and kitchen furniture	Thos. McKinney	$301

----- Land -----

3 1/2 leagues of land on Oyster Bayou together with the crops, provisions, farming utensils, etc.	John P. Coles	$1150
1/8 league of land out of the Boliver league	Thomas McKinney	$ 100
??? land on which there is a Sugar plantation, mills etc.	Zeno Phillips	$1000
? league of land adjoining the sugar plantation, above	John P. Coles	$1000
1/2 do. do. granted to Robt. Elder	William H. Wharton	$100
1/2 do. do. on St. Bernard near the mound	Zeno Phillips	$100
1 do. do. granted to Irons	Ditto	$500
2 do. do. on which is the Bernardo plantation, together with its crops, farming utensils, Blacksmith tools, provisions, 2 cotton gins, etc.	Zeno Phillips	$10000
1 league of land opposite the Bernardo planation	Ditto	$300
1/2 do. do. adjoining the above granted to Smeathers	William H. Wharton	$170
1/2 do. do. East side of Brazos ganted to Coats	Zeno Phillips	$395
1/2 do. do. do. do. granted to Mouser	William H. Wharton	$165
1/2 do. do. do. do. granted to Best	Zeno Phillips	$400
1/2 do. do. do. do. granted to Stevens	Thomas F. McKinney	$201
3 do. do. do. do. known as Groces Retreat	Ditto	$1200
1/2 do. do. do. do.do. granted to Brown or Williams	Zeno Phillips	$110
1 labor on the west side of the Brazos granted to Bright	John Henley	$100

[33] Austin County Deed Records CA/2/625

[34] The main house at Bernardo was known to have been extensively expanded and remodeled in 1838, perhaps the event to which Wm. Wharton Groce referred to in this description.

[35] "Wm. Wharton Groce" by Sarah Groce Berlet, Groce Family Papers, CAH.

[36] Groce had purchased this league from William C. White on March 8, 1828 [Austin County Deed Records CA/2/645.

[37] Austin County Deed Records CA 2/600: The Irons league on the left bank of the Brazos River, the White league less the 400 acres given to Julia Bracey, the Isaac Best league on the left bank of the Brazos(acquired on October 18, 1828), the Thomas Stevens league on the left bank of the Brazos adjacent to Retreat (acquired September 9, 1825), one-half of the James Hensley league on the east bank of the Bernard River (acquired from H.H. League on October 18, 1828), and one-half of the Andrew Robinson league on the left bank of the Brazos (from John Hall, administrator of the estate of Robert Elde on December 4, 1827, witnessed by Robert Peebles).

[38] The John Hall league on the left bank of the Brazos (acquired October 18, 1828), the lower one-third of a league originally granted to William Harris on the Brazos River and (acquired by Groce on October 18, 1828), One-half of the D. Mouser league on the left bank of the Brazos (acquired April 5, 1828), The lower one-fourth of the Smithers league, One of the original three Retreat leagues adjacent to Isaac Jacks, and 1000 acres in the upper part of the John Hall grant on the left bank of the Brazos (acquired March 27, 1829 from W.D.C. Hall [CA/2/609].

[39] Austin County Deed Records CA/2/621

[40] Austin County Deed Records CA/2/56.

[41] The Austin County record book "Probate Minutes 1837 - 1850" contains "Index to Probate and Succession Records" which on p. 47 has two entries: (1) Estate of Jared E. Groce filed March 1839   File # 20 (9)   Succession Volume B (pages 153-159, 215 - 220, 516 - 518;   Volume D (1-20, 292 - 296);   Vol. E (1-27); Probate Minutes B (81,129,192); C (16,17,80,81,82,83,84,85), and (2) Estate of Jared E and Barbara M Groce   File # 21 (8)   Succession Volume E (75-87, 231 - 256, 614); H (288-293, 298 - 301); K (120-125. 164-167). Each of these two files is a manila folder containing many original documents related to the two estates. The Groce brothers' partnership contract is in the first of these folders.   It states that the Bernardo Two Leagues division "having been agreed on will more fully appear & be understood by a separate instrument between the parties."

There are no page numbers nor an index to these files, although they are generally arranged in chronological order.

[42] Day, Donald and Harry H. Ullom, January 29, 1837 letter to Anna Raguet. "As to the new seat of government, I cannot speak advisedly, but reports are favorable to the situation of the place, and though it was not my choice, I am satisfied with it. I would have preferred much to have had the seat of government at "Groce's Retreat", but as I was interested in that place, I did not intimate my wishes on the subject."

[43] TSL Archives Box 2-9/25   Folder 13   Montgomery County papers

[44] this inventory is a handwritten document, faded and hard to read, in the Groce Papers at the Center for American History.

"1/6 of Bolivar ?	740	Brazoria Cty.
Plantation (sugar)	1000	"
Hall League	4444	"
Bernardo	2222	"
Irons	4444	Austin Cty.
Bernardo	4444	"
Sheppard	4444	Fayette Cty.
2/3 Botts	3000	Austin Cty.
1/4 Smithers	1111	"
1/4 Mitchell	1111	Washington Cty.
1/6 Parker	740	Austin Cty.
1/2 Coats	2222	"
Mower	4444	"
Best	4444	"
1900 acs. J. Hall	1900	"
Thom. Stevens	4444	"
Retreat	4444	Montgomery Cty.
LWG headright	3444	"
Widow Coates	4444	"
	57,486	
McKinney's	3000	Austin
	60,486	
1/2 Lawrence ?	2222	Washington
	62,708	
JEG [III] headright	4444	Austin
	67,152	
740 acres Whiteside	740	Austin

[45] Groce Probate Record File 20 (9)

[46] White, Gifford, pp. 2-4

[47] De Bow, p. 72: "Col. Jared E. Groce was the very first commencement of planting in Texas. This first cotton was in the prairie: after that year Groce planted in the Brazos bottom. The first year or two Col. G. sold his cotton to some neighbors, but afterwards gave it to the settlers who carried it down the river in flat boats. In 1825, Col. G. put up the first cotton gin in Austin's colony, on the plantation where his son, Col. L. W. Groce, now lives. The first cotton shipped from Texas was in 1831, in which year Col. Groce and Mr. Thomas McKinney took a crop to Matamoras by a schooner from the mouth of the Brazos, which, we believe, was sold for about 62 1-2 cents per pound. After that year, Col. Groce and his son, with Mr. Thos. F. McKinney, began to send cotton to San Luis Potosi, shipping it to Tampico and thence on pack mules to its destination. It was of course put up in small bales suitable for packing on mules. This trade was continued until the disturbances between Mexico and Texas broke out in 1835. Col. Groce at first procured his cotton baling and rope of Mr. Seymour, a merchant in the Red Lands of Eastern Texas; but subsequently he procured these articles from San Felipe. It is believed there was one cotton gin and only one in Texas before the one erected by Col. Groce, and that was built by Mr. John Cartwright, of the Red Lands."

[48] Looscan, Adele B., "The Pioneer Harris's of Harris County", Southwestern Historical Quarterly, Vol. 31, p. 366, and "Traditions, Memories, Romances, Tragedies of pioneer life in Waller County, Texas", ACCO Press, Anderson, Clayton & Co. Houston, Volume XVI, No. 6 June, 1936.

[49] Oglisby, p. 2

[50] Austin Papers, Vol. 1, p. 825 - 828; also Barker, "The Life of Stephen F. Austin", p.202.

[51] Barker, Eugene C., "The Influence of Slavery in the Colonization of Texas", Southwestern Historical Quarterly Vol. 28, July 1924, pp. 1 - 33.

[52] Campbell, p. 136.

[53] Barker Center for Texas History, Bexar Archives Manuscript Series for documents dated 10/19/1822 and 11/30/1823.

[54] Groce Family Papers at the Briscoe Center for American History in Austin (Herein abbreviated CAH) and Handbook of Texas Online, "John Cartwright".

[55] CAH Box 3S193; Texas General Land Office (GLO) Spanish Archives, Vol. 54, pp. 9-18; summary in Austin Papers, Vol. 2, p. 1275, English translation: "First Census of Austin's Colony - 1826" by the Texas General Land Office at CAH.

[56] Jackson, "Texas by Teran", pp. 63 - 65 ; 143 - 145.

[57] Berlandier, p. 324.

[58] Sanchez y Tapia, pp. 273, 274.

[59] "A machine has been built at the house to comb or gin this product. It consists of two moving wheels turned by horses. One of these [wheels], with its corresponding attachments, is devoted to grinding corn. The other one, by means of two other smaller wheels, sets in motion a wooden cylinder a foot or slightly less in diameter and four or five feet in length. It is set in a horizontal position and spins on its axis. Around the cylinder are inserted thin iron strips in the manner of a saw. There is one every two inches, and they stick out from the cylinder another inch. Another hollow iron cylinder, with slits for the saw blades to enter, is firmly attached by its convex side along the length of the first [cylinder], and in the concave part of the former, covered with wood in the manner of a box, they place the cotton. The teeth of the metal strips enters its fibers, which are deposited free of seeds under the cylinder."

[60] New agricultural land was cleared by "girdling" trees - cutting a circumferential notch through the bark and epidermis which prevented water transpiration up the tree and resulted in its death. The dead trees were left in place and crops planted around them.

[61] E.H. Barker, "The Life of Stephen F. Austin", p. 202.

[62] "EARLY COTTON - A day or two since, Mr. George Allen presented us several green cotton stalks, one of which was 27 inches in length, and had a dozen forms, which were ready to bloom. It was picked from the field of Mr. L. Groce on the 26th inst. The others were between 20 and 26 inches in length, well supplied with forms; they were picked from the field of Capt. T. Howard, whose plantation adjoins that of Mr. Groce. We are informed that these gentlemen have about 500 acres under cultivation, and plants through the fields are nearly as large and promising as these. … A spirit of generous rivalry has sprung up the many planters of the Brazos, and they are all striving to excel in the culture of this article. We are rejoiced to learn that they will be amply rewarded for their exertions, as we are assured that the crops in that section are the most promising ever known, and the most extensive. It is estimated that the crop of cotton of this year will be triple that of any previous season."

[63] Handbook of Texas Online: "James W. Robinson"

[64] "The American Farmer" magazine, published by S.Sands & Son., April 1858, p. 355.

[65] Campbell, p. 209.

[66] "Value of Texas Lands", 1873 Texas Almanac

[67] Elliott, Claude, "The Freedman's Bureau in Texas", Southwestern Historical Quarterly, Vol. 56, July, 1952, pp. 1-5

[68] Groce Papers, CAH

[69] Brazoria County Historical Museum.

[70] Waller County Deed Records 1/314 - 315.

[71] Waller County Deed Records 4/15-17

[72] Waller County Deed Records 5/139 - 141.

[73] Miller, p. 24.

[74] Woodrick, "Austin County", p. 154. "These two proposed counties (Waller and Gregg) are in area largely less than the constitutional limit, and they also leave the counties from which they are taken of such less area, but as they passed both houses of the Legislature by a vote very considerably larger than the constitutional requirement of two-thirds, I have not thought it advisable to return them with objections. But the creation of such counties is clearly contrary to good policy; the county organization must necessarily be too weak for efficiency, and will probably continue so for many years, this remark applying to the newly created counties as well as the counties from which they are taken. It must be remembered that there are scarcely a half dozen counties in the State having good jails and court houses, and the excuse for this is constantly given that the counties are too weak in population and wealth. I seriously doubt whether the people in the old or new counties affected by these changes have any particular desire that they should be made. At any rate, I would make the suggestion that the question of the creation of these two counties be submitted by a supplemental bill to a vote of those people before they are allowed to take effect. The same suggestion might apply to the other counties created as this session. I ask consideration of this matter by the houses".

[75] Glasscock, p. 165.

[76] photo CGH-3-87 from archives of the Natural Resources Conservation office (U.S. Department of Agriculture) office in Bellville, Texas.

[77] The nine children of Jared (I) and Sarah Sheppard Groce were Lucy (b. April 25, 1768, d. Oct. 28, 1849, married Robert Bannister Harper in Halifax County), Sarah (1770, died before December 1803, Sheppard (b. 1772, d. 1824 in Lincoln County, GA), Edmund, Jared Ellison II, Sally, Polly, Betsy and Patsy.

[78] The two children of Jared II and Annie Groce were Frances Ann (born Nov. 26, 1815, died 1821). and Waller William (born Jan. 10, 1818). William was born in the town of Jackson, Alabama, where his mother had fled from the Indians. When he was six weeks old she returned to Fort Groce where she died soon thereafter on March 30, 1818.

[79] details in chapter on Enslaved African Americans

[80] details of Groce's 1818 slave acquisition are given in the chapter on Enslaved African Americans, and in Appendix 1.

[81] "Jared E Groce to James Coleman, Deed, 1 January 1818, Two thousand five hundred dollars, 425 acres on Henly's and Ninety Six Creeks of Saluda River being SW part of tract late property of Tolaver Bostick deed adjacent to lands of Thomas Chiles, Littleton Myrick, heirs of A G Dozier, Jonathon Moore, Isaac Bunting, and land laid off by Thomas Chiles, Johnathin Moore, William P. Brooks, commissioners for that purpose. Wit Willis Bostick, Tale. Levingston, B.F. Whitner. /s/ Jared E Groce Proven 24 January 1818 by Willis Bostick; Nathan Lipscomb JQ. Rec. 26 Jan 1818." [p. 441];   and "Sheriff Harcher to Jared E. Groce. 7 October 1817, at suits of John Campbell, James Coleman and Franklin Scott against executors of Tolaver Bostick, land to be sold at public auction, struck off to Jared E Groce, Three thousand nine hundred two Dollars, 600 acres on Ninety Six Creek adjacent to lands of Thomas Chiles, esqr, Jonathan Moore, James Coleman. Wit. Wm. Lomax. Lyttleton Myrick, Jas Coleman /s/ J Hatcher SED Proven 1 January 1818 by Lyttleton Myrick; Catlett Corner JP Rec. 26 January 1818." [p. 444].

[82] Berlet, "Autobiography of a Spoon", p. 42.

[83] minutes of the ayuntamiento de San Felipe: "Town of Austin, March 21, 1829. The ayuntamiento of the jurisdiction of Austin met for the election of the officers of the civil militia of this jurisdiction, constituting a battalion of four companies. The following citizens were elected officers of the companies composing the battalion of Austin. For the first company, Abner Kuykendall, Captain; Thomas Alley, Lieutenant; Jesse Grimes, Lieutenant; Leonard W. Groce, Sub-lieutenant; Randall Jones, Sub-lieutenant; Thomas H. Borden, First Sergeant; John York, Second Sergeant; Joshua Parker; Francis Holland; Brazilla Kuykendall."

[84] Sarah Berlet's accounts of Edwin Groce changed over time. She first thought that he was the son of Jared's second wife, and in this quote erroneously said he was "a lad of sixteen" in 1831. He was actually 23 years old in that year. Later Berlet discovered other documents that showed that Jared's second wife had only two children and they both died young - neither was Edwin.   Finally she discovered a family bible that gave the proper birth date of Edwin.

[85] Sarah Berlet wrote "In 1831 Edwin Groce ... came out to Texas, and the family circle was complete for the first time since 1822. Mrs. Wharton, with her husband and small son John, came up from Brazoria County to visit her father, and there was a merry family reunion. When she returned home, Edwin accompanied his sister, but the return voyage was a disastrous one. ... In crossing the swollen stream [the Brazos] at the home of Mr. Dave Handon, the boat overturned. Mr. Wharton swam to shore with his wife and child, but when he turned to assist Edwin, the boy was not in sight. He was a good swimmer, so it was supposed that he was knocked unconscious by a piece of drift wood [and drowned]."

[86] Family lore says Muldoon performed the second marriage. No record of a Groce marriage by Muldoon has been found.

[87] Jared Fulton (Nov. 2, 1832), Sarah Wharton (July 22, 1835), Edwin Waller (Sept. 12, 1837; name later changed to William Wharton Groce upon request of Sarah Ann Groce Wharton, in memory of her late husband), Mary Henrietta (April 15, 1840), Eliza Ellen (June 16, 1842), Leonard Waller Jr. (Sept. 27, 1844), John Harris (1846), Martha Flint (Sept. 12, 1848), Bibb Marcus (1850), Charles Courtney (October 10, 1852) and Ellison Kirby (1854 at Liendo).

[88] Handbook of Texas Online: "John Sharp"

[89] Frances Ann was born on October 23, 1834 at her mother's parent's "Ever Green" Plantation. She died on August 31, 1836 of congestive fever in Louisiana. Jared Ellison IV was born on May 28, 1837 at "Ever Green", married Nevaline Hopson of Houston; they had a son Jared Ellison Groce V who was born December 18, 1870 at Pleasant Hill. Jared V married Venice McDAde and one of their children was Jared VI. Barbara Mackall Groce was born on July 7, 1838 at Pleasant Hill and married Phillip Clarke.

[90] Dixon, Samuel H., "Men Who Made Texas Free", pp. ???? book only in HRC Dobie F390D57

[91] Edward; Wooten, p. 237.

[92] Cantrell, p. 179.

[93] see Appendix V for the Clara Chappell slave narrative.

[94] Glasscock, p.31.

[95] Groce Probate Record File 20 (9)

[96] "Oh, horrible, horrible, most horrible! The devoted friend and brother-in-law of Leonard W. Groce, Col. William H. Wharton, died on the 14th day of March 1839, at the residence of L.W. Groce, from an accidental wound recd. in his left hand and breast, when drawing his pistol from the holster to examine it, on the morning of March 4, at the residence of L.W. Groce, when he and some friends were on the eve of leaving for his residence, "Eagle Island", near Velasco. By request of his much afflicted wife, his remains were started on the evening of this death to his residence for interment, in the care of his devoted friends, Dr. Branch T. Archer and Judge Edwin Waller. Col. Wharton has left an almost distracted wife, one son, and my self, unfortunate me, to mourn over his lamented loss. (signed by) Leonard W. Groce"

[97] from various reminiscences of Willliam Wharton Groce as told to Sarah Berlat.

[98] Hunter Rose Collection, image #s 2-132-002 and 2-132-003, in the Harry Ransom Humanities Center at the University of Texas in Austin.

[99] Carroll, "Custer in Texas", pp. 90 - 97.

[100] Custer, pp. 150 - 167

[101] Handbook of Texas Online: "Richard Rogers Peebles"

[102] Austin County Deed Records Vol. C p.137-139.

[103] Jared Groce I will (written March 2, 1803) "I give and bequeath to my sons Edmund and Jarred six negroes, York, Sook, Rachal, Nancy, Elbert, and Delphy an their increase forever, the above six negroes and their increase to be divided between my two sons Edmund and Jarred after my decease."

[104] Berlet, "Jared Ellison Groce", 361 - 363. Augmented by additional information found in "Life Among the Negroes at Bernardo" as told by Captain William Wharton Groce, The Groce Family Papers, CAH and "Reminiscences of my Early Life" by Wm. W. Groce.

[105] This sketch is found in the Groce archives at the Brazoria County Museum library. It is a reverse (negative) image and hard to read. The sketch shown in this book has been scanned from the negative image, traced and retouched as a positive image for clarity.

[106] Dated inventories of slaves at Bernardo and later, Pleasant Hill, are listed in Appendix IV.

[107] Zuber, "Life of Jared Groce"

[108] Austin Papers, Vol. I, p. 936. November 9, 1824. Through Coles, Groce requested Austin to visit him so the two could discuss Bernardo's operation and how that meshed with the manner Austin wanted to run his colony. Groce assured Austin that he would cooperate with Austin's wishes.

[109] Famed folklorist John Lomax and his wife Ruby recorded this song in 1940 in Sumterville, Alabama as sung by Harriet McClention, and by Irene Williams in Rome, Mississippi. The recordings are stored in the American Folklife Center of the Library of Congress at accession numbers: McClention (AFC 1940/003; AFS 04025 B01) and Williams (AFC 1940/003; AFS 04011 A03).

[110] "Samuel Wardleworth of Abbeville District to Jared E. Groce, 7 April 1817, Negroes, Six thousand three hundred seventy four dollars: Negro slaves Pompey, Worley, Stephen, John, Flora and two of her children Mary and Willis, and Sally and her child Rose; it is expressly understood that the Negroes are only mortgaged. Condition that Samuel Wardleworth is to sell two negroes named Harry and Henry, and Groce holds a bond on said Wardleworth executed 31 october 1816 for Six thousand three hundred seventy four dollars due 1 December 1817 with interest from date. [Other provisions here omitted]. Wit Jno S Jeter, Isaac Randolph. /s/ Saml Wardleworth. Proven 8 April 1817 by John S. Jeter; M Mimms CCP. Rec 8th April 1817." [Ref: Edgefield County, South Carolina Deed Records Books 34 and 35; p. 64]

[111] Austin Papers, Vol. II, p. 700, 701: "I have this day hired three negroes from Jared E. Groce, to wit a negro woman named Sally, a negro man called lame Jack, and one called Kelly. - the woman at eight dollars pr. month and the men at fifteen each. The hire to commence on the first day on November next, and continue for one year from that date, and I hereby oblige myself to pay said Groce the amt. of said hire at the expiration of the year. A boy called Fields [Fielding] is to be furnished to take care of Sally's child. The negroes are to be well treated by me, and said Groce is to clothe them. Should they run away or die, the loss is to be Groces - sickness to my loss --   Brazos River, October 19, 1823, Stephen F. Austin   -- the negroes is to be returned when the hire ceases. S.F. Austin (Rubric)"

[112] Campbell, pp. 88 & 89.

[113] Leonard Groce diary, entry of January 31, 1867. Groce Papers, CAH.

[114] US Census, 1870, Montgomery County p. 9. Lorenzo Dow was listed as black, age 45, born in Louisiana.

[115] Austin County Clerk's Office, Book "Miscellaneous B"

[116] Kuykendall, J.H., pp. 35, 36.

[117] Austin Papers, Vol. II, p. 700.
"Stephen F. Austin, Esqr To Jared E. Groce Dr.

2 yds Cloth at 10$	$20
2 Black Silk Hdkfs at 2$	$ 4
5 yds Castinette at 3.50	$17.50
3 yds Green Cloth at 7$	$21
2 yds Lindan at 1$	$ 2
3 1/2 yds Lining at 75c	$ 2.63
2 doz. buttons	$ 2
4 small do.	$ .75
6 skeins Cold. thread	$ .24
15 do. Black Silk	$1.75
6 do. Cold do.	$ .60
3/4 vest pattern	$2.75
2 yards Cottonade	$2.20
To cash	$100
To an order of Cap. Pettus	$70
To a order of H. Chrisman's	$12
To an order of Seth Ingrams	$9.12
To your Due Bill	$50.12
[new total inc. carryforward]	$326.49

Gave Groce a receipt for the above sum as so much received towards the payment of his land.   October 18, 1823
    [signed] S.F. Austin"

[118] Cantrell, p. 179

[119] "Memoires du Commandant Persat - 1806 - 1844", by Gustav Schlumberger, Paris, Plon-Nourrit Et. Co, 1910]. Excerpts translated from French by Bob Skiles.

[120] Austin Papers, Vol. I, p. 1525 and Vol. II: pp. 1595, 1596

[121] Center for American History, UT Austin, Bexar Archives Manuscript Series, for date September 2, 1827.

[122] Lutz, p. 190

[123] Henson, pp. 7-9.

[124] Thrall, p. 631. Thrall wrote: "Williams was a native of Baltimore; while young spent several years in Mexico, where he acquired a thorough knowledge of the language. He met in Mexico Colonel Jared E, Groce, who invited him to Texas. He arrived in the mouth of the Colorado in 1822, in the same vessel with Jonathon C. Peyton, Mrs. Eberle, Messrs. Clopton, Claire and other colonists. At the opening of the land office in San Felipe, in 1824, Mr. Williams became the Secretary, and he kept the records of the Land Office for Austin's Colony during the whole colonial period ". In fact, Williams learned Spanish while living in Argentina, not Mexico.

[125] Austin Papers, Vol. II p. 699.

[126] Texas State Historical Association, Handbook of Texas Online, "Samuel May Williams".

[127] Brindley, Anne A., "Jane Long", Southwestern Historical Quarterly, Volume 56, p. 235.

[128] Jackson, "Almonte's Texas", p. 205: "Some of these problems (between Austin and Wm. Wharton) were likely of a personal nature, for William had wooed and wed Sarah Ann Groce, whose hand Austin had once supposedly sought."

[129] Austin Papers, Vol. II:1075.

[130] Austin Papers, Vol. 3, p.12

[131] Austin Papers, Vol. 1, p. 207

[132] Wortham, p. 279.

[133] Charlton, p. 235.

[134] Williams and Barker, pp. 229-230.

[135] Handbook of Texas: "James Bowie"

[136] Glasscock, p.165

[137] Day, James M., pp. 472, 670, 684

[138] Austin Papers p. 666:
"Hotel Bill
Mr. Jarrot V Groce [Jared E. Groce]
To Warren D.C. Hall, Dr.
1823 August 3

To supper himself and friend	$ .75
" " for three negroes	$ .75
" Five Horses one night	$ 3.75
" two lodgings at 2/ [bits]	$ .50
" Breakfast himself and friend	$ .75
" " for three negroes	$ .75
" Cash lent	$11.00
" Ferriages for three negroes and five horses	$ 4.00

1823 August 4

To Two Dinners at 4/	$ 1.00
" " suppers at 3/	$ .75
" " lodgings at 2/	$ .50
" " Breakfast at 3/	$ .75
" " Diner at 4/	$ 1.00
	$26.25
Received Cash	$20.00
	$ 6.25

Province of Texas 2nd Novr. 1823
    Received the balance due from John W. Hall"

[139] "Reminisces of Jesse Burnam", SWHQ Vol. 5 p. 14

[140] Gambrell, Herbert, "Anson Jones, The Last President of Texas", (Austin, University of Texas Press, 1946), p. 176.

[141] Pearson, P.E., "Reminiscences of Judge Edwin Waller", Southwestern Historical Quarterly, Vol. 4, No. 1, pp. 33 - 54)

[142] Austin County Deed Records B/157.

[143] Hales, Douglas, "A Southern Family in White and Black - The Cuneys of Texas", (College Station, Texas A&M University Press, 2003).

[144] Handbook of Texas Online, "Jared Ellison Kirby"

[145] Jenkins, p. 310. confirm this.

[146] Telegraph and Texas Register, March 17, 1836 and March 24, 1836

[147] Jenkins Papers #1141

[148] Jenkins Papers, #1833

[149] "Pleasant Hill Feby 3d 1836
"Dear Sir
    "I send to you by my sun a package of letters that governor Smith gave to me and requested of me to send them by Mr Mann or my sun as he was afeared that someone would get them and you would not get them sum gentle men in San Fellipee saw me receive them and offered me one hundred dollars to let them intercept them but I cannot be bought by munney when I see you I will tell you who the persons are the same persons replied that you had designed against them and the Govt and people two but you General doo not drop a hint from me as I am all most afeared of my life we now have our wagons lowdded to move to the neighbourhood of Washington we hope we can get a house in town we send you by my sun fifty dollars to get Corn from Col Groose and you get it and tell Col Groose to delever it to Mr Manns order or mine the independance ticket went the hole hog in this presenct and the present majority this then was but nine votes for the Constetutiun in San Fellipee votes was nearly eaqual but I believe the Constetution beat a little Forgive bad spelling
                                                  Yours with Respect

"Major General S. Houston   Mrs. P. Mann"

[150] Jenkins Papers #248; Hogan; Anonymous

[151] Jenkins Papers #1838.

[152] Haley, James, pp. 120 - 122.

[153] Groce Probate records, Austin County Clerk's office. Invoice dated April 21, 1838 from E.M. Struit of Alexandria to Jared Groce: "Please pay Thos. Hooper [Courtney Ann Groce's step father] ten dollars for your account of 1836 and March obligations." Marked paid by Hooper.

[154] Gray, pp. 126 - 129.

[155] Dixon, pp. 415 & 416.

[156] Austin papers, 2558 & 2746

[157] Daughters of the Republic of Texas archives

[158] Zuber, "My Eighty Years in Texas", pp. 71-77.

[159] Day, James M., p. 148

[160] Austin Papers, #2525

[161] Jenkins Papers, #2676.

[162] TSL, Republic of Texas Archives

[163] Winkler, E.W., "Twin Sister Cannon 1836 - 1865", SWHQ, July, 1917, 21:63

[164] *Telegraph and Texas Register*, September 8, 1838.

[165] old ref. #18 needs to be defined

[166] Texas State Library, Republic of Texas Claims, #03800600

[167] Brooks, "History of an Old Clock"

[168] TSL, Republic of Texas Claims, #338/03800621

[169] Anonymous

[170] Barker, "Recollections of the Campaign", p.301

[171] Schiwetz, p. 67

[172] Jenkins Papers, #s 2653 and 2913.

[173] The invoice from Wells to the Groce brothers is in the Groce Probate File 20 (9). The service documents mentioned here all are housed in TSL's Republic of Texas records.

[174] TSL documents filed as Military, Actual Services

[175] TSL Republic of Texas Claims #233/23300088.

[176] Summary of the inventory of Groce lands in 1849:
1. 3528 acres in Grimes County, the upper league of the Retreat Tract less 900 acres.
2. 2952 acres in Grimes County in the Hannah Connancy grant and sold by her to Jared II.
3. One league in Fayette County originally granted to W.W. Shepherd.
4. lower half of the league on Brazos east bank in Austin Co. granted to Thomas W. Stevens.
5. One league on east bank of Brazos in Austin County granted to Daniel Mouser.
6. upper half of a league on Brazos east bank granted to M. Coats.
7. lower half of league in Austin County, east bank. granted to Wm. Whitesides and adjacent to the original Bernardo two leagues.
8. One league on the Brazos east bank granted to John Irons.
9. One league and one labor in Austin County lying east of the leagues granted to Coats and Whitesides, being the headright of Jared III.
10. 2552 acres on the Brazos west bank in Austin County being part of the Wm. C. White league.
11. one half of the league on the east bank of the Bernard River in Brazoria County granted to Henessey being the same half conveyed to Jared III.
12. Two undivided thirds of a half league less 100 acres in Grimes and Brazos Counties being part of the league originally granted to Henry Whitesides.
13. 1894 acres in Austin County lying back of the league originally granted to David Mouser being part of the league originally granted to James Hall
14. About 3000 acres in Austin County being part of the Liendo survey.
15. About 2000 acres on the Brazos east bank in Austin County being all that part of the two leagues known as Bernardo that lies south of Pond or Donaho's Creek.
16. One league of land in Brazoria County known as League No. 11 east of the Brazos being the upper of two leagues granted to John W. Hall.

[177] Waller County death records for May E. Groce, file # 2218734, born May 13, 1868 and died December 10, 1947 in Hempstead, and for Bertie Groce, file # 2117177, born. October 1, 1867 and died February 27, 1963 in Hempstead.

[178] Waller County Probate Records, Book F, George and Abner Groce. Wills list children by name.

[179] Williams, Henry M., "Jared Ellison Groce, Entrepreneur - An Investigation into the Activities of Jared Ellison Groce in Texas from 1822 - 1836", Master's thesis, Texas Southern University, August, 1959.

[180] interviews supported by and on file with Community Archaeological Research Institute.

[181] White, Frank Edd, (add page #); Hollbrook, p. 361.

[182] On March 23, 1867, Congress passed legislation that called for a registration of qualified voters in each military district. The commanding officer in each district was required to have, before September 1, a list of these voters from each county. These lists would be used to determine all who would be eligible to vote for any proposed Constitutional Convention in the state. The registrant had to take an oath stating that he was not disqualified by law from voting. Those ineligible included Confederate veterans with a rank of major or above; any person who had previously taken an oath as a member of Congress, as an officer of the United States, as a member of any state legislature, or as an executive or judicial officer of any state, to support the Constitution of the United States, and who later engaged in insurrection or rebellion against the
United States, or gave aid or comfort to the enemies thereof, and whose "disability" had not been removed by a two-thirds vote of both houses of Congress.

Local military authorities often interpreted this prohibition to include anyone who held any type of office or who in any way benefited from either Confederate state or federal government patronage, thereby preventing a number of otherwise eligible citizens from voting.

The 1867 Voter Registration includes names of voters who registered in the period between 1867 and 1869. A few entries date from 1870, but these occur infrequently.

[183] Source: 1867 Voters' Registration Lists, Austin County, Texas; compiled by Michael Hait, Hait Family Research Services; Laurel, Maryland; 2009

[184] Bruseth, et. al.

[185] Houston *Chronicle,* "Archaeologists search for Texas plantation remains Site was also a staging area for Sam Houston", August 23, 2009
Houston *Chronicle*, "Digging Texas History", Dec. 27, 2009
Cherokee *Herald*, Dec. 16, 2009
Katy *Sun*, "Archaeologists Unearth Bernardo Plantation", December 24, 2009
Houston *Tribune*, Archaeological Field Work at Historical Bernardo Plantation in Waller County Making Texas History", January, 2010.
Waller County *News Citizen*, Archaeology Uncovers Bernardo Plantation", Dec. 12, 2009.
Cumins, Light, "Finding the Site of Bernardo and Pleasant Hill Plantations", Texas State Historian website, August 27, 2009

[186] "Archaeologists Excavate Historic Plantation Site", THC newsletter, January 2010.
Bruseth, Jim and Pat Mercado-Allinger, "Collaboration for Discovery", *Current Archaeology in Texas*, April 2010.

[187] Bruseth, et. al. "Remote Sensing and Archeological Testing at the Bernardo Plantation's Main House" *Bulletin* of the Texas Archaeological Society, 2011. ; The Sarah Berlet sketch is found in her manuscript "Groce and Kindred Families" in archival Box 2Q248 at CAH.

[188] Woorick, James and Robert Marcom, "History and Archaeology Come Together at Bernardo", *Bulletin* of the Texas Archaeological Society, Winter, 2011.

[189] Woodrick, "Archaeological Activities at 41 AU 82, Houston's "Camp West of Brazos"", Bulletin of the Texas Archaeological Society, Volume 82 / 2011, pp. 379 - 394.

[190] The Fondren Library at Rice University, "Groce Family Correspondence" contains several letters to and from family members dated 1824 - 1850's.

[191] [Ref: "Papers Concerning Robertson's Colony in Texas", Volume I: 504 - 517, compiled and edited by Malcolm D. McLean, 1974. Available online at www.lonestar.texas.net].

[192] Harvard Historical Studies, Vol. I. "The Suppression of the African Slave Trade to the United States of America 1638 - 1870" by W. E. B. DuBois (Cambridge Univ. USA Press, 1896).

[193] Texas State Library map #0917

[194] GLO Book 2, p. 120, Book 1, p. 136, GLO "Atlas" Map Collection, Counter 79.

[195] Unfinished Padilla title, Texas GLO Spanish Collection, Box 104, Folder 6, GLO digitized document 1034030.

[196] Austin County Book I, pp. 305 - 315

[197] GLO #4847

[198] letter in "Groce Family Correspondence", Box 240 at the Woodson Research Center, Fondren Library, Rice University, Houston, Texas.

[199] Ref: "Texas Department of Agriculture Bulletin, Year Book 1909", No. 13, May-June, 1910.

[200] Braman, D.E.E., "Braman's Information About Texas", (Philadelphia, J.B. Lippincott & Co., 1858) p. 164; available online from Google Books.

[201] Index to Executive Documents, Senate of the United States, First Session, 23rd Congress, 1853 - 54, Volume 12, Document No. 84. Available online from Google Books.

[202] Slave Narratives from the Federal Writers' Project, 1936-1938, contains more than 2,300 first-person accounts of slavery and 500 black-and-white photographs of former slaves. These narratives were collected in the 1930s as part of the Federal Writers' Project of the Works Progress Administration (WPA) and assembled and microfilmed in 1941 as the seventeen-volume Slave Narratives: A Folk History of Slavery in the United States from Interviews with Former Slaves. The interviewer states that Clara Chappel was born Clara Williams, and was at the time of the interview residing at the rear of 803 Beaver Street, Brownwood, Texas and when interviewed was in prayer.

Made in the USA
Middletown, DE
18 December 2016